Jesus Matters

Jesus Matters

150 Years of Research

C. J. den Heyer

TRINITY PRESS INTERNATIONAL
Valley Forge, Pennsylvania

Translated from the Dutch *Opnieuw: Wie is Jezus? Balans van 150 jaar onderzoek naar Jezus*, published 1996 by Uitgeverij Meinema, Zoetermeer, The Netherlands.

Copyright © Uitgeverij Meinema, Zoetermeer 1996

Translation © John Bowden 1996

First U.S. edition published 1997
Trinity Press International,
P.O. Box 851, Valley Forge, PA 19482-0851

Trinity Press International is a division of the Morehouse Group.

First British edition published 1996 by SCM Press, London.

Library of Congress Cataloging-in-Publication Data
Heyer, C. J. den, 1942-
 [Opnieuw,wie is Jezus? English]
 Jesus matters: 150 years of research / C.J. den Heyer.
  p. cm.
 Includes bibliographical references and index.
 ISBN 1-56338-195-8 (alk. paper)
 1. Jesus Christ—History and criticism. 2. Jesus Christ—History of doctrines—19th century. 3. Jesus Christ—History of doctrines—20th century. I. Title.
BT301.9.H4813 1996
232'.09'034—dc20   96-42948 CIP

Printed in the United States of America

97 98 99 00 01 02 03   8 7 6 5 4 3 2 1

Contents

Introduction

Jesus of Nazareth continues to preoccupy theologians and non-theologians alike. His name resounds in the churches, but it is also mentioned outside them. He is a source of inspiration, a sign of hope, a living demonstration of God's love and faithfulness. In a secularized world, believers and other interested people hope to form a picture of the man who lived as a Jew two thousand years ago, and died on the cross in Jerusalem.

Historical investigation has to be carried on within clearly defined limits. Creativity and imagination are indispensable for a historian, but first and foremost the historian is dependent on sources. For this reason our knowledge of the past is limited. We see and hear only those things which our sources have selected and preserved. They allow us to look with their eyes and listen with their ears. Much more happened, but the sources pay no attention to it. Perhaps they did not know about it, or put it aside as unimportant.

In the New Testament, four evangelists tell stories about Jesus Christ. On the basis of the dogma that from the first to the last page the Bible is the 'Word of God' there is no reason to doubt the historical reliability of the Gospels. But anyone who takes the trouble to read the stories about Jesus accurately and to compare them with one another will discover that sometimes they are by no means identical. However, for centuries that was not felt to be a serious problem. The Bible remained intact. There could be no mistakes or imperfections in the Word of God. Human beings make mistakes, and human understanding is imperfect. Moreover, that is where the heart of the problem lies. Contradictions in the Bible are only apparent contradictions, and differences can be explained. Even on closer inspection, everything proves to be in harmony.

During the eighteenth and nineteenth centuries there was an increase in the number of those who were no longer content with this 'pious' explanation. Their view of the Bible changed. They also noticed the *human* aspects of the book which for centuries had stood on an unassailable footing. As so often, one thing led to another; indeed we can even talk of a snowball effect. Anyone who reads the Bible with new eyes is going to evaluate the Gospels in a different way, and will soon cease to be content with attempts to harmonize the differences between them.

Around 150 years ago 'the historical Jesus' was born. Exegetes began to look behind the traditional picture of Jesus Christ as he is presented in creeds and dogmas, for the 'real' Jesus, the *human being* Jesus of Nazareth who had lived among the Jews of Palestine at the beginning of our era. During their quest, they found themselves confronted with the question whether the Gospels in the New Testament were sufficiently trustworthy as sources for a reliable historical picture of the life of Jesus.

Since that time, 150 years have passed. It is difficult not to be overwhelmed with feelings of discouragement. Does it make sense to continue along a course which seems to have become such a well-trodden path? 150 years of scholarly investigation into the life of Jesus has produced an impossibly large quantity of books and articles. Production in the last century was already impressive enough, but in our time the flood of literature has already become overwhelming. It is impossible to read everything that appears all over the world in this sphere of theology.

Can any surprisingly new voice be heard in this cacophony of thousands? Is there an area in which pioneering investigation remains possible? It is easier to ask the questions than to give the answers. So much has already been said and written in 150 years that it is unwise to have the illusion that one can add a completely new hypothesis. Those who claim that they are doing this usually prove to have insufficient knowledge of the past. In New Testament scholarship developments usually take place slowly, and it is only rarely that much attention is paid to them. However, looking back over a period of 150 years we can talk of 'progress'. Nevertheless, anyone who hopes for sensational discoveries will put the present book aside with feelings of disappointment; on the other hand, those who understand that New Testament scholarship can only go forward cautiously will, I hope, enjoy the following chapters.

The world changes, but the New Testament does not. Since the 'canon' (the list of authoritative books) was established during the third/fourth century, no books have been added to the list or removed from it. The book has not changed, but modern readers read it with different eyes. Since the last century our knowledge of the world in which Jesus lived has increased considerably. Theologians have discovered the Jewish tradition and realized that Jesus did not live in a vacuum. By chance, sometimes writings have surfaced which have proved to come from the period around the beginning of our era. Archaeological discoveries which were made shortly after the Second World War in two places in the Middle East – a Gnostic library in Nag Hammadi in Egypt in 1945 and the Qumran writings by the Dead Sea in 1947 – created a sensation.

For centuries, confessions and dogmas had left no doubt that a 'high' christology was the only good way of describing the meaning of Jesus Christ: he is the unique Son of God. In the course of the nineteenth century there was a radical transformation in reflection on christology. Gradually the *humanity* of Jesus came more markedly into the foreground. The consequence was that the ways of exegesis and dogmatics increasingly ceased to run in parallel. During the second half of this century, the discovery of the humanity of Jesus has been followed by the discovery of his *Jewishness*. The high and exalted Christ of confession and dogma underwent a far-reaching metamorphosis. Anyone who sets out to sketch a profile of Jesus today no longer begins 'above', in heaven, but 'below': in Jesus of Nazareth, a Jew living among Jews in Palestine at the beginning of this century. Presumably he was initially a member of the Pharisaic movement – since the Qumran discoveries, some scholars have even supposed that for a time he belonged to this sect of priests; he had remarkable gifts and properties: he was a healer, an exorcist, a teacher, a man whose eyes were open to the needs of others, an apocalyptic prophet; a man of good will who nevertheless was regarded as a danger to the peace by both the Roman and the Jewish authorities. He died on the cross as though he were the leader of a rebel movement.

150 years is a long time. A great deal has happened over this

period. Does it make sense to rake up the past and compare it with the present? I was stimulated to write this book – this stocktaking of 150 years of theological and historical investigation – by the discovery that in English-language theological literature there is a wealth of books about Jesus, academic studies of Jesus of Nazareth which seem to reach a wide audience. To begin with, I thought that I could easily dismiss this as 'old news'. But slowly I sensed that it is worth spending time over this remarkable development. The historical Jesus has again become the focus of interest. It even seems possible to look at him with new eyes.

Jesus of Nazareth, the Son of God

The Nazarene

Who is Jesus? This question is not a new one. The Gospels tell us that the debate already began during Jesus' lifetime. He is called the Nazarene (Mark 14.67; 16.6). He got this name because he came from Nazareth in Galilee (Mark 1.9), an ordinary place which in the Old Testament period did not play any important role. The villagers knew who he was and had no difficulty in identifying him: 'Is not this the carpenter, the son of Mary, and the brother of James and Joses and Judas and Simon? And do not his sisters belong here among us?' (Mark 6.3). It's a small world. People know one another from their youth upwards. So the appearance of Jesus among his fellow townspeople causes scandal and indignation (Luke 4.14–30).

Jesus grew up in a small village in Galilee. He was a countryman and not a city-dweller. He never went beyond the borders of Jewish territory. He never visited the great world cities of this time, Rome and Athens. He was a typical Galilean. Moreover, that is how the inhabitants of Jerusalem also saw him, as a miraculous pilgrim from Galilee (Matt.26.69); some attributed prophetic characteristics to him, in jest or in earnest (Matt.21.11; 26.67–68).

Who was this Galilean from Nazareth? His activity attracted the attention of many people. The things that he said provoked differing reactions. There was joy over the openness which he offered, but he also caused perplexity. Some even found him scandalous because he spoke his mind and moved in circles which the pious people of his time found disreputable. Jesus had special powers. He healed the sick and freed the demon-possessed from the spirits that were tormenting them. People wondered at him, but he also met with opposition and came into conflict with religious leaders who thought that he should not go against traditional points of view. His name became known, first in Galilee but soon also in Judaea and in adjacent areas (Mark 3.7–8). People with their pains and their questions came to him and seldom left him alone (Mark 1.36; 2.1–2). In the company of his followers and usually surrounded by a great host of the sick, the needy and the curious, he first wandered around Galilee and finally embarked on a journey to Jerusalem as a pilgrim.

Who is he?

This question dates right back to the time of Jesus. People in his home town of Nazareth thought that they knew him, but he surprised and scandalized them. He was a human being among human beings. Moreover, that is how he was seen by his contemporaries; however, those who encountered him had the feeling that they were dealing with a special person. He was different, and dared to go outside the well-trodden ways. He told stories and made people think. His interpretation of scripture was sometimes original, and his view of the imminent coming of the kingdom of God (Mark 1.14–15) was exciting. Would the immediate future prove him right or show him up as a dreamer?

Jesus felt called to go in search of those people who had left the ways of the Lord and risked getting lost (Luke 15). Why did he do that? In the Gospels such questions are often put to him. There is amazement over the power which Jesus seems to have over the evil spirits (Mark 1.27–28). People are dumbfounded at his interpretation of the commandments of the Torah and say that he has more authority than the scribes (Matt.7.28–29). Pious Pharisees are surprised that Jesus seems to have no hesitations about eating with sinners and tax collectors (Mark 2.16). In Jerusalem the authorities want to know with what authority Jesus acts (Mark 11.27–33), and during his trial before the Supreme Council the interrogation is finally focussed by the high priest in the question 'Who are you?' (Mark 14.61)?

Who is Jesus? The Gospels do not make it easy for readers to answer this question in a simple, unambiguous way. Jesus reacts cautiously and even with restraint to questions about himself. Evil spirits who say that they know who he is are punished and are mercilessly muzzled (Mark 1.25; 3.12); in many cases those who have been healed by Jesus are told that they must not tell anyone else about this happy event (Mark 1.44; 5.43; 7.36; 8.26), and those who witness a miracle get no reaction at all to their amazed exclamation, 'Who is this, that even the wind and the sea obey him?' (Mark 4.41; cf. Matt.14.33).

An unexpected Messiah

The evangelists relate that at a crucial moment in his life Jesus asks his disciples, 'Who do men say that I am?' (Mark 8.27–28)? Different answers seem possible: John the Baptist, Elijah or a prophet like Moses (Deut.18.15–18), and moreover in one Gospel the name of the prophet Jeremiah is also mentioned (Matt.16.14). Then Jesus puts the same question personally to his disciples, 'What do you say?'. Peter replies, 'You are the Christ' (Mark 8.29). Did the one who was later to become an apostle really know at that time what he was saying? The sequel to this conversation shows that Peter has an image of the Messiah which bears little relationship to Jesus' own view of his messiahship. That difference in insight leads to a harsh confrontation between the teacher and his disciple. When Jesus says that he will suffer and die in the near future, Peter reacts furiously to his words (Mark 8.31–33). He wants to know nothing of a suffering Messiah.

Is Jesus the Messiah? The evangelists do not conceal the fact that even his disciples do not know how to answer this question. Sometimes he reminds them of influential figures in the history of the people of Israel and they venture to interpret the 'great' sayings with reference to him. Even then they usually have little or no idea of what they are saying. Miraculous stories about Jesus go the rounds. Through his father, the carpenter of Nazareth, he is said to be a descendant of no less than the great king David (Matt.1.1–17). Is he perhaps the 'Son of David' who is expected in the imminent future, the Messiah of Israel who will put an end to the domination of the Roman occupation forces? Anyone who hopes for the coming of such a Messiah receives a harsh awakening from Jesus' announcement of his suffering and death in Jerusalem (Mark 8.31; 9.31; 10.32f.).

3

Is this Jesus, an offshoot of the family of David, the Messiah, the new king of the Jews? After his striking entry into Jerusalem (Mark 11.1–11) the situation soon becomes a grim one. Outside the city a great deal was possible and deviant behaviour was more easily tolerated. At the centre of power, words had to be weighed carefully and any public demonstration was watched with eagle eyes.

By objective, reasonable standards, the public appearance of Jesus in Jerusalem cannot be said to have been particularly diplomatic or well-considered. He challenges both the Jewish and the Roman authorities in an unmistakable way. He enters Jerusalem as though he cherishes kingly pretensions and his action in the temple suggests that he thinks that he can act in the spirit of Old Testament prophets like Jeremiah (Mark 11.15–19).

Who is this man from Nazareth? Is he a fool or a fanatic, a dreamer or a charismatic, an irresponsible figure who leads the people astray or a rebel who hopes by a carefully prepared surprise attack to put an end to the Roman occupation? The passion narratives in the Gospels repeatedly say that the authorities take pains to track down Jesus' true identity. At the beginning of his stay in Jerusalem, the Jewish leaders interrogate him about his 'authority' (Mark 11.27–33). This point is also a central one in his trial before the Sanhedrin: 'Jesus, tell us precisely who you are' (Mark 14.61). The Roman procurator goes about things less circumspectly. Unfamiliar with Jewish religious expectations and ideas, Pontius Pilate gets right to the point, 'Do you think that you are the king of the Jews?' (Mark 15.2). The high dignitary who expects to be given a clear answer is disappointed. Even at this dramatic moment Jesus does not make things clear for his interrogator, 'You say so.' This is an answer which can be taken to mean 'That's what you say', or 'I leave it to you'.

In the Roman empire it was customary to reserve the abhorrent death of crucifixion for runaway slaves and for all those who had rebelled against the rule of Rome. Pontius Pilate condemns Jesus because he thinks that he is a rebel. The soldiers play a macabre game with the pretender to the throne who has been condemned to death (Mark 15.16–21). Even the Jewish leaders mock him (Mark 15.29–32). They can be content. Thanks to their swift intervention, at this Passover – the feast of liberation – there are no serious disturbances.

Jesus dies alone (Mark 15.33–37), mocked by bystanders, and left in the lurch by his disciples. When he had been arrested earlier in Gethsemane in the early hours, Peter and the other disciples had taken flight (Mark 14.43–52). The evangelists say nothing about the reactions of the crowds – people who followed Jesus with their problems, marvelled at him, and were fascinated by his words and actions. Certainly they note that women were witnesses to this terrible event from afar. These women seem to have accompanied Jesus on his pilgrimage to the city of Jerusalem (Mark 15.40–41). The readers of the Gospels can only be amazed that their presence has not been mentioned earlier (Mark 15.42–27).

Risen from the dead

Who is this crucified Jesus? After his execution by Roman soldiers he could have been included in the incalculable series of innocent people who have been tortured and killed in the course of the centuries: the gentle and the peacemakers, those who fought fiercely for a just society and uncompromising prophets. Jesus died on the cross because in Gethsemane he had arrived at the insight that God, his 'abba' (an intimate Aramaic word for father), required this sacrifice of him (Mark 14.32–42).

After Easter the Christian community began to look at the recent past with new eyes. It confessed that God had raised Jesus from the dead on the third day (I Cor.15.3–4). The cross was not the last word, and the tomb did not prove to be the place where this human life definitively ended. The 'crucified one' became the 'risen one'. The apostle Paul gives Jesus a unique place in history. As the 'crucified', he is one of the righteous sufferers and martyrs; as the 'risen one' he is a new creation and stands at the beginning of a new time: 'the firstfruits of those who sleep' (I Cor.15.20). From Easter onwards, a surprising new light falls on the cross. It is no longer the tragic end of a man of good will, but forms the overture to a new episode in the history of God and the world.

Easter is of essential significance for Christian faith. Anyone who lives and believes after Easter knows more than the very first

5

followers. They did not know the future and were groping in the dark about the way which Jesus thought that he had to follow. After Easter, the Christian community broke the silence and unrestrainedly called Jesus the Christ, the Messiah of Israel and the world. Supported by the Spirit, it began to look in scripture and tradition for the best and clearest words, concepts and images with which to confess Jesus.

The first answers to the question 'Who is Jesus?' are to be found in the New Testament. In his letters Paul concentrates on the suffering of Jesus. The apostle puts the crucified Christ at the centre of Christian faith (I Cor.2.2). The four evangelists follow the traces further back. They not only relate Jesus' passion and death but are also interested in his life, in his words and actions, in his travels through Judaea and Galilee, in his miraculous charismatic powers and in his interest in people who risked getting lost.

Son of God

In Jerusalem Jesus of Nazareth died on the cross. God raised him from the dead. Who is this Jesus? Why did God make an exception for this crucified man? In those days men were regularly nailed to a cross because they had been condemned to death and were executed in this terrible way. Without Easter, Jesus would have gained a place in the long series of righteous sufferers and all those who were prepared to die as martyrs for their convictions.

In the New Testament the humanity of Jesus is not denied, but it disappears into the background, because the early Christian community seems above all to be interested in his relationship to God. Apostles and evangelists do not hesitate to speak of a unique relationship. Jesus lives closer to God than ordinary mortals. In Gethsemane he wrestled with his task and at that dramatic moment addressed God as his 'abba', his 'father' (Mark 14.36). At the end of the Gospel readers are again reminded of the beginning. When Jesus was baptized by John the Baptist, a voice resounded from heaven which called him 'my beloved son' (Mark 1.11).

Can a human being be addressed as 'son of God'? The roots of the New Testament lie in the Old Testament–Jewish tradition. Those are called son of God who are chosen by God to fulfil a special task.

6

Israel, the chosen people, is son of God (Ex.4.22; Hos.11.1). The king, as representative of the people, is also given the title 'son of God' (II Sam.7.14; Ps.2.7). However, there is no question of divinization. In Israel the king remains a vulnerable human being with faults and crimes.

At the baptism of Jesus it emerges that God has again made a choice. As one human being among others Jesus is son of God. In his letter to the Galatians Paul writes briefly and tersely, 'But when the time had fully come, God sent forth his Son, born of a woman, born under the law' (Gal.4.4). Jesus is a human being – like all other human beings he is 'born of a woman' – but at the same time he is the Son who is sent by God the Father. For the Fourth Gospel, such a view of things is of essential importance. Jesus is the 'only-begotten Son' who is sent into this world by God the Father (John 3.16). Father and Son are so much one (John 17.22) that Jesus can say, 'He who has seen me has seen the Father' (John 14.9).

Is Jesus human or divine? This question is certainly raised in the writings of the New Testament, but it is not given an explicit answer. Jesus is the Nazarene, but he is also the beloved Son of God who is sent by the Father. He is said to come from the family of David (Matt.1.17; Rom.1.3–4), but Mary, his mother, is told, 'The Holy Spirit will come upon you, and the power of the Most High will overshadow you' (Luke 1.35). Two of the four Gospels – Matthew and Luke – relate that Jesus was born in Bethlehem (Matt.2.1–12; Luke 2.1–7), whereas the 'city of David' plays no role in the Fourth Gospel (John 7.40–44), because the reader is challenged to look towards heaven. Jesus comes 'from above'. He is the Word that 'was in the beginning with God' (John 1.1–2) and 'was made flesh' (John 1.14).

The evangelist John teaches his readers to use two words about Jesus: in him 'flesh' and 'glory' come together (John 1.14). He is the man Jesus of Nazareth and knows human emotions (John 11.33): after a long journey he sits wearily by a well (John 4.6). But he is also the Son of God who knows what is awaiting him (John 13.1); his arrest does not surprise him (John 18.1–11); he bears the cross himself (John 19.17); and even as he hangs on it he is the one who is in charge (John 19.25–30).

7

Who is Jesus? The preaching of the gospel of the crucified and risen Jesus seems to have found a hearing, first within the limits of Jewish territory, and then also in the world of the Gentiles. In a number of successive journeys, Paul went through Asia Minor and Greece. In great metropolises like Ephesus, Corinth and Athens he preached the gospel of the crucified Christ and founded Christian communities. The book of Acts ends by giving an account of the journey which Paul makes to Rome. The gospel of Jesus Christ also resounded in the centre of the gigantic Roman empire (Acts 28.11,31). Paul was fond of travelling, and his achievements command respect, but he was not the only missionary. In early Christian writings the name of Thomas also appears repeatedly. Whereas Paul travelled from Jerusalem in a westward direction, Thomas may be called the apostle of the East: he is said to have gone to Syria, ancient Mesopotamia, Persia, and perhaps even India and China.

People come and people go. The disciples and apostles also grew old and died. On their retinas they still had a picture of Jesus. However, by the beginning of the second century the number of eye-witnesses had been reduced to virtually nil. With the disappearance of the very first followers, the value of the writings which they had left behind increased. Here new problems arose, since the production of texts continued undiminished. New Gospels appeared in the name of well-known apostles; so did letters which were said to have been written by disciples of Jesus, acts and apocalypses which were attributed to Christians of the first generation. Which writings were authentic and which were not? The selection of 'canonical', authoritative writings proved a long process. At the beginning of the second century the New Testament was by no means complete, in a volume that could be read out in church and cited in dogmatic discussion. Initially the 'canon' had an 'open' character: books were added and books were removed. Only in the fourth century was the canon of the New Testament definitively fixed.

Those who steep themselves in the apocryphal writings of the New Testament will note with surprise the many details of the life of Jesus which are mentioned. Do these authors really know more than the authors of the canonical writings? It seems a topsy-turvy world. The further people are removed from the time in which Jesus lived, the more they think they know about him. The sobriety of the canonical Gospels has totally disappeared. We are told with verve about the virginity of Mary, about Jesus' birth, about the childhood years in which he emerged as a precocious child with remarkable gifts. In these stories his humanity disappears further and further into the background.

In the second century, 'pious fantasy' created events in the life of Jesus which the canonical Gospels do not know. The new stories met a need. Because deep differences of opinion emerged in the church, theologians felt called to create more clarity about Jesus' divinity. Thus dogma began to form a welcome supplement to the writings of the New Testament. The apocryphal Gospels in their turn projected dogmatic developments back on to the life of Jesus.

The christological debate begins at a very early stage of church history. That is understandable, since the New Testament seems multicoloured, and the successful missionary journeys of people like Paul and Thomas created a need to translate Christian belief from its original Old Testament Christian context into words and images which were comprehensible to pagans. In this fascinating struggle for clarity, the person of Christ was the centre of interest. Here the dispute focussed on the interpretation of the title 'son of God'. In the world of the ancient Near East and classical antiquity this term was not unknown. Rulers like pharaohs, emperors and kings saw themselves as 'sons of God', and the title was also given to people with special gifts, like magicians, miracle-workers and soothsayers.

The church needed to react in a balanced way to the question whether Jesus was also such a 'son of God'. Merely a negative answer here would not have been understood. The notion of sons of God offered the church the opportunity to build a bridge towards the world outside the Jewish tradition. Jesus too had miraculous powers and had appeared as a charismatic. According to Christian conviction, here just the very edge of the veil covering the mystery of Jesus' origin was lifted. The bridge provided by the idea of sons of God made it possible for the church to show the pagan world that Jesus is 'son of God' in a completely unique way. It is for this reason that the Gospel of John sets such a lofty tone: 'In the beginning was the

Word, and the Word was with God and the Word was God' (John 1.1).

The Fourth Evangelist invites his readers to go on speaking of Jesus Christ, the Son of God (John 20.30–31), with two words: he is divine and human at the same time. 'The Word was made flesh' (John 1.14), but he is and remains the unique Son of God; he shows who God is (John 1.18), and in this manner shows the only way to the Father (John 14.4–14).

The Chalcedonian Definition

The New Testament raises questions, and challenges the Christian church to look for answers. In the first centuries of church history there was a fierce debate over christology. In the framework of this study it is neither possible nor necessary to sketch out this debate in detail.[1] At the time of the Council of Chalcedon in 451 a formula was accepted which proved to be of great significance for christological reflection in subsequent centuries. This formula also spoke of Jesus using two words: he is both truly God and truly man, in such a way that he is one and the same Christ, the only-begotten Son and Lord. In him, in one person and being, two natures come together, a divine nature and a human nature, and the two natures are *unconfused and unchanged, indivisible and inseparable.*[2]

Did this formula solve the problem for good? Church history shows that this was not the case. Dogmatic formulae rarely, if ever, proved to be the end of all opposition. The Chalcedonian Definition can be said to be wise and understanding, because those who made it deliberately imposed limitations upon themselves and did not try to have the last and definitive word. They set down limits – four words beginning with 'un- or 'in-' – and thus respected the mystery.

Despite this attempt to create calm and space, the debate continued. The desire to know more and to decipher the mystery gained the upper hand. If two natures come together in one person, what then is the relationship between the two natures in this one person? In the christological dispute after Chalcedon the human nature of Christ seemed to be made quite simply and even obviously subordinate to his divine nature.

In retrospect, it is not surprising that the process of reflection developed in this direction. By definition a divine and a human nature are unequal partners. The 'logical' consequence is that Jesus' personhood is above all connected with his divine nature, whereas his human nature is seen as impersonal. He was more divine than human. He was more the Son of God who had descended from heaven than the human being Jesus who came from Nazareth. He knew more than a human being could ever know. In this divine splendour his humanity faded.

Soteriology

After Chalcedon, the christological debate lost its edge. The dispute seemed settled. During the Middle Ages the view prevailed that the fathers of the Council of Chalcedon had found a satisfactory solution to an extremely complicated problem. There was virtually no discussion any longer about the question whether a divine and a human nature could come together in one person – *unconfused and unchanged, indivisible and inseparable.* In the sixteenth century, Rome and the Reformation were entangled in a life-and-death feud, but in principle they did not differ over the value of the Chalcedonian Definition.

In classical dogmatics it is customary to make a distinction between 'the person of Christ' and 'the work of Christ'. In the first centuries of church history the question of the *person* of Christ was central. In the long run it became necessary to arrive at a definition of the meaning of the *work* of Jesus Christ (= soteriology). In this reflection, the dogma about the two natures of Christ also proved to be quite useful in soteriological terms.

Since the fall of Adam and Eve in Paradise, the whole of humankind has been living in sin and will not be able to avoid the punishment of God (Gen.3). No one is in a position to resist or to overcome evil, and no individual can bear the sins of another. In fact the human situation is hopeless and there is no way out. However, the Bible reveals that God is not only a righteous God – who will punish sin – but also a God of love and grace. It is this love for human beings which led God to send his only-begotten, beloved Son to earth (John 3.16). As the human being Jesus of Nazareth, on the cross he 'vicariously' bears the punishment for the sins of human beings. He can do this because as Son of God he is without sin and therefore is also without guilt. For this reason he can 'pay for others' on the cross, and is the one who brings about reconciliation between God and human beings (II Cor.5.16–21).

The dogmatic system in which the 'person' and the 'work' of Christ were connected in the way indicated above was normative for centuries in theology and the church. The chapters which follow will show how problems arose when in the nineteenth century critical questions came to be asked about the doctrinal statement about the divine nature of Christ. To the present day it is a live question how far soteriology is robbed of its foundation once it is denied that Jesus Christ is the Son of God in the classical sense of the word.

Summary

Who is Jesus? The New Testament does not seem to give an unambiguous answer to this question. Paul wrote letters in which he reacted to current problems. The Gospels tell of the words and actions of Jesus, in stories about his life and his passion and death. The New Testament is not a collection of studies on christological themes, and it contains no dogmatic formulae. In the midst of confusion, opposition and chaos, however, the need for clarity and certainty grew in the church. Hebrew words and concepts needed to be made comprehensible for people who had grown up in a world dominated by Hellenistic Greek and Roman thought. The christological dispute was carried on in these circumstances, and theologians and church leaders who suggested that they could say more about Jesus than the authors of the New Testament writings believed that they were providing what was wanted. The consequence was that the multicoloured Bible was transformed into a strict dogmatic system. Anyone who could not accept it was declared a heretic by the church leaders and expelled from the Christian community. The church leaders thought that they were in the right, and they did this in the name of the Son of God, who, as Jesus of Nazareth, went around Jewish territory in search of people who risked getting lost.

2

Holy Scripture under Discussion

Back to scripture

Who is Jesus? The Reformers of the sixteenth century did not formulate any new answer to this question. Luther and Calvin, like their fellow Reformers and disciples, aimed at a thorough reform of theology and the church, not a total change. The Chalcedonian Definition was not disputed and the dogma of the two natures of Christ was not changed. Anyone who had asked the Reformers in the sixteenth century 'Who is Jesus?' would have been given a traditional answer: he is the Son of God who died for our sins on the cross.

The Reformers wanted to reform the church, purge it of any ideas, notions and customs which concealed and obscured the heart of the matter. Consequently the supporters of the Reformation, following the ideals of the Renaissance and humanism, went 'back to the sources' and put Scripture at the centre *(sola scriptura)*. In contrast to Roman Catholicism they denied the value of church tradition and regarded the Bible as the only source from which the church and theology could draw their wisdom. Dogmatic formulae and church customs without sufficient biblical backing lost their authority: these included the veneration of Mary and other saints, the power of the Pope in Rome, the mass and purgatory.

The Protestant 'purification' of theology led to iconoclasm – in many places in Europe the statues and paintings in the churches were physically destroyed. The exposition of Scripture was central at worship in the Reformation churches. With *sola scriptura* the Reformation stated that sinful human beings can only be saved through faith in Christ *(sola fide)*, who died on the cross for the complete remission of all our sins.

In the previous chapter I pointed out that it is not unusual to make a distinction in dogmatic reflection on christology between the 'person' and the 'work' of Christ. As far as the 'person of Christ' was concerned, the Reformation accepted the classical dogmas and confessional writings; by contrast, in 'the work of Christ' it accentuated an aspect which had been pushed into the background in Roman Catholicism: Jesus Christ is the only redeemer (= *solus Christus*): 'I am the way and the truth and the life; no one comes to the Father but by me' (John 14.6).[1]

The Reformation thought that it could respond to the question 'Who is Jesus?' with a simple reference to scripture. It was convinced that christological dogma does not add any new elements, but is in fact a summary of the biblical statements. Bible and dogma are on the same wavelength. It is one of the tasks of the exegete to safeguard the biblical foundation of dogmatic statements. It is no coincidence that leading Reformers like Luther and Calvin were primarily skilled exegetes and biblical theologians.[2]

A book from a distant past

The clarity of the Reformation position left nothing to be desired. Anyone who wants to know what Jesus said and did must be content with what scripture relates. No other source can add anything to this: no church tradition, no Pope or bishop, no council or theological school. However, in the long run the Reformation position proved vulnerable.

The Old and New Testaments are not recent books but were written centuries ago and recount a distant past. The urgent question is what significance these old, 'antique' writings can still have for generations which live centuries later. Human words are dependent on the time and situation in which they are spoken. After the course of years they lose meaning and importance. They disappear from memory and get forgotten. Does the Bible also run this risk? It seemed possible simply to answer this question in the negative. In scripture the Reformation thought that it had found a firm and unassailable foundation for faith. The Old and New Testaments do not contain 'time-conditioned' human words. The Bible contains God's revelation and as such is the Word of

God. Human words may pass away, but God's Word has eternal value.

Prophets and psalmists, chroniclers and wisdom teachers, evangelists and apostles, set down the words of God in writing over the course of centuries. They did not do that on their own authority but were inspired by the Spirit of God (II Tim.3.16). Here, too, it proves that any solution to a problem keeps raising new questions. Biblical authors were inspired by the Spirit of God – but precisely how did that happen? Did the Spirit of God completely exclude the human spirit? These are questions which could not be answered in a simple way that would satisfy everyone. The Bible may be the Word of God, but human beings set down the word of God in writing. Did they do so 'mechanically', so that in fact they were little more than the pen which was moved by the Spirit of God? Or did the Spirit give them freedom to express the Word of God in their own words and images?

From the Reformation to the Enlightenment

The dispute between Rome and the Reformation in the sixteenth century was a serious dispute over the truth, but the bloody wars of religion which were the result of it had a negative effect on the credibility of Christendom. In the seventeenth century in philosophical and theological circles in Western Europe fierce criticism developed of the Christian creeds and dogmas which had been recognized as authoritative for centuries. In European cultural history these intellectual developments are usually described as 'the Enlightenment'.[3] The choice of this word is very significant. The leading spokesmen of the Enlightenment had the feeling that they were at last emerging from the darkness of the Middle Ages and entering a new 'enlightened' time.

There is a classical saying that 'nothing comes from nothing'. Ideas and thoughts in world history do not drop from heaven. They are a continuation of, and often a reaction to, patterns of thought from previous generations and are always inspired by them. The 'Enlightenment' was critical of church tradition, but at the same time it formed a continuation of a social development which was set in motion by the Reformation. The powerful church of Rome in principle had a hierarchical structure: the top of the hierarchy determined what people had to believe and what they were to reject. In Protestantism, thanks to the emphasis on *sola fide*, faith took on a very personal character: faith was primarily understood as *my* faith. Assertions and statements by church leaders and theologians, princes and other civic authorities, could be disputed by anyone, from the top to the bottom of the social ladder, with a reference to scripture and to personal belief or conscience.

A 'rational' faith

The Reformation appealed to the Bible and attached great importance to the faith of the individual. The Enlightenment went further down that line and made a connection between faith and understanding: human faith may in no way conflict with 'reason'.

If understanding – 'reason' – was also to triumph in church and theology, that meant the end of all those forms of religion which prevented people from coming of age,[4] which belittled them, caused them anxiety, and blamed them unnecessarily. It meant the end of intolerance and fanaticism, of wars of religion and the church's misuse of power, of dogmatism and legalism. Ultimately a Christian belief was to survive which could be described as 'rational'. Anyone who believed in this way did not need to do violence to his capacity for understanding.

For the Christian church in Western Europe this 'enlightened' view had far-reaching consequences. Here I shall limit myself to those which the radical change in thought had in the sphere of biblical exegesis and christological reflection. Since the eighteenth-century Enlightenment, modern men and women have become aware that they live in a different world from that of the generations which populated the earth before them. Access to the past is definitively closed. It is a fiction to suppose that 'enlightened' Europeans could enter into the thoughts and feelings of someone from antiquity.[5] Anyone living in the cultural world of antiquity, but also in that of the Middle Ages, was aware of being surrounded by gods and spirits, by saints and witches; and metaphysical (= supernatural) notions were accepted as a matter of course.

Rational thought 'disenchanted' this ancient word. It is true that many people did not immediately and definitively write off belief in a deity, but the traditional Christian image of God certainly lost its power of conviction. Belief in a personal God who guided history and, when he thought it desirable, actually intervened in the course of history, seemed hardly compatible, if at all, with the regularities which science thought that it could discover in nature and human history. The logical consequence was that God slowly but increasingly disappeared into the background and the tension between faith and science increased.

The creation of human beings and the world by God is central to the first chapters of the biblical book of Genesis. However, scientific discussion of the origin of the universe begins from a Big Bang, an event which is said to have taken place millions of years ago and is to be regarded as the beginning of everything. Human beings are no more than a tiny part of the evolution of life on earth. Adam and Eve have countless ancestors, and if it was possible to put all these human beings in a line, then it would emerge that their appearance slowly changes, the further back into the past we go.

The Bible tells the splendid story of paradise, but science begins from the fact that in the history of the world the right of the strongest has always prevailed everywhere. No paradise fits into such a view of reality. Anyone who believes in God as the Creator is well aware of the 'riddle of the good creation' and wrestles with the problem of the 'fall'. The creation story, in the figures of Adam and Eve, makes the whole of humankind responsible for the sin and evil in the world. By contrast, the natural sciences raise the question whether the idea of collective guilt is real at all. Creation does not become bad through human faults. Creation 'evolves'. In christological reflection, traditional soteriology gave an answer to the problem of human error. But what significance can the suffering and death of Jesus take on in a picture of the world which is not characterized by the fall, but by evolution?

Historical criticism

In the sixteenth century, the Reformation put the Bible as the Word of God at the centre of church and theology: *sola scriptura*. In the theological debate, considerably more value was attached to biblical texts than to the age-old statements of church fathers and councils, popes and bishops. The exegesis of the text took precedence over tradition, over dogmas and encyclicals. In the course of the seventeenth century adherents of 'Enlightenment thought' not only freed themselves from church tradition, from dogma and confessional writings, but also ventured to attack Scripture. They saw the Bible no longer as the 'infallible' Word of God, but as a collection of writings by human beings who had lived centuries earlier.

The Reformation stimulated interest in the Bible; the Enlightenment intensified the critical study of it. The Reformation strove for a theology which was founded on scripture. The Enlightenment was sponsor to the historical criticism of scripture. Thanks to the Reformation, exegetes could make an important contribution to the dogmatic debate. The consequence of the Enlightenment was that a deep and wide gulf began to form between exegetes and dogmatic theologians. 'Enlightened' exegetes came to see the *historical* character of the Bible and did not hesitate to study this book – like other books written by human beings – *critically*, with human reason as a starting point.

Believers thinking 'rationally' began to look on the Bible with other eyes. The 'Enlightenment' had made them aware of history as an unmistakable factor in thought. Many centuries earlier, people in the Middle East had written books which had gained a place in the canon of the Bible. Other books were also written which were not included in this same canon. 'Enlightened' believers also came to see the time-conditioned character of scripture. Moreover they raised critical questions about the extent of the biblical canon.

One significant feature of 'rational' belief was that people were no longer satisfied with a reference to the work of the Spirit. That also meant that they no longer felt compelled to defend the unity of scripture. Any unprejudiced, careful reader of the Bible had to come to recognize that there were tensions between the Old and the New Testaments and that it was not difficult to summarize the obvious difference within the New Testament: between the four Gospels, and between the Gospels and the letters of Paul.

In the seventeenth and eighteenth century, Enlightenment thought shook Western men and women awake and made them aware of living in a world which was not dominated by supernatural interventions. The Bible seemed to have been written by people who lived in another culture and in a far distant past. Even Jesus of Nazareth was not an 'enlightened' citizen of Western Europe, and the same applied to apostles and evangelists. Past and present were separated by a deep gulf. The discussion of christological dogma in the first centuries of church history took place in a climate of thought completely alien to those living in an 'enlightened' world. Anyone who wanted to have a rational faith found it very difficult to conceive of the combination of a divine and a human nature in one and the same person. They had no alternative than to bid a painful farewell to the dogma of the two natures of Christ.

The connection between the 'person' and the 'work' of Christ indicated earlier implies that 'enlightened' believers also had great difficulty in accepting the classical soteriology. Opposition to this dogma was further strengthened by a growing awareness of the problem of history. How can the death of a man in the distant past have meaning for generations living centuries later – and even bring about reconciliation with Christ?

Some Enlightenment theologians resorted to age-old mysticism and spoke of 'the ideal Christ' and the incarnation of the eternal Christ in human existence. However, they challenged the notion that the 'ideal Christ' had become incarnate only once in history in the human being Jesus. Whereas from antiquity emphasis had been placed in church tradition on the *extra nos* (outside us, without us) and the confession of the vicarious action of Christ (he died on the cross 'for us'), some adherents of Enlightenment thought emphasized the idea of *Christus in nobis* (= Christ in us). What was of decisive importance for our redemption was not the knowledge of historical facts but the 'indwelling' of the eternal Christ in us: 'Though Christ were born a thousand times in Bethlehem and not in you, then you are for ever lost.'[6]

The discovery of history made Christian faith vulnerable. There are no immediate possibilities of escape; it is difficult to find a safe haven in historical debate. Even the 'Christ in me' has to be linked in one way or another with the Jesus who was born long ago in Bethlehem. Far less does the Bible offer any solace. Enlightened thought also 'disenchanted' the Word of God. The Bible is a human book.[7] So it may be read just as critically as other books by authors past and present. And very soon that is precisely how it came to be read.

3

A 'Rational' Christology

In quest of the 'authentic' Jesus

Who is Jesus? In their answer to this question, 'enlightened' theologians no longer made use of classical dogmatic concepts like the pre-existence and incarnation of the Son of God, his divine and human natures and his virgin birth. Nor was there room in their 'rational' belief for the traditional doctrine of reconciliation. They did not deny the historical fact that Jesus died on the cross, but they rejected the notion that this event had to be interpreted as an 'atoning death'.

As a consequence of Enlightenment thought, for the first time a distinction was made between the human being Jesus of Nazareth and the Christ of church tradition. Theologians dared to go back and look behind creeds and dogmas for the 'real' Jesus, the man Jesus of Nazareth who had lived among Jews in the first century after the beginning of our era. After centuries of church history people hoped that they would rediscover this 'undogmatic' Jesus, freed from dogmas and other ecclesiastical 'adornments'.

In theological literature, after a while the term *the historical Jesus* arose as a synonym for the 'real Jesus'. It is worth pausing for a moment over the word 'historical'. The life of Jesus was 'historical' because it could be described as an 'authentic', tangible and perceptible reality, without supernatural intervention. In the nineteenth century the term 'the historical Jesus' was deliberately used in confrontation with the orthodox, dogmatic picture of Christ. 'Enlightened' theologians tried to look behind church dogma for the 'authentic', the historical Jesus.

The twentieth century saw a shift of meaning here. Because the ways of dogmatics and exegesis had meanwhile moved so far apart, the battle had to be fought on another front. Exegetes trained in historical criticism no longer regarded dogma as a presupposition for their investigation. In this new context the term 'historical Jesus' was applied above all to events in the Gospels which can be shown by objective historical investigation really to have happened. On the basis of such investigation the modern exegete may be expected to be in a position by means of scientific methods to sketch out a reliable picture of the historical Jesus. However, caution and modesty are needed in the drawing of any conclusions. Anyone who makes use of historical methods can only create a 'historical Jesus'. By definition, the result of the investigation is limited. Beyond question, much more can be said about Jesus of Nazareth, but such statements lie beyond the scope of reliable scientific methods.[1]

Another Jesus

The dogma of the two natures of Christ was arrived at in the first centuries of church history. In the eighteenth century, Enlightenment thought created the historical Jesus. The moment when he was 'born' can be fixed precisely. It happened in May 1778, and from this date alone the historical Jesus may rightly be called 'a child of the Enlightenment'.[2]

In 1778 the well-known philosopher and writer Gotthold Ephraim Lessing (1729–1781) caused a great scandal with the publication of the last part of the posthumous work of a certain Hermann Samuel Reimarus (1694–1768). Little is known about the life of this scholar. He was not a theologian by profession, but taught oriental languages. The ideas of the Enlightenment had a great attraction for him and brought him into conflict with traditional Christianity. His ideas were not the subject of fierce polemic during his lifetime. Reimarus himself took care not to attract public attention. Probably for fear of reactions from orthodox circles, he did not publish the writings in which he had set down his fierce criticism on paper. Lessing knew Reimarus personally and thought his ideas so valuable that some years after his death he took the initiative of publishing his work posthumously.[3]

The last study to appear, which had been given the challenging title 'The Intentions of Jesus and his Disciples', is important for our theme. In it Reimarus argues that the origin of Christianity in fact rests on deceit. During his lifetime Jesus had a different 'intention' from that of his disciples after his death on the cross. He saw himself primarily as a political Messiah who regarded it as his most important task to liberate the Jewish people from Roman oppression. However, he failed, and with his cry on the cross, 'My God, my God, why have you forsaken me? (Mark 15.34), he acknowledged his failure. The disciples refused to recognize the destruction of their dreams and therefore they created belief in the resurrection of Jesus and exalted him to be the Son of God.[4]

Reimarus answered the question 'Who is Jesus?' in a way which differed markedly from previous answers. He went back not only behind dogma, but also behind the texts of the New Testament. From the perspective of historical scholarship, even the Gospels must be regarded as 'suspect'. Jesus himself left no writings. All that is known about his life is written in the Gospels. However, these works cannot be historically reliable, because they were only written 'in retrospect', after the execution of Jesus. Out of disappointment at the failure of their leader his disicples decided to put the recent past in another light. They deliberately blurred the boundaries between dream and reality, between their wishes and the historical facts. So they manipulated history and created a new image of their teacher. The result of this was that the Jesus whom we meet in the Gospels is someone other than the 'historical' Jesus of Nazareth who lived among the Jews at the beginning of the first century and was executed for his revolutionary attitude on the orders of the authorities.

Reimarus introduced a notion which since then has become one of the most important issues in the discussion of the historical Jesus. Whereas for centuries the continuity between the life of Jesus and the preaching of the early Christian community had been taken utterly for granted, Reimarus emphasized the discontinuity: in reality Jesus will have been a totally different Messiah from the Christ figure who is described in the Gospels.

A mythical Jesus

Who is Jesus? Reimarus and Lessing confronted theology and church with a question which touched the heart of Christian faith. At

23

all events, their 'attack' needed to be taken seriously. Is there no alternative than to choose between the Christ of dogma or the rebel Jesus who was nevertheless a failure, and whom Reimarus thought that he could discover behind the texts of the New Testament? From what follows it will prove that New Testament scholars sought possible ways of avoiding this dilemma.

Some decades later the problem became topical again with the publication of a book which provoked storms of protest. In 1835, *The Life of Jesus Critically Examined*[5] appeared, written by the young and learned David Friedrich Strauss (1808–1874). As a pupil of the eminent church historian and historian of dogma Ferdinand Christian Baur (1792–1860), who can be regarded as the great advocate of a theology which uses consistently historical methods,[6] Strauss not only trod in the footsteps of his teacher, but also thought that he could offer a solution to the dilemma mentioned above. He fought on two fronts. He denied the traditional view that the four Gospels present a true picture of Jesus Christ. But he also turned against the 'enlightened' theologians who, following Reimarus, thought that a distinction had to and indeed could be drawn between the historical Jesus and the Christ of church tradition.

In the footsteps of F.C.Baur, David Friedrich Strauss was a firm champion of the radical historical-critical investigation of the Bible. However, at the same time he was convinced that such biblical criticism could not pose a fundamental threat to the nucleus of Christian faith. Evangelists and apostles did not seek to publish dogmatic discourses, far less did they engage in historical investigation. They were not Christian dogmatic theologians, nor were they 'enlightened' historians either. They lived in a 'mythical world'. They knew its thoughts and ideas and they spoke its language. That was the context in which they wrote their Gospels and tried to put into words the meaning of Jesus Christ. Anyone who is content with a quest for the historical Jesus encounters a Jesus who is not essentially different from other human beings and who can be fitted into normal, human frameworks without too much difficulty.

However, Jesus was not 'ordinary'. He was unique. The evangelists expressed his unusual qualities 'mythically', by means of supernatural terms and images. Those who put questions to the Gospels which the authors never raised and to which they never wanted to give an answer may perhaps develop an attractive picture of Jesus which satisfies them, but in the end that will have little to do with the Christ who comes to us in the mythical language of the Gospels. Strauss thought that in this way he could 'rescue' Christian faith. He declared it in fact to be 'immune' to historical investigation. Moreover it was not very difficult for him to recognize the deep differences between the four Gospels. He did not see it as an obstacle that these differences make it almost impossible to produce a chronology of the life of Jesus. Christian faith is not dependent on a reconstruction of the past. It is not focussed on the historical Jesus, but towards the mythological Christ. Of course the mythical language of the New Testament is time-conditioned, but it does express the nucleus of Christian faith: the conquest of the natural by the spiritual, the temporal by the eternal, history by 'the idea'. Thus biblical myth gives expression to the 'Christ idea', in other words the eternal Christ. This eternal Christ has taken temporal form in the historical Jesus, but that is not the whole story. History goes on: the historical Jesus is a figure of the past, but the eternal Christ remains. The 'enlightened' person must learn to see that not one human being but the whole of humankind is central to the progress of world history.

The 'mythical dismantling' of the gospel by Strauss, and his spiritualization and dissolution of the historical, provoked a reaction. His battle on two fronts led to an attack on him from various sides. He was maligned in orthodox circles, but he was also criticized by 'enlightened theologians' who regarded historical criticism as a valuable means of investigating the Bible. They felt challenged to set their historical Jesus on a less disputed foundation.

In search of the earliest Gospel

Thus the investigation into the history of the four Gospels was given a powerful impetus. For centuries, the status of the Gospel of John was above all doubt. It was supposed to have been written by no less than the 'beloved disciple', of whom it was said that he 'reclined on Jesus' breast' (John 13.23) at the last supper of Jesus with his disciples. He appeared as the key witness. He was present by the cross at the death of Jesus (John 19.25–37).

It is not surprising that to an important degree the Fourth Gospel defined the classical view of Jesus and formed the basis of christological dogma. Jesus is the Son of God, one with the Father and sent by the Father, come down from heaven and made 'flesh' (John 1.14). Thus a divine and a human nature are united in one person. It was not seen as any great difficulty that the word 'nature' did not occur with this specific meaning anywhere in the New Testament.

The other New Testament writings did not seem to clash with this picture and moreover were also used as welcome supplements. The Gospel of Matthew was also rated highly for centuries. It was even given the honorific title of the church's Gospel. This was no coincidence: the Pope in Rome was fond of referring to Jesus' words of praise to Peter in support of his authority (Matt.16.13–20). Like John, Matthew too, the toll collector who was called and converted, was regarded as an important eye-witness to the life of Jesus. This was not true of the third evangelist, Luke, and already at an early stage of church history the shortest of the four Gospels, the Gospel of Mark, was held in least repute. The influential church father Augustine called this Gospel a summary of Matthew[7] and this statement seemed to be the final judgment. Why should one attach much importance to a work which was hardly more than an abbreviation – and moreover quite a bad abbreviation at that: no birth narratives, no Our Father, and so on – of a work which was also in the Bible?

During the nineteenth century, historical criticism of the Bible led to a decisive change in the traditional picture of the origin of the four Gospels. This development is worth noting, because it has consequences for the discussion of the historical Jesus. In the first place, already in the first half of the nineteenth century doubts began to grow about the historical reliability of the Fourth Gospel. If both John and Matthew had been eye-witnesses – as church tradition claimed – was that a satisfactory explanation for the deep-seated differences between the two writings? Increasing attention was paid by exegetes to the special character of the Fourth Gospel. It differed notably not only from Matthew, but equally from Mark and Luke. This produced the first dilemma with which historical criticism of the Gospels found itself faced: the three synoptic Gospels on one side and John on the other. Which writing(s) is (are) historically most reliable?

Slowly John, the supposed eye-witness, lost his normative position in this debate. The Fourth Gospel was not written by one of the very first disciples, but by a theologian from the early Christian community, a man who had written his work towards the end of the first century. He was convinced that the life of Jesus had meanwhile become completely a thing of the past. The unknown evangelist looked back, not to give an accurate historical account, but to offer his readers a helping hand with theological reflection on the past. New Testament scholarship, too, has its changes of fashion, but this view of the Fourth Gospel is still subscribed to by most exegetes.

That gave rise to a new question: if John cannot have the last word, then who can? The three synoptic Gospels also pose problems to the exegetes. After Johann Jacob Griesbach (1745–1812) produced his *Synopsis* of the Gospels according to Matthew, Mark and Luke in 1774, New Testament scholarship was more than ever before 'plagued' with the synoptic problem: anyone who compares Matthew, Mark and Luke will discover a complex combination of agreements and differences. There is no doubt that there are specific connections between the Gospels, and that the evangelists used one another's works as 'sources' – but which Gospel was 'source' and which evangelist used whose writings?

A maze of possibilities offered itself. Finally the view prevailed – the logic is attractive – that the shortest Gospel must also be the earliest. At any rate it is more likely that fellow evangelists added stories than that the author of the Gospel of Mark omitted parts, like the birth narratives and discourses of Jesus. This logical reasoning led to a notable rehabilitation of the short Gospel of Mark. From the middle of the nineteenth century it was no longer undervalued as a less successful summary of the great Gospel of Matthew. On the contrary, the 'little' Mark was in fact the creator of a new literary genre, the Gospel.[8]

Mark on Jesus

In 1863 a young scholar of thirty-one published a pioneering study on the synoptic Gospels.[9] His name was Heinrich Julius Holtzmann

(1832–1910). We shall meet him again later as one of the teachers of Albert Schweitzer in the theological faculty of the University of Strasbourg. Holtzmann may be seen as a scholar who put a very important stamp on developments within New Testament study in the second half of the nineteenth century. His study of the synoptic Gospels is still regarded as a milestone in their investigation.[10] He built on the discoveries of others, summed up their results and created a clear and convincing scientific foundation for the view that the Gospel of Mark is the earliest of the synoptic Gospels. Moreover, his investigation supported the notion that the evangelists Matthew and Luke used not only Mark but also a second common source. Holtzmann did his work so thoroughly that since then, when reading his term 'two-source hypothesis' many scholars have been inclined tacitly to scrap the word 'hypothesis' or to put it in brackets.[11]

Thanks to Holtzmann, investigation into the life of Jesus had gained some firm ground under its feet. From then on decisions could be made on the basis of a reliable historical document: the earliest Gospel. This solution to the synoptic problem had far-reaching consequences for christological reflection in the nineteenth and twentieth centuries. It is no exaggeration in this connection to speak of a definitive 'break' with the past. From the first centuries of church history it had become customary in dogmas and confessions to describe Jesus Christ as the truth 'from above': he is the pre-existent Son of God who has become man. 'Little' Mark necessitated a fundamental revision of traditional points of view. In contrast to the Fourth Gospel (John 1.18), Mark does not begin 'above', in heaven, but 'below', on earth. The evangelist bursts straight in. Nothing is said about the pre-existence of Jesus or about a special birth. Mark begins with the story of the adult John the Baptist, who attracts a great deal of attention. Those who have themselves baptized in the Jordan by John include a certain Jesus who comes from Nazareth in Galilee (Mark 1.9–11).

Who is this Jesus? The readers of the Gospel are given answers to this question, but these are not answers which allow them to develop a christology in the classical sense of the word. Rather, they are pointers which suggest that this Jesus of Nazareth is a special person. After his baptism in the Jordan a voice is heard from heaven which calls him 'my beloved son' (Mark 1.11). The man from Nazareth is addressed as 'son of God'. Is dogma then right, and is the Chalcedonian Definition a good solution to a complicated problem?

Theologians influenced by Enlightenment thought refused to give a positive answer to this question. A human being cannot be a 'Son of God', and a divine and a human nature cannot come together in one person. Jesus was a human being, a historical figure who lived at a particular moment in history. He differed from other human beings in being aware of living in a direct and close relation to God. He did not seek to found a new religion or a church. He proclaimed the imminent coming of the kingdom of God.

The kingdom in this world

It may be said to be typical of theological discussion in the second half of the nineteenth century that Jesus' preaching of the coming kingdom of God was interpreted in a totally new way. The 'enlightened' man could not longer accept the thought that the kingdom of God would appear like 'a thunderbolt from a clear sky'. In this situation theologians looked for possibilities of giving a new topical significance to age-old expectations about the future. They bade farewell to the classical notion of the sudden coming of the kingdom 'from above', like an unexpected flash of lighting which stops people in their tracks. It would not come as the consequence of a divine intervention in the course of events. Far less would it lead to a radical and dramatic change in heaven and earth.

Jesus preaches the coming of a kingdom which is realized within the framework of human history. It develops in this world in a slow process, lasting for centuries. 'Enlightenment' theology has an optimistic mood. The kingdom is not an unreal dream or a beautiful utopia, but an attainable ideal. Despite all wars, natural disasters and other terrors which can befall human beings, there is progress. History has a purpose. The human spirit is developing. 'Reason' is overcoming chaos; the understanding is overcoming ignorance and is abolishing those forms of religion which try to keep human beings in tutelage. Thus the kingdom of God is growing in this world: it is the final purpose of history.

Enlightened thought created an optimistic picture of human beings and the world, and theology developed in the same direction. The human being Jesus of Nazareth, a specially gifted personality, a religious genius, a man in whom the spirit of God was at work, was seen as the teacher of this kingdom of God. In scholarly literature this theological trend is usually described as the 'liberal theology' of the second half of the nineteenth century. In this connection the word 'liberal' means 'free', i.e. free from dogma and church authority and tolerant of other views and religious expressions. In this connection, there was also talk of 'culture Protestantism'. These developments were taking place above all in Germany.[12]

The life of Jesus

Who is Jesus? In the period of liberal theology it seemed relatively easy to answer this question. The classical dogma had been pushed aside, and thanks to historical criticism of the Bible a consensus had been arrived at over at least one literary source – the Gospel of Mark – which was regarded as historically reliable. The quest of the historical Jesus began from this position in the second half of the nineteenth century. This really was an exciting episode in the history of New Testament scholarship. Anyone who wants to examine the question of the historical Jesus cannot do so without going in depth into this investigation of the life of Jesus in the nineteenth century.

Of course it is neither necessary nor possible to sketch the results of this investigation in detail. A good deal has been forgotten and has disappeared under the rubble of history. However, at least one title seems to be an exception to the rule. In 1863, around 130 years ago, the French historian of religion and philologist Ernest Renan (1823–1892)[13] published his notorious *Life of Jesus*.[14] The book proved to be a best-seller of the first order. Reprints followed in France in rapid succession, and the work also aroused attention abroad. Ernest Renan was admired, but even more vilified and challenged in every conceivable way. To the bewilderment and wrath of many who had been accustomed to think and believe in traditional patterns, he described Jesus not in dogmatic terms as the Son of God but as a human being of flesh and blood, though he was a quite special man and moreover an unsurpassed preacher of a religion without dogmas. Renan did not proclaim any insights which could be said to be completely new, but he attracted attention from far outside the circle of initiates because he had literary style. He wrote a highly readable book about Jesus. His romantic, sentimental description did not fail to make a deep impression. However, his clear style also proved to have disadvantages. It was not difficult for his opponents to criticize his heretical ideas: 'Ernest Renan drove Jesus out of heaven.'

130 years ago a battle was fought over an issue which is still a live one today. What ideas about Jesus are justified by scripture and what 'pictures' of him definitively exceed the limits of what is theologically admissible and should be rejected as being in conflict with scripture and confession? Ernest Renan's book did not just cause difficulties in conservative circles. Theologians who were as attracted as he was by the quest of the historical Jesus expressed disappointment at his description of the life of Jesus. In contrast to the representatives of orthodoxy, these 'modern' theologians did not find him too critical, but felt that he had not been critical *enough*. In their view Renan was not meeting the requirements of historical criticism, and as a result it was impossible for him to give a good and reliable account of the life of Jesus in his book. He did not base himself on the synoptic Gospels, but sketched a picture of Jesus which more or less corresponded with that of the Fourth Gospel,[15] albeit stripped of its metaphysical features and overlaid with all kinds of contemporary feelings which had their roots not in the New Testament but in Romanticism.

This sharp, justified criticism of Ernest Renan was stated as early as 1864 by the Protestant theologian Timothée Colani (1824–1888).[16] He was active in Strasbourg in the 1860s, first as a preacher and later also as a professor of theology. Albert Schweitzer speaks with respect about Colani and calls him the spokesman of a new critical trend in French theology. The geographical location of Strasbourg on the border between France and Germany put Colani and those of a like mind in a position to keep up with developments in German theological faculties. As a young man he had been attracted by the quest of the historical Jesus.[17] His deep disappointment with Ernest Renan's 'romance' is to be explained by his efforts with the help of historical criticism to reconstruct a life of Jesus that was historically reliable and thus could be secured against the attacks of radical-critical scholars.[18] Colani had already won a prize at the age of twenty-three with a critical discussion of the famous book by David Friedrich Strauss. Certainly this work aroused more opposition than the study by Ernest Renan. For Strauss his 'success' had tragic consequences: he was not given a post at any of the German universities.[19] By contrast, Renan's life did not end in tragedy, though as a result of his ideas and books he initially forfeited a professorial chair. In 1870 he was rehabilitated and appointed professor of Semitic languages in Paris. In this position he made a name as a leading historian of religion and an expert in the languages of the ancient Near East. His nomination as a member of the Académie Française in 1878 indicates that he was respected and had made a career in the scholarly world.

At the end of this chapter we can note that the tensions were increasing. Differences of opinion were becoming greater. A consensus seemed more remote than ever. Faith and reason were virtually incompatible. There was a deep abyss between church dogma and historical criticism. If the first centuries of Christianity were dominated by the christological dispute which issued in the doctrine of the two natures of Christ, since the rise of Enlightenment thought in the seventeenth and eighteenth century a new 'christological' dispute had arisen: the problem of the historical Jesus. This dispute boiled up furiously. A satisfactory solution was still a distant ideal.

4

A Vain Quest for the Life of Jesus

Jesus in our image

Who is Jesus? Nineteenth-century liberal theology was convinced that classical christological dogma gave an unsatisfactory, out-of-date and time-conditioned answer to this question. It was necessary to follow the traces backwards and look behind dogmatic formulae for the authentic, historical Jesus. In this way a quest started in which many joined. They produced a sea of literature. This included academic studies which were mentioned and quoted in theological circles with respect, but also works which were based more on fantasy than on accurate investigation and at best could be described as historical romances. However, different though all these books were, their authors were striving after the same goal: they were trying to reconstruct the life of Jesus and they thought that it was possible to give a reliable description of the past. There was no unanimity over the literary sources that could be used. Exegetes opted predominantly for the two-source hypothesis and based themselves primarily on the Gospel of Mark. They represented the mainstream in the investigation, but they could not prevent other voices from also being heard.

In this context it is not necessary to discuss this literature at length. That was already done admirably a century ago. The polymath Albert Schweitzer (1875–1965), theologian, physician and musician, has shown convincingly the shortcomings and the failings of this investigation into the life of Jesus.[1] In a long book which appeared around the turn of the century he surveyed dozens of studies of the historical Jesus. His conclusion was that each author constructs his own 'Jesus'. There are as many authors as there are Jesuses. Anyone who is inspired by the ideals of socialism will sketch a portrait of

33

Jesus which makes him a forerunner of socialism. Anyone who belongs to the well-to-do middle-class and does not want to turn the existing order into chaos will not describe Jesus as a revolutionary. Anyone who thinks that society could be improved by a bloody revolution in which those in power definitely get what is coming to them will also look in the Gospels for stories which suggest a revolutionary disposition in Jesus. Romantics have a romantic Jesus; dreamers know Jesus as their 'master dreamer'; those who like beautiful things and have an aesthetic sense regard Jesus as an aesthete; those who want to turn their back on society and lead a wandering existence will point out that Jesus, too, had nowhere to lay his head.[2]

An apocalyptic Jesus

Albert Schweitzer wrote a gripping book, but in the end his readers were left with mixed feelings. Why have all the creativity and efforts of so many led to such a disappointing result? In his survey Schweitzer put his finger on the weak point. All authors, novelists and scholars made the same fundamental mistake. They sought the historical Jesus, but they saw him as their contemporary and did not take sufficient account of the fact that they were living centuries later. They were 'enlightened' men from Western Europe, whereas Jesus was born in a Jewish milieu at the beginning of our era. He grew up in a world which was dominated by scripture and tradition, and his trust in God had not yet been shaken by scientific thought. Anyone who believes it possible to 'modernize' Jesus without difficulty discovers that at the same moment Jesus escapes his or her grasp. Jesus disappears and returns to his own time.

Schweitzer emphasized that Jesus is a stranger to those who live in nineteenth-century Western European society. Those who have no eye for this 'stranger' create a Jesus in their own image: only those who are really aware of the distance that separates them from modern times will be able to find their way back to the historical Jesus. In his book, Albert Schweitzer called his own view of the life of Jesus 'the solution of thoroughgoing eschatology'.[3] This is a term which clarifies a good deal but can also give rise to misunderstand-

34

ing. Given the further course of the discussion it would be better had he spoken of 'thoroughgoing apocalyptic' rather than 'thoroughgoing eschatology'.

Schweitzer paints a fascinating picture of Jesus. He sees him as an apocalyptist who is completely driven by belief in the imminent coming of the kingdom of God. Jesus lived and died in this apocalyptic expectation of the future. He gradually arrived at the insight that by his suffering he could play a decisive role in the final apocalyptic drama that was in process of unfolding. For a good understanding of Schweitzer's view we need to pause a moment over his idiosyncratic view of the history of the origin of the synoptic Gospels.

Albert Schweitzer was a thinker who was not afraid to go his own way and to adopt a standpoint which did not fit easily with established views in scholarship and society. Among other places, he studied at the theological faculty of the University of Strasbourg and there went to lectures by the influential New Testament scholar Heinrich Julius Holtzmann, whom we have already met and who had written a fundamental study on the priority of the Gospel of Mark and the two-source hypothesis. Anyone with a teacher of this calibre might have been expected to follow him in every respect. However, it was inconceivable for a critical and independent student like Albert Schweitzer that he should limit himself to an attitude of reverent admiration and slavish imitation. In his autobiography *My Life and Thought*[4] he relates how he arrived at the discovery that the two-source hypothesis defended by Holtzmann could not be correct. While fulfilling his duties, in his free time he produced an essay which he presented to Holtzmann. Intensive study of Matthew 10 and 11 made him realize that an adequate description of the life of Jesus can be given only on the basis of 'thoroughgoing eschatology'. Jesus sends his disciples out after giving the mission discourse contained in Matthew. He charges them to go round the Jewish territory in order to proclaim the gospel of the kingdom of God there. They do not have much time, since Jesus seems convinced that the apocalyptic end of the world is near: 'When they persecute you in one town, flee to the next; for truly, I say to you, you will not have gone through all the towns of Israel, before the Son of man comes' (Matt.10.23).

35

This quotation has been called a key text in Albert Schweitzer's view. According to him the mission discourse in Matthew 10 contains a historically reliable account of the words and thoughts of Jesus. Schweitzer thought that he could see clear agreements with comparable pericopes in Jewish apocalyptic writings from the same period.[5]

Disappointing experiences

Jesus was a thoroughgoing apocalyptist who lived in a tense expectation of the imminent coming of the kingdom of God. It must have been an extraordinarily disappointing experience for him when his disciples returned without the kingdom of God having come. From that moment, Jesus increasingly felt that he himself *had to* risk his life for the sake of the coming of God's kingdom (Matt.16.21). In the apocalyptic expectation of the future the suffering of the pious and the righteous is seen as a necessary stage on the way to the end of the world. Just as the birth of a child is preceded by pangs which the mother must suffer, so the coming of the kingdom of God is preceded by 'messianic woes', the pain which the world and humankind, but above all the pious and the righteous, must suffer. It was this apocalyptic 'dogma' that Jesus applied to himself when he had the deep disappointment of his disciples returning without the apocalyptic scenario having been realized in one way or another. At that moment Jesus saw it as his task to go the way of suffering. In this way he hoped to force the coming of the kingdom of God.

That was the mood in which he went to Jerusalem, and on the way he prepared his disciples for the worst. After a powerful inner struggle, he finally accepted the way of suffering once for all (Matt.26.36–46). He died in unshaken trust in the coming of the kingdom of God. He refused the drink which could have dulled his pain, because at that decisive moment he wanted to retain complete consciousness. Jesus counted on the coming of the kingdom of God to the very last. Even on the cross his hope had not yet completely disappeared.[6] He died, but the kingdom of God still had not come. His suffering and death did not change the course of events. History went on as before.

A tragic failure?

Did Jesus make a wretched mistake? To this tricky question, in the first instance Albert Schweitzer gives a positive answer. Within the presuppositions of the Jewish apocalyptic expectation of the future Jesus indeed made a mistake. Despite his suffering and death the kingdom of God did not come. So must the whole of Jesus's life be described as a tragic failure? To this question Schweitzer gives a negative answer. The 'strange', apocalyptic Jesus who lived in the land of the Jews at the beginning of our era and died on the cross can at the same time be significant for people who, many centuries later, live in a completely different world. The stranger he is to us, the more we seem to be able to learn from him. The more we see him as a 'child of his time', the greater his significance for our time becomes.

Jesus gave the coming kingdom of God a central place in his life. He refused to make compromises, but wanted only to respond to commandments which would apply in the coming kingdom. In a unique way he was far ahead of his time. He already lived in the kingdom, though it was not yet a reality. But he dared to anticipate this future and give the kingdom form in word and deed. Albert Schweitzer was deeply convinced that the attitude of Jesus is of great importance and remains so for all times and all peoples. Moreover it is not surprising – and a cause for no less admiration – that Schweitzer decided to devote his life to the poorest people in Africa. Soon after the outbreak of the First World War he left Europe and founded a hospital in Lambarene.

Albert Schweitzer's 'thoroughgoing eschatology' had consequences for his christological views. In classical dogma there was no place for the idea that Jesus made a mistake over the coming of the kingdom of God. For centuries Jesus had been presented as the Son of God who knew what awaited him and did not seek and accept suffering in a desperate attempt, but saw it as his task to die on the cross for the sins of humankind. In orthodox circles the name of Schweitzer was mentioned with respect, but generally speaking people made no secret of the fact that they saw his view of christology as a prime example of freethinking and rejected it out of hand. Schweitzer felt that he could no longer believe in the Christ of confession and dogma, but he was inspired by the apocalyptic Jesus who seemed ready to allow his life to be governed completely by the coming kingdom of God.

From a study published posthumously it seems that the large amount of criticism which Schweitzer had to endure made little impression on him. He remained true to himself to the end of his life.[7] However, with one exception,[8] theologians could not accept his view of Jesus as the apocalyptic prophet of the kingdom of God. The dilemma which Schweitzer had put before theology and the church was clear: did Christian dogma have its roots in the apocalyptic *expectation* of God's judgment, or did it find its origin in the belief that the cross and resurrection may be said to be the *fulfilment* of the saving promises of God?

No renewal

Albert Schweitzer did not create a school, but nevertheless his investigation of the historical Jesus had a decisive influence for a long time. His own view found little echo, but his writings were taken to heart. His acute analysis of the result of the investigation into the life of Jesus during the nineteenth century is mentioned in every christological study down to the present day. While people adopted an uncritical – not to say naive – approach at that time, this can certainly not be said to be the case today. That is the lesson that Schweitzer has taught us. Thanks to his book, every theologian needs to realize that it is irresponsible to commandeer Jesus all too easily and as a matter of course for the views and standpoints of our day.[9]

Schweitzer did not have much of a following. He came under fire from two sides. His apocalyptic Jesus was a source of scandal for orthodox believers. However, because he had adopted an idiosyncratic standpoint over the solution of the synoptic problem, he gained little approval from the circle of historical-critical exegetes either. Despite all the appreciation that people had of him, he was accused of having in fact done the same thing as all those whom he had criticized. In his book he did not call for an end to the investigation of the life of Jesus. Contrary to his words of warning, he continued to think that the Gospels make it possible for us to have access to the historical Jesus. His option for the Gospel of Matthew was remarkable, but the way in which he used this writing as a source did not differ from the way in which his contemporaries used the Gospel of Mark.

When Albert Schweitzer completed his study of the quest of the historical Jesus, the twentieth century was just dawning. In more than one respect he found himself on the frontier of two worlds. It is tempting to give him a place at the beginning of a new period of theological investigation. However, that does not seem advisable. Schweitzer's view of the possibility of reconstructing the life of Jesus ultimately stamps him as a man of the nineteenth century. He criticized his predecessors sharply, his warnings were justified, but he brought no renewal.

5

From Optimism to Scepticism

The source Q

A historian needs sources. The past cannot be mapped out without documents: archives, accounts, chronicles, letters, personal testimonies, etc. Here the researcher is confronted with the difficulty that not all sources are equal and that they do not have the same value or significance. Moreover, historical investigation cannot avoid the assessment of sources, 'weighing' them and classifying them. The New Testament scholar who wants to describe the life of Jesus in a scholarly way is confronted with a similar task. Choices have to be made. Those who opt for the two-source hypothesis face a new and burdensome dilemma. Central to this hypothesis is the presupposition that the evangelists Matthew and Luke made use of *two sources*: the Gospel according to Mark and a second common source which is indicated in scholarly literature by the letter Q.[1]

What can be said about the *content* of the Q source? Was it a writing comparable to the four canonical Gospels? Unfortunately no satisfactory answer can be given to these questions. New Testament research must necessarily move in the realm of speculation and hypothesis. It is not even certain whether there ever was a written Q source. And if that was the case, then yet other problems arise. Supposing that the Q source consisted of the texts which Matthew and Luke have in common and which are not in the Gospel of Mark, then Q would have been a 'Gospel' without a passion narrative. Is that conceivable?

It is also possible that Matthew and Luke made selections from Q, each in his own way. In that case the original Q source could have been considerably more extensive than the reconstruction which Matthew and Luke now allow us to make. Moreover this reconstruction, too, raises countless problems. When Matthew and Luke together follow the Gospel of Mark, they seem to show more agreements with each other than when they use Q as a source. On the basis of this fact there are exegetes who imagine the Q source not so much as a rounded written text but rather as a dynamic process of tradition, a 'stream' of both oral and written tradition. Within the 'fluid' Q source it is said to be possible to distinguish different 'levels', the result of ongoing theological reflection.[2]

Mark or Q?

The possession of two sources presents the historian with new problems. There are no problems when the sources do not contradict each other, but when they do, a choice has to be made. Which of the two sources is the most reliable? To begin with, it did not seem difficult to choose between the Gospel of Mark and the Q source. It was natural to give Mark priority. His Gospel was the earliest writing, and there was every reason to suppose that it was also the earliest source. In the second half of the nineteenth century, interest in Q increased and the possibility was no longer ruled out that the Q source could be earlier than the Gospel of Mark. This dilemma is not without significance for the question of the historical Jesus. Anyone who reads the Gospel of Mark alongside a reconstruction of Q will discover striking differences between the two sources. Mark tells *stories* about Jesus: Jesus healed the sick, drove out evil spirits and did miracles; he did not shun the company of sinners and tax-collectors; he engaged in disputes with Pharisees and representatives of other religious groups and parties in the Jewish world of those days. Moreover Mark gives a detailed account of the suffering and death of Jesus in Jerusalem.

In the texts which Matthew and Luke presumably derived from Q, another Jesus takes the stage. Nothing is said about his suffering and dying. He does not deliver any long monologues, but by means of short sayings makes his audience think and arouses them to conversion. On closer inspection the picture of Jesus in the Q source is remarkably ambivalent. He is characterized as an apocalyptic prophet who lives in the awareness that the end of the world is near;

41

however, he is also a wisdom teacher who does not concentrate on the future but on the present.

Who is Jesus? Is his life to be reconstructed on the basis of the Gospel of Mark or on that of Q? After reading what has been said above, readers will understand that research in fact has to face a burdensome dilemma. On the basis of the earliest Gospel Jesus can be described as a preacher of the approaching kingdom of God, a man with special gifts, a charismatic, a miracle-worker and exorcist. He provoked opposition and he came into conflict with the established powers. Therefore he was condemned and died on the cross. A description of Jesus on the basis of the Q source produces a different picture of him. Nothing is said of his suffering and dying. The cross plays no role. The *words* of Jesus are central in the Q tradition. Anyone who takes these words to heart will be saved.

Adolf von Harnack[3]

In the winter semester of 1899/1900 an event took place in Berlin which must be mentioned in any survey of the discussions of the historical Jesus. The date is highly symbolic. The nineteenth century was almost over and the twentieth century was at the door. Was there reason to regard the new century with great optimism? In the nineteenth century New Testament scholarship had freed itself from the constricting bonds of dogmatic presuppositions and gone in search of the authentic, the historical Jesus. Now that this century was over, it made sense to draw up a balance sheet.

This event which calls for our attention is also significant for people living almost a century later. It may be regarded as the high-point of 'liberal theology' in Germany. Before an audience of around 600 students from different faculties, Adolf von Harnack (1853–1930) gave a series of sixteen lectures on 'The Essence of Christianity' (in the English translation, the book arising from these lectures was called *What is Christianity?*). Beyond question the speaker was one of the great theologians of his time. He produced countless authoritative studies relating to early Christianity and the history of dogma. However, although he enjoyed international fame in academic circles, his position in the church in Germany was controversial.[4]

Harnack was regarded as one of the most important representatives of modern theology. In the 1880s he had provoked a storm of protest when he took sides in a conflict over the ongoing importance of the Apostles' Creed.[5] In his contribution to the discussion he declared quite publicly that some passages in the Apostles' Creed had become unacceptable to modern Christians. Here he referred in particular to the statement about the virgin birth of Jesus. There was great indignation in orthodox circles and his reputation was permanently tainted there. That was clear when at the end of 1887 there was a proposal to appoint Harnack as professor of church history and the history of dogma in the theological faculty of the University of Berlin. This proposal immediately provoked opposition. However, Harnack's academic qualities were so great that the nomination could not be prevented, though his opponents succeeded in creating alongside him – as a kind of counter-balance – a new chair which was occupied by a scholar who enjoyed the trust of church circles: Adolf Schlatter (1852–1938), an orthodox figure who was respected by friend and foe in the sphere of the scholarly exegesis of the New Testament.[6]

Without exaggeration it can be said that in the autumn of 1899 the man speaking in the lecture hall in Berlin could be regarded as the embodiment of the special combination of German culture and theology expressed in the term 'culture Protestantism'. Harnack's lectures were also regarded as a special event by his contemporaries. He spoke without notes, extempore, as he so often did, but to his surprise his words were preserved for posterity through a stenographic account made by one of those present, without his knowledge. There was much interest in the printed text. The book went through more than fifteen reprints and was translated into fourteen languages.

'The kingdom is in your midst'

It is no coincidence that Harnack's lectures on 'the essence of Christianity' provoked memories of the famous *Speeches on Religion* which Friedrich Schleiermacher (1768–1834) had written a century earlier in 1799, and which was at first published anonymously. Schleiermacher, too, had concentrated on the nucleus of Christian faith, and he intended his 'speeches' for 'cultured' people, i.e. people who were already so influenced by 'enlightened' ideas that they tended to look down on church and religion as outdated phenomena.[7] A century later Harnack was in fact pursuing the same, apologetic,[8] aim. He, too, hoped that he could convince his audience, consisting of students from different fields of study, that the Christian faith, once purged of unacceptable notions, is still worth the attention of modern, educated, men and women. In his own words, he surrendered all kinds of strongholds of Christian tradition – like belief in miracles, in the resurrection, etc. – in order to be able to defend the last stronghold.

Unconcernedly, Adolf von Harnack distanced himself from classical dogma and then called on his audience to return to the source of Christian faith: the gospel of Jesus Christ. This programme seems simple, but the way to the goal proves long and complicated. At the beginning of the series of lectures Harnack gives his view of the sources available for the investigation. He can be brief about the letters of Paul: they play no significant role in this question. The same is true of the Fourth Gospel. Here Harnack does not hesitate to point out the great significance of this work for the study of early Christianity. It discloses the 'effect' of the gospel of Jesus Christ on the Christian community. Finally, Harnack explains that his description of the historical Jesus is based on the three synoptic Gospels. Remarkably, he does not dwell further on the synoptic question, though he did go into this problem in a study which was published later, and into the possibility that the Q source could be earlier than the Gospel of Mark.[9]

Harnack was an eminent scholar, but like all human beings he was also a child of his time. For him, as a typical representative of liberal theology, the essence of Christian faith was Jesus' preaching of the kingdom of God. At the centre of this preaching stood not the person of Jesus Christ but the God whom Jesus chose to address as 'Father'. In the fierce discussions provoked by his comments in the first years of the twentieth century, Harnack was sometimes accused of having excised Jesus from the gospel. He could not deny this charge, but nevertheless brushed it aside with an easy conscience. He was convinced that Jesus' preaching concentrated on the realization of the kingdom of God. Nothing is to be found in his words of all the thoughts and ideas that the early Christian community and the later dogmatic tradition thought that it could attribute to him.

Adolf von Harnack and Albert Schweitzer seem to be kindred spirits, but they were not. Both scholars gave the kingdom of God a central place in the preaching of Jesus, but they interpreted it quite differently. Harnack opposed the notion – which Schweitzer defended forcibly – that God's kingdom has to be regarded as an eschatological or even an apocalyptic concept. In his lectures Harnack emphasizes that the kingdom develops within human history. It does not come suddenly in the future, but is already present in this world now. A text which Harnack was fond of citing appears in the Gospel according to Luke, 'For lo, the kingdom of God is within you' (Luke 17.21).

An 'un-Jewish' Jesus

In fact, Albert Schweitzer and Adolf von Harnack were not kindred spirits. It does not do either of them an injustice to put them at opposite poles. For Schweitzer, Jesus was an apocalyptist who was a complete stranger to modern, Western European men and women. By contrast, in his lectures Harnack prefers to describe Jesus as a teacher of exalted ideals, a prophet of progress in the Western world, who proclaimed a kingdom of God which may not be depicted in apocalyptic colours, but is realized in our world and therefore can sometimes even be seen or felt.[10]

As an influential representative of German 'culture Protestantism', Harnack was an optimist. He looked hopefully to the future and believed that humankind could attain a higher spiritual level. He gave the preaching of Jesus a place in that 'contemporary' view of the world. The expectation of the kingdom of God indeed came from the Old Testament, but in the words of Jesus it took on a deeper spiritual meaning. Harnack drew an unmistakable distinction between the two Testaments. He did not begin from any continuity, but emphasized the discontinuity. The New Testament is not only different from, but is also more than, the Old Testament. Jesus' preaching of the kingdom of God has a universal focus, and in it he goes beyond the limits drawn by the religious customs and ideas of ancient Israel and those described in the Old Testament. Moreover, the conclusion must be that the 'essence' of Christianity has a loftier content than the 'essence' of Judaism. The Old Testament was given only a marginal role in Harnack's lectures. He showed just as little interest in the early Jewish writings from the inter-testamental period and spoke negatively about the Judaism of the time of Jesus.[11] In theological terms he was regarded as progressive, but in his negative evaluation of the Old Testament and Jewish tradition he was a child of his time. The book which he published at the beginning of the 1920s is typical of his view: a magisterial but also controversial study of Marcion,[12] the man whom the church declared a heretic in the second century, because he defended the view that the Old Testament could not function within the Christian community as Holy Scripture. Marcion regarded himself as a follower of Paul and thought it his task to bring out the consequences of the apostle's letters. Starting from the radical opposition between 'law' and gospel, Marcion stated that it was impossible for Jesus Christ to have been sent by the God of the Old Testament. In the words and actions of Jesus he thought that he found a 'strange' God, hitherto unknown, a God who unlike the God of the Old Testament made mercy, love and grace prevail over punishment, justice and vengeance. However, the world has been created by the God of the Old Testament. This God has put his stamp on the stories in the Old Testament writings, which are stories full of horrors and atrocities, stories about a world dominated by a thirst for blood and violence. They are realistic stories which reflect reality, but offer no hope of change and renewal. Other stories are told in the New Testament, stories about redemption and liberation brought about by a gracious God who loves the sinner.

Harnack admired Marcion, but he did understand why Marcion was declared a heretic by the church in the second century. The man was too far ahead of his time. It was far more difficult for Harnack to accept that Luther in particular had not drawn the final consequences of his rediscovery of the central place occupied by God's grace in the letters of Paul. At the time of the Reformation the church should have resolved to reject the Old Testament as scripture. This did not happen, so Harnack argued that this decision should be taken in the twentieth century. The time had come to tread resolutely in the footsteps of Marcion and finally bid a definitive farewell to the Old Testament.[13] This plea was a logical consequence of his view of the origin of Christianity. Certainly Jesus was born a Jew, but with his preaching of the kingdom of God he emphatically went beyond the bounds of the Old Testament and the early Jewish tradition.

An end to optimism

Around the turn of the century, Albert Schweitzer and Adolf von Harnack, each in his own way, brought to an end the optimistic period of the investigation of the life of Jesus. Adolf von Harnack did so by sketching out with great conviction and glittering words a picture of Jesus as a prophet of social progress who proclaimed a gospel that was more than the 'legalism' of the Old Testament and the early Jewish tradition. Harnack had a great deal of success. When his lectures appeared as a book it became a real bestseller. However, he met not only with approval but also with a great deal of criticism. His views caused indignation, and numerous opponents put down their objections on paper.

Around ten years later Europe had turned into a terrible battlefield. All dreams of progress were suddenly forgotten, and optimistic feelings died a horrible death in the trenches of the First World War (1914–1918). Another picture of Jesus became current. He no longer pointed the way to high ideals, but issued a summons to comradeship and a readiness for sacrifice: 'Greater love has no man than to lay down his life for his friends' (John 15.13) – quite specifically, these friends could be comrades in the trenches.

Albert Schweitzer brought the period of the investigation into the life of Jesus to a close by showing its shortcomings. He contrasted an 'assimilated' Jesus with his apocalyptic Jesus. Thanks to Schweitzer, in the twentieth century Jesus' preaching of the kingdom of God has become one of the most important themes in New Testament scholarship. Schweitzer's contribution to the discussion called for a reply. His 'thoroughgoing eschatology' may rightly be described as a stone in the theological pool. His portrayal of an 'apocalyptic' Jesus made an impact, but also provoked opposition, and in this way for many people proved a stimulus to go once again in search of the significance of the expectation of the kingdom of God.

47

Albert Schweitzer was a man who could not be content with treading well-trodden paths. The other side of the coin is that his influence on New Testament theology remained limited. His view of the origin of the Gospels found little or no echo. At present, no one any longer seems to defend his view that the discourse in Matt. 10 is the way to the historical Jesus.[14] But all this does not mean that after a century Albert Schweitzer's book is only valuable as an antique and is no more than a collector's item for those interested in the history of New Testament scholarship. His voice admonishing caution can be heard in almost every study devoted to christology, whether written from an exegetical or from a dogmatic perspective.[15]

Anyone familiar with the results of Schweitzer's investigation will know that it is impossible to sketch out a biographical portrait of Jesus on the basis of the four Gospels which is free from presuppositions, from personal hopes and desires. Thanks to Schweitzer, and thanks also to the 'form criticism'[16] of the New Testament, there is a widespread realization that the Gospels are not biographies – at least in the modern sense of the word.[17] They are not suited to serve as sources for the reconstruction of an objective and historically reliable picture of Jesus.

The consequences are obvious. Albert Schweitzer's warnings against optimism in the second half of the nineteenth century led to pessimism in the twentieth century. Little could be said with certainty about the life of Jesus, and from a scholarly point of view it seemed advisable for people to keep silent about those things of which they could no longer be certain.

6

The Kerygmatic Christ

The sources under fire

Which source is historically reliable? Is it Mark, is it Matthew or is it Q? Around the turn of the century the optimism of the nineteenth century was slowly drowned by pessimistic voices. Historical-critical investigation of the Bible did not stand still. Knowledge about the origin of the Gospels increased. Exegetes increasingly realized that in the light of new developments within New Testament scholarship the answer to this question of reliability had to be a complicated one. Three names need to be mentioned in this connection.

First, William Wrede (1859–1906). He challenged the most important pillar in the quest of the historical Jesus in the nineteenth century. As we know, the Gospel of Mark was given much credit as a historically reliable document. The two-source hypothesis regarded it as the earliest of the synoptic Gospels, and as such it was said to be a possible basis for a reconstruction of the life of Jesus. Wrede produced objections to this view. He thought that he could show that even the earliest Gospel did not contain an objective historical description of the past. Thus it seemed typical of Mark that Jesus consistently avoided the question of his messiahship. He constantly required silence not only from his disciples (Mark 8.30), but also from the sick whom he healed (Mark 1.44; 5.43; 7.36) and the evil spirits which seemed to know him (Mark 1.25; 3.12). From this Wrede deduced that Mark was not particularly interested in an accurate description of historical events but that on the basis of his belief in the Risen Lord he was giving a theologically coloured interpretation of the past. The evangelist created the 'dogma' of the 'messianic secret' as a last resort.[1] In this way Wrede sought to offer an explanation of the enigmatic fact that Jesus had not presented himself as Messiah during his lifetime. He refused to claim this role and he asked others to be silent because he feared being misunderstood. He saw it as a real danger that his contemporaries would want to see him exclusively as a 'political' Messiah.

The second name which deserves mention is that of the influential biblical scholar Julius Wellhausen (1844–1918). Although he was originally an Old Testament scholar, Wellhausen produced important results in the historical criticism of the New Testament. He thought that the Gospels must be seen as sources for the history of the early church. He did not deny that they could also be of value for the reconstruction of the life of Jesus,[2] but this was a secondary matter. With his thesis he paved the way which was explored later by Rudolf Bultmann, who introduced great changes in the process.[3]

Finally, I should mention the pioneering work of Karl Ludwig Schmidt (1881–1956). In 1919 he published a study which formed the basis of the 'form-critical' investigation of the New Testament. Schmidt showed that by far the greatest part of the three synoptic Gospels – an exception needs to be made for the passion narratives – consists of pericopes which show little connection between one another. They are like the beads or pearls on a necklace the clasp of which has been broken. It is thanks to the redactional activity of the evangelists that readers of the Bible nevertheless think that they have an undamaged chain and regard the Gospels as an account of the actions and life of Jesus in chronological order. They collected 'loose' stories about Jesus from oral tradition and then gave them a framework, ultimately producing an apparently consecutive whole with verses in which they gave largely fictitious geographical and other details. Beyond question Karl Ludwig Schmidt's study sounded the knell for the quest of the historical Jesus. Whereas in the nineteenth century exegetes were inclined to accept the facts in the 'frameworks' as historically reliable, Schmidt pointed out that the facts in these verses could not form a basis for a reconstruction of the life of Jesus.[4]

The 'so-called' historical Jesus

Historical investigation needs sources, the reliability of which can be checked. With this ideal the New Testament scholars of the nineteenth century also went in search of the historical Jesus. Around the beginning of the twentieth century doubt arose as to the viability of this investigation. The sources proved less reliable than had been supposed. All the evangelists wrote after Easter. They were believers, and so they too looked to the past, to the time before Easter and the life of Jesus. Their accounts of the past could not be 'objective'. Thus slowly the awareness penetrated New Testament scholarship that historically speaking exegetes were groping in the dark. Jesus lived, but the historical Jesus remains unattainable and it is impossible to portray him. In the end the historian stands with empty hands.

In 1892, and thus well before the lectures of Adolf von Harnack and Albert Schweitzer's account of 'the quest', a remarkable book appeared which did not receive at this time the attention which it deserved. It was written by Martin Kähler (1835–1912), a theologian who moved on the frontiers between New Testament, biblical theology and dogmatics.[5] Kähler gave his book the evocative title *The So-called Historical Jesus and the Historic, Biblical Christ.*[6] The Bible formed his starting point in another work, too, and he argued for biblical-theological solutions to modern questions. Thus in the debate over the value of the Old Testament for the Christian church – a topical theme in those days – he tried to provide a christological basis for defending the unity of the two Testaments. In any case, Jesus had regarded the Old Testament as his Bible and used it. Moreover, the Old Testament writings relate that God's saving work in Jesus Christ has been prepared for in the history of the people of Israel.[7]

In the discussion of the historical Jesus Kähler seeks where possible to avoid the well-known dilemma of 'Enlightenment thought' – either the 'authentic', historical Jesus or the 'dogmatic' Christ. In the title of his book Kähler speaks with good reason of the *so-called* historical Jesus. In his view, it is a misconception to think it possible and necessary to tread the path into the past. Christian faith cannot and may not be made dependent on historical investigation. Moreover, the Gospels are not suitable to serve as the basis for a scientifically reliable biography of Jesus. The evangelists did not write historical studies, but through their Gospels hoped to arouse and strengthen faith in Jesus Christ.

According to Kähler, theology and church must not allow themselves to be drawn into the debate over this 'so-called historical Jesus'. It is no longer possible to go back behind the Gospels to the 'real' Jesus. Therefore Christian faith needs to concentrate on the *biblical* Christ'. The foundation is not historical investigation, far less later dogmatic reflection, but the biblical testimony to Jesus Christ. Those who follow this way free themselves from the straitjacket of history and dogma. According to Kähler, what is ultimately central in the New Testament is not Jesus' preaching of the kingdom of God, but the message of the crucified Christ. On the basis of this it could be said that the doctrine of reconciliation and justification is the nucleus of biblical theology.

In his time, Martin Kähler stood comparatively alone in his view of the significance of 'the biblical Christ'. Some decades later his ideas were taken over and further developed by Rudolf Bultmann. Albert Schweitzer showed the failure of the quest of the historical Jesus. Martin Kähler went further. He criticized the presupposition of ninteenth-century liberal theology that it was possible to give Christian faith a historical foundation. For this reason he propounded a 'third' way.[8]

Rudolf Bultmann

The name of Rudolf Bultmann (1884–1976)[9] has already been mentioned once in this book. That is not surprising, since he was a decisive influence on developments in twentieth-century New Testament theology. Almost all the lines from the past come together in him, and he inspired many people to go further along the way that he marked out. He was so influential that he founded a school. For all these reasons it is worth giving a more detailed account of his views.

First Bultmann occupied himself with the origin of the Gospels. Together with Karl Ludwig Schmidt, who has already been mentioned, and Martin Dibelius (1883-1947), Bultmann formed a trio which in the 1920s and 1930s pioneered the 'form-critical' investigation of the Gospels. As we already saw, the synoptic Gospels – passion narratives apart – are constructed of originally loose pericopes which were linked by the evangelists to form a consecutive account of the life of Jesus. The conclusion is unavoidable: form criticism marks the end of the quest of the historical Jesus. The evangelists were not historians in the modern sense of the word. They collected stories and provided them with linking texts. Only a small number of these stories will go back to the time before Easter. The majority arose in the early Christian community as an answer to questions of faith and as a legitimation of its deviations from the Jewish tradition and their rejection of some commands in the Torah (like the observance of the Sabbath and certain regulations about purity). Therefore nothing can be found in these – literally unconnected – stories which can provide any kind of reliable account of the psychology of Jesus, of developments in his thought or of any growing awareness of a special relationship with God.

A Messiah who did not want to be Messiah

Bultmann was more aware than anyone that the Gospels in the New Testament may not be read as biographies of Jesus. However, that did not prevent him from writing a book of his own on Jesus in the 1920s.[10] It was published in a series of biographies of influential figures from human history. Bultmann remained sceptical, but nevertheless he thought it possible to sketch out a profile of Jesus on the basis of the synoptic Gospels.

Time passed. Since then seventy years have elapsed. But it is still worth reading this Jesus book. Bultmann criticized the quest of the historical Jesus, but at the same time he stood in the tradition of nineteenth-century liberal theology. So he, too, began from Jesus' humanity. The result was that all those facets of the Gospel texts could be rejected as unhistorical which have a metaphysical character and are difficult if not impossible to reconcile with modern scientific thought. That applies to Jesus' pre-existence and virgin birth, his miracles and his resurrection and ascension. None of this was completely new. In the nineteenth century, exegetes trained in historical criticism had already arrived at more or less similar statements.

Starting from the humanity of Jesus, moreover, Bultmann thought that he had to deliver a negative verdict on the historicity of the three announcements of the passion in the synoptic Gospels (Mark 8.31;

9.31; 10.32–33). He came to the same conclusion about the texts in which Jesus' messiahship is presupposed (Mark 8.29–30; Mark 14.61–62). Bultmann was certain that the man Jesus could never have foreseen or announced his suffering and death in Jerusalem, and that the biblical texts which suggest this must be attributed to the early Christian community. According to him, the announcements of the passion were put into the mouth of Jesus by the community after the cross and resurrection.[11]

Bultmann treated statements about Jesus' messiahship in the same way. Among other things, it can be argued from Paul's letters that after Easter it very soon became customary to add the title 'Christ' to the name Jesus. Moreover this title was projected back on to Jesus' life: he died as the crucified Christ (I Cor.15.3–4; I Cor.2.2), he lived as Christ (II Cor.5.16), and he was also born as Christ (Matt.1.18). Thus the proclaimer of the kingdom of God subsequently became the Christ of the Christian proclamation, and the early Christian community put the 'un-messianic' life of Jesus in a 'messianic' perspective.[12] According to Bultmann, it was impossible for Jesus to have seen himself as the Messiah. He emphatically distanced himself from such expectations because he had another view of his task. His Jewish contemporaries pinned their hopes on the coming of a royal Messiah, an offshoot of the family of David with the political aim of fighting against the Roman occupying forces and restoring the famous dynasty of his distant forefather.[13] Jesus did not seek this battle. He was not the leader of a group of guerrillas. He certainly did not want to be such a Messiah. Royal pretensions were alien to him, nor did he die on the battlefield. The fact that he died on the cross should be seen as a tragic mistake: he was executed as a political rebel, which was not what he wanted to be.

Eschatology

Jesus did not see himself as the Messiah. He was a human being and not 'son of God'. In his Jesus book Bultmann primarily describes him as the prophet of the coming kingdom of God. Now one might naturally conclude that what Bultmann was saying was not much of an advance on Albert Schweitzer. And indeed one could also call Bultmann's interpretation of Jesus' proclamation of the kingdom of

God 'thoroughgoing eschatology'. However, there is a striking difference between the two theologians. I wrote earlier that the use of the term 'thoroughgoing eschatology' by Albert Schweitzer was to give rise to misunderstandings and would have been better replaced by 'thoroughgoing apocalyptic'.

Bultmann agrees with Schweitzer that the proclamation of the coming kingdom of God has a central position in the life and thought of Jesus. But Bultmann refuses to regard Jesus as an apocalyptist. To avoid any misunderstanding he opts for the term 'eschatology' – and at the same time creates new misunderstandings. He describes Jesus' expectation of the coming kingdom of God as 'eschatological'. By that he means that Jesus, unlike Jewish apocalyptic, is not particularly interested in the 'signs of the times', but puts all the emphasis on human actions. Moreover, Jesus' preaching is not concerned with these 'signs' – Bultmann attributes texts in the Gospels with such an emphasis, like Mark 13, to the later community. Jesus does not draw the attention of his contemporaries to 'signs of the times', but summons them to convert in view of the approach of the kingdom of God (Mark 1.14–15).

The cross

The material is complex. Bultmann is writing a Jesus book, but he does not think the question of the historical Jesus of essential importance for Christian faith. His view was that historical research cannot and may not either confirm or deny faith. Moreover, he saw no reason to regret the fact that the image of Jesus often becomes so vague as to be not much more than the shadow of a prophet who had announced the imminent coming of the kingdom of God. In the confrontation between the historical Jesus and the Christ who is proclaimed in the Bible, Bultmann allied himself with Kähler, and opted for the biblical Christ. Unlike Kähler, he did not speak of 'the biblical' Christ but seems to have preferred the term 'the kerygmatic Christ' – the Greek word *kerygma* means proclamation: Christ in the proclamation of the early Christian community. The Gospels are not historical accounts but Easter stories. On the basis of its belief in the Risen Lord the Christian community did not turn to the past, but to the present. Therefore the Gospels gives us no access to the historical Jesus, but offer a picture of the faith of the early Christian community in the kerygmatic Christ.[14]

In his criticism of the theological relevance of the nineteenth-century quest of the historical Jesus, Bultmann thought that he could count on the support of no less an authority than Paul.[15] In one of his letters the apostle had written a passage which is both striking and mysterious: 'From now on, therefore, we know no one after the flesh. If we once knew *Christ after the flesh*, now we know him so no longer' (II Cor.5.16). The question is: precisely what did Paul mean by the words 'know Christ after the flesh'? This is a phrase which can be interpreted in more than one way: does 'flesh' belong with 'know' or with 'Christ'?[16] Anyone who opts for the second possibility has to give an explanation of the term 'Christ after the flesh'. Was the apostle already warning against the misconception that historical research could be of importance for theology? Was Paul really so far ahead of his time?

As Schweitzer taught us, Jesus did not live in the nineteenth or twentieth century, and the same is of course also true of the apostle Paul. Those aware of the cultural distance which separates Paul from our time will be on their guard against too easily declaring him a congenial spirit. Even if it is true that in the phrase 'Christ after the flesh' he was opposing people who in his view attached too much importance to 'the life of Jesus', he was not doing this because he had learned by experience the historical scepticism of New Testament scholars in the second half of the twentieth century. There must be another reason why Paul is so silent about events from the life of Jesus. Of course it is natural to seek an explanation in the fact that he was not a member of the circle of the first disciples. And there is no doubt that this biographical aspect played a role in his theological reflection on the past.[17] But this explanation is not completely satisfactory. The heart of the matter lies deeper. Even Rudolf Bultmann recognized that. In fact we may think it fortunate that the Gospels cannot give us any historically reliable picture of Jesus, since according to Paul we would be going wrong if we made our faith dependent on historical investigation. In fact the message of the cross prohibits us from clinging to faith in the humanity of Jesus. For Bultmann, the judgment on all that is human is made in the cross:[18] in other words, all humankind and everything human – including Jesus – comes under the verdict of the cross.

Implicit christology

Rudolf Bultmann unmistakably stands in the tradition of the theology of the 'Enlightenment'. He is aware of the problem of history, and in his works he repeatedly posed the question how our faith could be dependent on more or less chance events from a distant past. Despite his historical study of Jesus, his view was that the quest of the historical Jesus cannot be of essential importance for faith. With an appeal to Paul, Bultmann concentrates on the cross and interprets that as the end of all human certainties. Anyone who goes in search of the historical Jesus is seeking certainty, and anyone who ventures with the crucified Christ in the footsteps of Paul will discover what faith really is.

Jesus was the prophet of the coming kingdom of God. He did not regard himself as the Messiah, and when he spoke of the coming of the Son of Man he did so in the third person. From this it can be deduced that he expected someone else. How did a faith arise after Easter of the kind that is expressed in the letters of Paul and the Gospel of John? Bultmann has no problem with the gulf between the historical Jesus and the kerygmatic Christ. He suggests a certain continuity despite all the discontinuity. The summons by Jesus to his contemporaries to repent with a view to the coming kingdom of God implies that he was aware that he could and might speak in the name of God. This awareness could be described as an 'implicit christology'; it functioned as a starting point for christological reflection within the early Christian community.

7

Renewed Interest in the Historical Jesus

Demythologizing

In 1942 Rudolf Bultmann produced a study in which he argued for the 'demythologizing' of the biblical message.[1] In the world of the ancient Near East 'myths' played a central role in human life. Myths were age-old stories which were handed down from generation to generation; stories full of miraculous, strange, and sometimes also terrifying events; stories telling of the world of the gods, of heaven and creation, the past and the future. Mythological ideas answered questions about life: the purpose and meaning of human existence; the riddle of a good creation, the origin of evil and the devastating powers of sin. The biblical authors lived in this 'mythical' world and they too made use of mythological notions.

Bultmann was not the first theologian to be aware of the mythological character of biblical stories. However, the conclusion he drew from this discovery differed from that of those who in the nineteenth century called the Bible a mythical book. Their verdict was a purely negative one. They regarded the myths as outdated, with no relevance for modern 'enlightened' men and women. Bultmann, too, began from the scientific picture of the world, but he did not argue that the biblical mythology was insignificant. Anyone who wanted to scrap the myths would have little left, but anyone who took the trouble to demythologize the age-old stories – to strip them of their mythological garb – would discover a core, a message, which is not time-conditioned but seems to be surprisingly topical.

To clarify this, here is a typical example. A large number of New Testament writings speak unmistakably of a cosmic catastrophe which is rapidly approaching, a change in heaven and earth which will be as sudden as it is radical (Mark 13.24–27; Luke 17.22–37; I

Thess.5.1–11; Rev.20–22). According to Bultmann this *eschatological* expectation fits completely into a mythical view of the world. For people in the twentieth century, eschatological notions are a great stumbling block in the way of taking the Bible seriously. People can no longer make anything of stories about the destruction of heaven and earth, the appearance of the Son of Man with the clouds of heaven, a thousand-year kingdom, a final judgment at which the evil will be punished and the good rewarded, and finally the coming of a new Jerusalem. Modern men and women know the laws of nature and have difficulty in believing in a supernatural, divine intervention in history.

Does this mean that the biblical message has become insignificant? Bultmann did not draw this conclusion. Through his demythologizing of these time-conditioned, eschatological ideas he identified the 'kerygma', the message, which was put in mythological language. 'Eschatology' calls for 'conversion'. Human beings need to take a decision, a radical decision which will fundamentally change their lives 'here and now'.

In this spirit, Bultmann now also interpreted Jesus' preaching of the approaching kingdom of God. We already discovered earlier that he was opposed to the notion that Jesus had been influenced by Jewish apocalyptic expectations of the future. In this connection Bultmann preferred to speak of the 'eschatological' preaching of Jesus. Jesus did not confront his contemporaries, in the style of Jewish apocalyptic, with a large number of deterrent and terrifying notions about the end of time. He had something else in view. He did not direct his gaze to the future, but to the present, and by his preaching of the coming kingdom of God hoped to move people to make a radical change in their lives *now*.

Bultmann made a virtue of necessity. It is certainly true that he thought that his programme of demythologizing was legitimated by the preaching of Jesus. That was why he was so enchanted by the Fourth Gospel. The author of that work already translated Jesus' proclamation of the coming kingdom of God into images which exclusively focus on the present (John 3.3,5). In this way he took a decisive step towards changing 'futuristic eschatology' – centred on the future (the kingdom of God is coming soon) – into 'realized eschatology', centred on the present: the kingdom of God is already here.[2]

The preaching of the kerygma

After the Second World War Rudolf Bultmann wrote his *Theology of the New Testament*. The opening sentence is devastating: 'The message of Jesus is a presupposition for the theology of the New Testament rather than a part of that theology itself.'[3] I first read that sentence in the middle of the 1960s, and thirty years later I still remember vividly how much I puzzled over it. This was totally new. I had never seen or learned anything like it. One sentence put a series of question-marks against things that I had accepted completely as a matter of course. The preaching of Jesus is not the heart of the New Testament, but only a presupposition. Bultmann even implies the plural: Jesus' preaching is one of the presuppositions of the theology of the New Testament. Other presuppositions can be mentioned, like the belief of the disciples in the resurrection of Jesus; the early-Jewish expectation of the coming of the Messiah; mythological notions in the world of the ancient Near East and the Hellenistic Greek world. In the following chapters Bultmann sketches out the theology of the New Testament as a conglomerate of all kinds of influences.

Anyone who looks at the past with historical methods will discover a Jewish prophet who lived in the first century, who believed in the nearness of the kingdom of God and who finally died on the cross. These are interesting historical facts, but Christian faith cannot live by them. So theologians must not allow themselves to be seduced into constantly pursuing the 'phantom' of the historical Jesus. They must not be preoccupied with the past, but with the kerygma. That has constantly to be interpreted and proclaimed anew. The apostle Paul sums up the kerygma as the justification of the sinner – despite his critical position Rudolf Bultmann was a disciple of Luther and remained one!

Bultmann's influence extended further than the sphere of New Testament scholarship. His programme of demythologizing the biblical message led to a 'hermeneutics' – the translation of the kergyma into the present – which also found an echo in systematic theology. In Ebeling's view God's revelation cannot be limited to a particular historical event – not even to the event that took place in the first decades of our era in a Jewish setting. The revelation is not closed, but constantly takes place anew where the kerygma is preached.

Criticism of Bultmann

The name of Rudolf Bultmann will always be associated with developments in twentieth-century theology. His influence is evident to the present day not only in Germany, but also outside it. His views are not undisputed. Above all those theologians who do not want to share his historical-critical presuppositions have fundamental difficulties with them. They refuse to make a distinction between the historical Jesus and the Christ of the church's faith, a distinction which was also alien to the New Testament. In accord with a tradition of centuries, they emphasize that Jesus saw himself as the Messiah and also as the Son of God. The continuity between the period before and after the cross and resurrection is even such that one can rightly speak of 'Christ on earth'.

Critical voices against Bultmann's views are also heard from groups of New Testament scholars who are not at all opposed to historical criticism of the Bible. But they do challenge the presupposition that the majority of the stories in the Gospels were created by the early Christian community. In his view of the origin of the Gospels Bultmann hardly paid any attention to the role of the disciples. That is strange, since in the period before the cross and resurrection the disciples had been eyewitnesses to the actions of Jesus and had heard his words, and after that Peter and his companions played a prominent role in early Christianity as apostles. With a remarkable mixture of dryness and irony an English theologian once asked whether Bultmann did not believe that the disciples had disappeared from the earth with their teacher for good after his resurrection. In this situation the early-Christian community would have had to take refuge in the creation of new stories about Jesus and a 're-creation' of the past.[4]

On this point a critical evaluation of Bultmann's position was indeed desirable. Jesus' disciples did not disappear from the scene, but after the death and resurrection of their teacher played an important role as apostles in the early Christian community. Beyond question their persons guaranteed some degree of continuity between the time before Easter and the time after Easter. But the last word on the nature of this continuity is far from having said. The disciples had accompanied Jesus in person; they had heard his words and seen his actions. His picture was engraved on their minds. After the cross and resurrection they were the ones who could tell of the past. However, their stories took on another tone. Easter had opened their eyes to a new and unexpected reality. With a feeling of shame they recalled their incomprehension during the lifetime of Jesus. They had followed him, indeed, but sometimes they were groping in the dark about the meaning of his words and actions.

The evangelists are not reporters who follow the actual event with sharp eyes. They are writing after the event, indeed quite some time later: it was around forty to fifty years after the death of Jesus that they collected the stories in circulation in the early Christian community and revised them to fit their theological concept. That is how the evangelists describe the life of Jesus. They do so with the help of sources, but they did not hesitate to work over these sources to a greater or lesser extent. Bultmann was too critical. He had too little of an eye for the continuity between the time before and the time after the cross and resurrection. However, anyone who challenges him runs the risk of going to the other extreme: having too little of an eye for the discontinuity between the life of Jesus and the kerygma of the early Christian community. It is by no means easy to find the golden mean between the two extremes. It is certainly true that Jesus' disciples guarantee a certain degree of continuity. After Easter they formed the circle of apostles, the leaders of the community that was being built up. Doubtless they will have recalled the recent past, but their recollection was 'coloured' by their belief in the Risen Lord.

Back to the past

The way to the past proves a difficult one to take. Bultmann saw the dangers and warned against misunderstandings and against drawing conclusions which fail to do sufficient justice to the complexity of the problem. While taking these warnings to heart, some exegetes nevertheless ventured to embark on this way into the past. This group included the German New Testament scholar Joachim

Jeremias (1900–1979). Jeremias was anything but an opponent of historical criticism of the Bible;[5] he practised the method himself in his scholarly studies. In contrast to Bultmann, he thought that it must be possible to use historical criticism to find traces of the historical Jesus. Jeremias had a balanced view of Bultmann's theology. At all events he found it a positive feature that Bultmann in his plea for the priority of the kerygmatic Christ had returned to the centre of the Protestant confession: Paul's preaching of the crucified Christ and the justification of the sinner. However, Jeremias made no secret of the fact that he felt it necessary to warn against some less positive aspects of Bultmann's thought. If the option for the kerygmatic Christ ultimately seems to be taken at the expense of the remembrance of the historical Jesus, theology runs the risk of the incarnation becoming spiritualized. It must never be forgotten that 'the word *really* became flesh' (John 1.14) and that God acted concretely, *truly,* in the history of the people of Israel and the words and actions of Jesus of Nazareth. Jeremias warned Bultmann and his disciples against docetism,[6] against a christology in which the humanity of Jesus is pushed into the background and even threatens to become unimportant. Finally he pointed to another danger. In Bultmann's theology the scales seem to have tipped to the other side and the preaching of the apostle Paul gets so much attention that it totally overshadows the message of Jesus.[7]

Those who wants to avoid the dangers indicated by Jeremias must once again concern themselves with the past. But is that possible after all that was said by Albert Schweitzer, Martin Kähler and Rudolf Bultmann in particular? Jeremias recognizes that the four Gospels cannot put us in a position to write a biography of Jesus. At the same time he also believes that these very sources compel us to follow the trail back to the historical Jesus and his proclamation. The Gospels leave no doubt that the ultimate origin of the Christian faith does not lie in the kerygma of the earliest community or in the Easter experiences of the disciples but in a historical event: the activity – both in words and deeds – of Jesus of Nazareth, who was hung on the cross on the orders of Pontius Pilate with the complicity of the Jewish authorities.

Secondly, Jeremias argues that not only the literary sources but ultimately also the kerygma itself forces us to follow these traces. At any rate the kerygma of the community – God has reconciled himself with the world in the crucified Christ – unmistakably refers to a historical event. Anyone who talks about incarnation cannot avoid engaging in the quest of the historical Jesus, however difficult that undertaking is, and however incomprehensible Jesus remains.

Abba

Christianity has its roots in history. Without the historical Jesus Christian faith lacks any real grounding. The way to the past needs to be taken time and again. But is this way viable? The danger that the mistakes of the past will be made all over again is not an imaginary one. How is it possible to avoid once again constructing a picture of Jesus which totally fits our wishes and longings?

Jeremias answers such questions with striking optimism. The way back can be taken with confidence, because in contrast to the last century exegetes are no longer groping completely in the dark. The past is less a closed book than it used to be. Since the nineteenth century, interest in both the Jewish and the Roman, Hellenistic Greek world of the time of Jesus has increased enormously and intensive research has deepened and enriched our knowledge. For this reason, too, Jeremias is hopeful about the results of the quest of the historical Jesus. In a series of studies he attempted to demonstrate that study of Aramaic, the vernacular of Jesus and his contemporaries, makes the way to the past viable. Quite often the original Aramaic can still be heard behind the Greek words and expressions in the Gospels.[8] Thus Jeremias himself thinks that he can identify authentic words of Jesus.

The following example gives a good insight into his method of investigation. Moreover it is interesting, because it had a good deal of influence on christological discussion. In 1954 Jeremias gave a paper at a meeting of theologians in Berlin in which he drew attention to the particular significance of the Aramaic word abba. The term appears only once in the four Gospels: according to Mark, in his prayer in Gethsemane Jesus addressed God as his abba (Mark 14.36; cf. Rom.8.15; Gal.4.6). Jeremias demonstrated that this is not an isolated example, but that it was customary for Jesus to address God in such a 'familiar way'. Evidently Jesus had the boldness to see

God as his *abba*, his father (whom he could address in an intimate way). In the Aramaic of the time of Jesus the word *abba* predominantly functioned in the sphere of the family. Children said *abba* to their father. Jeremias regards the fact that Jesus dared to speak to God in such familiar terms as convincing proof of his uniqueness. There was a special bond between Jesus on earth and God in heaven.[12]

Jeremias opened up a good deal of material with this original contribution to the discussion. In a similar way he tried to prove the historicity of, for example, the announcements of the passion in the synoptic Gospels and the words of institution in the eucharist.[10] Is it in fact possible to go back like this and arrive at a picture of the historical Jesus? The work of Jeremias inevitably found both supporters and opponents. From the critical reactions it seems that sceptics have been little if at all convinced by his arguments. An exception needs to be made for his interpretation of the word *abba*. This theory also enjoyed a certain popularity outside the circle of those of like mind to Jeremias. I need only refer to the famous book on Jesus by Edward Schillebeeckx.[11] Agreement is not rapidly reached in the world of exegetes, but one can say that there has been something of a consensus over the 'abba' experience of Jesus (though in most recent times serious doubts have been raised, also on linguistic grounds).[12]

No discontinuity

Jeremias begins from the continuity between the historical Jesus and the kerygma of the early Christian community. In fact he will not accept a possible discontinuity. He warns against a 'one-sided' theology 'which limits itself to the preaching of Jesus and finally becomes a successor to Ebionitism; those who base themselves purely on the kerygma of the early Christian community run the risk of lapsing into docetism'.[13] I explained earlier what is meant by docetism. Ebionites were Jewish Christians of the second and third centuries. For them Jesus was primarily a new Moses.

Jeremias does not seem to be a conversation-partner who can easily be labelled. He is critical of Bultmann, but he also opposes those who make things too easy and think that they can pass over problems. As a scrupulous exegete he had little difficulty in summing up the differences between the message of Jesus and the proclamation of the Christian community. So he also warned against a simple 'levelling out' of the difference between the time before Easter and the time after. The gospel of Jesus is not precisely the same as the kerygma of the early Christian community. In his view, one relates to the other as 'summons' and 'response'.[14]

It need hardly be pointed out that on numerous points Jeremias and Bultmann are at opposite poles. Of course Jeremias will have nothing to do with Bultmann's thesis that the historical Jesus is only one of the presuppositions of the theology of the New Testament. For Jeremias, Jesus is the only presupposition of the kerygma of the early Christian community. There is no one else and nothing else.[15] The consequences of Jeremias' standpoint finally appear unmistakably when he defines the term 'revelation': revelation takes place in Jesus, in him and not in anything or anyone else, either in the proclamation of the early Christian community or in the preaching from the pulpits of churches somewhere in our modern world.[16] According to Jeremias a view which takes account of an 'ongoing revelation' is little different from Gnostic false teaching.[17]

Between historicism and docetism

The old debate about the meaning and meaninglessness of the quest of the historical Jesus still remained alive in the 1950s and 1960s. Unexpectedly in this period it was even given new and powerful stimuli, and inspired so many exegetes to write on it that within a short space of time an endless stream of literature was published.

The new discussion was opened by Ernst Käsemann. He came from the Bultmann 'school', but gradually emerged as an independent disciple. In earlier published studies Käsemann had given the impression of feeling at home in his teacher's camp. Thus he sharply and acutely criticized the position of Joachim Jeremias and accused him of an uncritical return to outdated theological insights from the nineteenth century.[18] Käsemann was not a man to limit himself to the viewpoints of a circle of like-minded scholars. He ventured to fight on two fronts. He accused Jeremias of 'historicism', but he warned Bultmann and his disciples against docetism.

Käsemann officially opened his attack in 1953 when at a meeting of Bultmann and his pupils he gave a lecture on the problem of the historical Jesus.[19] Käsemann turned against the usual scepticism and defended the view that investigation can indeed by carried on into the historical Jesus and that reliable results can be expected. There are various parts of the synoptic Gospels which exegetes must recognize as authentic if they want to be taken seriously as historians.[20]

Anyone who wants to follow this discussion must also pay attention to the details. Käsemann defended the view that the historical Jesus had not disappeared totally into the mist of the distant past. Bultmann did not fully disagree with this idea. We should not forget that he, too, had produced a book on Jesus in his younger years. Moreover, strictly speaking the difference between Bultmann and Käsemann is not about how many texts in the Gospels can be regarded as historical, but about the theological consequences which can be drawn from the knowledge about the historical Jesus that has been gained. Bultmann draws attention to the negative aspect: historical investigation cannot substantiate faith. Käsemann does not dispute this, but he also points to the positive aspects of historical research. He can do that because his view is that the 'historical' may not be completely irrelevant for theology. On the basis of this insight, Käsemann calls for a new debate on the historical Jesus. In contrast to his teacher, moreover, he thinks it important that a degree of continuity can be claimed between the message of the historical Jesus and the early Christian community's kerygma of the risen and exalted Lord.

It would take too long to describe the course of the discussion completely. Readers may be assured that the lecture by Ernst Käsemann cast a stone into an apparently peaceful pool. In a fierce debate, subtle differences can easily develop into far-reaching oppositions. The discussion between Bultmann and Käsemann extended over several years, and repeatedly one or the other claimed that his conversation-partner had not understood him properly, indeed had failed to understand him at all. Both scholars were agreed that historical investigation cannot prove faith, but Käsemann saw more use in historical investigation than Bultmann, because he attached more importance to the continuity between the message of the historical Jesus and the kerygma of the early Christian community. In Bultmann's view the 'that' remained central – for faith it is enough to know *that* Jesus lived and died on the cross – but he recognized that it had been meaningful to go on telling stories about the historical Jesus, because otherwise there was a danger that the person of Jesus would have become a mythical figure. Finally he seemed ready to agree with Käsemann that the earthly Jesus is both a criterion and a legitimation of the kerygma of the early Christian community.[21]

Word and action

The debate continues. In the discussion between Bultmann and Käsemann attention was constantly focussed on the possibility or impossibility of continuity between the message of Jesus and the kerygma of the early Christian community. Ernst Fuchs, another pupil of Bultmann's, emphasized a new aspect. Continuity is created not only by words but also by actions. So it is not enough to know that Jesus lived and what he said; at the same time explicit attention needs to be paid to the question 'what he *did*'.

In this connection Fuchs pointed to the remarkable and scandalous meals which Jesus had with sinners and tax collectors (Matt.11.19). They need to be described as 'eschatological' meals. In his preaching about the coming kingdom of God, Jesus did not stop at words alone. He did more than simply theorize about the future. He drew consequences for the present from his eschatological expectation, and in his dealing with sinners and tax-collectors he showed what God's coming kingdom could already mean on earth now.[22] Jesus actions form the key to understanding his message.[23]

Anyone who goes in search of an answer to the question 'Who is Jesus?' therefore cannot be content with listening to his words. The Gospel stories of his actions and way of life make the picture of Jesus complete. His words take shape in his actions and his actions are given meaning and significance by his words. His opponents accused him of being a 'glutton and a wine-bibber' (Matt.11.19). They were scandalized that Jesus did not avoid the company of sinners and tax-collectors and even regularly had meals with them (Mark 2.15–

17). On various occasions he provided the food needed by a large crowd (Mark 6.34-44; 8.1-10). Meals play an important role in Jesus' life. They can be described as 'eschatological meals'. Their deepest meaning was in fact only discovered after the event. In the last meal which Jesus held with his disciples,[24] he once more expressed in words and actions – the words which he spoke on breaking the bread and distributing the wine – that his life was completely dominated by 'being for others'. So he lived and so he died. What applies to Jesus' words also applies to his conduct: in this there is already *implicitly* present what was later explicitated in the kerygma of the early Christian community.[25]

A new Jesus book

Rudolf Bultmann's book on Jesus of Nazareth appeared in 1926. It seemed to mark the definitive end of any *theological* interest in the historical Jesus. It was no chance that the work appeared in a series about great figures from world history. Bultmann had no objection to giving Jesus a place in the past. This 'biography' had no significance for Christian faith. Afterwards there was silence in this sphere.[26] For a long time not a single pupil of Bultmann dared to write a study of the historical Jesus. It was legitimate to expect that in this situation after 1953 there would soon be a change. Käsemann opened the debate but did not write a book about Jesus. In 1956 his colleague Günther Bornkamm did.[27]

Again a pupil overstepped the limits which had been set by his teacher. Bornkamm, too, thought that the actions of Jesus were not of any lesser importance than his words in a search for the continuity between the time before the cross and resurrection and the time afterwards. Moreover he asked for attention to be paid to yet another facet in the discussion. In a short chapter he assembled from the Gospels all the events which have a biographical character. On the basis of this Bornkamm tried to give a sketch of the personality of Jesus. To avoid any possible misunderstanding, it should be remembered that he was a pupil of Bultmann and he knew what he was doing. He gathered these facts not in order to be able to write a historically reliable biography of Jesus, but in the hope that in this way he could give an impression of the effect that the words and actions of Jesus had on his contemporaries. These contemporaries sensed that they had encountered someone with special gifts: a man who acted with authority; a man who differed from their scribes and other experts in scripture and tradition; a man who made them think and sometimes prodded them into opposition.

Bornkamm's study met with mixed feelings within the circle of Bultmann's pupils and those of like mind. Was history repeating itself, and did an old battle have to be fought all over again? Among other things, Bornkamm was accused of having too easily attributed historical significance to kerygmatic statements.[28] Moreover in contrast to his teacher, Bornkamm was seeking the continuity between Jesus' words and actions on the one hand and the kerygma of the early Christian community on the other. That is shown by the last chapter of the book, which was given the programmatic title 'Jesus Christ'.

Jesus' self-consciousness

It is an age-old problem: Jesus of Nazareth proclaimed the coming of the kingdom of God, but after the cross and resurrection Jesus Christ became the central content of the kerygma of the early Christian community. Thus the proclaimer himself becomes the one who is proclaimed.

Albert Schweitzer called Jesus an apocalyptist, and Rudolf Bultmann seemed to have a preference for the term 'eschatology', but both were agreed that Jesus lived in expectation of the imminent coming of the kingdom. However, both scholars needed also to find a solution for the failure of the kingdom to come. Jesus died in disappointment on the cross and the Christian community made a virtue out of necessity. Certainly the kingdom failed to come, but there was so much spiritual force in the words and actions of the preacher that in early Christian preaching the disappointment could easily be assimilated.

Hans Conzelmann, who also came from the influential school of Rudolf Bultmann, asked himself whether the traditional way of looking at things described above did justice to reality. He argued that the eschatological message of Jesus should not be interpreted in the usual way in categories of time – 'temporally' – but rather 'christologically'.[29] Is this playing with words, or does it amount to a serious question?

Very much in the steps of his teacher, Conzelmann asserted that Jesus was not an apocalyptist. He was not concerned to give all kinds of information about the near future, but his whole preaching of the approaching kingdom of God needs to be understood 'existentially'. In this expectation Jesus – and thus no one else! – called on people to be converted and radically to change their lives. The preaching of the imminent kingdom 'cannot be had separately'. The words point to the person who spoke them. Jesus' life was already completely dominated by his eschatological expectation. Anyone who talks about the kingdom of God cannot leave out of account the one who proclaimed that kingdom. Therefore Jesus' eschatological preaching forms the starting point for christological reflection. In this connection, to avoid the misunderstanding that he wants to defend an orthodox standpoint, Conzelmann uses the term 'indirect christology'. Here he comes very close to his teacher, who in various publications pointed out that Jesus' call to conversion in view of the approach of the kingdom of God necessarily amounted to an 'indirect christology'.

Ultimately the circle seems to close again. The nineteenth century was the heyday of optimism and many people were roused to go in search of the historical Jesus. They even thought it possible to penetrate Jesus' mind, to trace his emotions and describe his psychological and religious development, almost in detail. Rudolf Bultmann in particular was sharply opposed to this 'psychologizing' of the investigation of the life of Jesus. The New Testament texts are so influenced by the kerygma of the early Christian community that they are of no use as a basis for a psychological study of the man from Nazareth.

As a result of the discussion started in 1953 it proved necessary once again to pay attention to the historical Jesus. Attention was first concentrated on his words, but very soon it became clear that his actions, too, were of significance for gaining a clearer picture of the continuity between Jesus and the early Christian community. Those who want to draw attention to someone's words and actions also want to know more about the reasons, motives and background to what that person said and did. Thus the way finally leads back to the question of the self-consciousness of Jesus. How did he see himself? Did he see himself as Messiah or as prophet?

For some time already in the Bultmann school there had been a consensus that Jesus did not see himself as the Messiah. However, this thesis did not bring the discussion to an end. Terms like 'implicit' and 'indirect' christology raised the question what Jesus did think about himself. Did he regard himself as a prophet in the spirit of the Old Testament? He unmistakably came forward as the prophet of the approaching kingdom of God. But how did he arrive at this notion? Why did he believe that God had given him this task?

Such notions can be found in the work of the dogmatic theologian Gerhard Ebeling, who has already been mentioned earlier. He speaks of a 'christology *in nuce*'. Jesus did not require faith in himself, but his conduct aroused faith in people. There again we have the question of the continuity between the time before and the time after the cross and resurrection. Before this time Jesus was the *witness* of faith in God, and afterwards he became the *ground* of Christian faith.[30]

8

A Jewish Rabbi

Schism

The life of Jesus mainly takes place within the frontiers of Jewish territory. His parents' home was in Nazareth and this place in Galilee is also called his 'father's city' (Mark 6.1–6). For some time he travelled around in the region bordering on the sea of Galilee, and finally as a pilgrim he undertook the long journey from the north to the temple in Jerusalem. The four evangelists leave no doubt that Jesus belonged to the Jewish people. The genealogies in the Gospels of Matthew and Luke do not agree at all points, but they are unanimous that Jesus is a distant descendant not only of King David but also of Abraham, Isaac and Jacob (Matt.1.17; Luke 3.23–38). As a Jew he could call himself 'son of Abraham', while as a descendant of the famous king he had the right to the title 'son of David', a title which meant that his life and death were asssociated with ancient messianic expectations. He was arrested and executed in Jerusalem. Pontius Pilate saw him as a foreign rebel who could pose a threat to the *status quo*. The Roman procurator had the inscription 'king of the Jews' (Mark 15.26) attached to the cross on which the supposed rebel died.

After Easter the circle of disciples and other followers began to develop into a community of people who believed in the resurrection of Jesus and called him their Lord and Saviour. However, this did not mean that immediately there was a radical break with Jewish tradition. Members of the early Christian community still went to the temple in Jerusalem (Acts 2.41–47) in the time after Pentecost. Others had gone before, but the apostle Paul was the first to devote himself consistently to spreading the Christian gospel in the Gentile world (Gal.1.11–2.10). He was successful, but at the same time created problems which were difficult to resolve. Was the Christian faith part of the Jewish tradition, or was it a new religious phenomenon? The question came to a head over circumcision. If Christian faith is part of the Jewish tradition, then the commandments of the Torah should also apply to Christians, and Gentiles who had attached themselves to the Christian community needed to be circumcised. Paul fiercely opposed this notion and himself seems to be ready to relativize the significance of the Torah (Gal.3.–4). He goes a long way, but not so far as to resolve to abolish the Torah (Gal.5.14), and in his letter to the community in Rome he presents an impressive argument in which he assures the Christian community that despite everything it is still rooted in Israel and abides in it (Rom.9.–11).

The destruction of the Jerusalem temple in 70 CE not only caused unspeakable human suffering but also had consequences for the Jewish religion itself and the relationship between Jews and Christians. From that moment on there begins a process which eventually led to the tragic split between Judaism and Christianity. In the world of the Gentiles the church sought and found its own way and gradually became alienated from its Old Testament and Jewish roots. In the christological dispute during the first centuries the Jewishness of Jesus became increasingly forgotten. That Jesus had been born and lived among Jews paled into insignificance in the light of the confession that he was sent into the world as the pre-existent Son of God, 'that the world should be saved through him' (John 3.17).

Cast out

During his lifetime Jesus regularly visited the synagogue (Mark 1.21; 3.1; 6.1; Luke 13.10). He was treated with respect there, read from the Scriptures and had occasion to expound his 'teaching' (Luke 4.14–30). Sometimes that led to difficulties, but there was never a break with the Pharisees.

Soon after the schism between Judaism and Christianity Jesus became a *persona non grata* in the synagogue. He was now an alien in the Jewish world. As a result of the place which he came to occupy in the Christian confession, Jews could not longer recognize him as

74

their brother. His name is hardly mentioned in rabbinic literature – Mishnah, Talmud and Midrashim.[1] He was cast out and ignored. He disappeared from the history of the Jewish people and no Jew wanted to hear of his Jewishness again. Jeshua from Nazareth had become Jesus Christ, a Christian and not a Jew.

Time went on. The Christian church became a powerful institution in Europe. Judaism and Christianity increasingly became alienated from each other and went their different ways. Moreover they became totally unequal: over against a small, powerless synagogue stood a great, influential church. In the Middle Ages, in periods of persecution, discrimination and oppression – more the rule than the exception – Jews sometimes broke their silence over Jesus. In a mixture of anxiety and anger they had recourse to mockery and scorn. Above all they rejected the Christian dogma of the 'virgin birth'. Behind the attractive stories in the first chapter of the Gospels of Matthew and Luke lay a totally different reality. Jesus was an illegitimate child. His mother, the Jewish girl Miriam/Mary, had been raped or had had intercourse with a Roman soldier called Panthera, and had been made pregnant. To rescue the honour of Mary and her family Joseph, the carpenter of Nazareth, was betrothed to her.[2]

The roots of this Jewish Panthera legend go far back into the past. In 178 a certain Celsus, a Roman philosopher of the school inspired by the thought of Plato, wrote a fierce attack on Christian faith, *Logos Alethes* (= The True Word).[3] His book has been lost, but its content is largely known because in 250 Origen published an extensive refutation of Celsus. In the writing of the Roman philosopher, too, Mary is accused of intercourse with Panthera, a soldier in the army of occupation. It is assumed that the name Panthera was formed as an allusion, mocking and sarcastic, to the Greek *parthenos* (virgin).

Recognition after alienation

The alienation lasted for many centuries. Christians thought that they owned the truth. Supported by Christian rulers, theologians summoned Jews to religious discussions and required them to recognize that Jesus was the expected Messiah.[4] According to the Christian exegetes, well-known messianic texts – like Isa.7.14 on the birth of 'Immanuel' and Isa. 53 on the 'suffering servant of the Lord' – made clear statements. The refusal of the rabbis to recognize that the Christians were right was seen as a proof of their stubbornness.

The mediaeval religious disputations were not of course an appropriate way of persuading Jews to adopt another view of Jesus. Quite the opposite. The rejection increased, and more than ever the name of Jesus Christ was tabu in Jewish circles. That is understandable, since in this name Jews in Spain had been sent to the stake and in countless European countries had been driven into ghettos; in Eastern Europe during pogroms they had been robbed, tortured and killed. What Jewish man or woman could still dare to speak this name?

But that happened in the nineteenth century. That it did is not the result of a changed attitude on the part of Christians. Christians did not change, but changes took place in Jewish circles. In the course of the nineteenth century interest in Jesus of Nazareth increased there. Threats, mockery and hatred gave place to curiosity and serious interest. In 1838 a book appeared in Paris written by a Jewish author, Joseph Salvador, which took a positive view of Jesus of Nazareth.[5] It is no coincidence that this book was published in France. Some decades earlier Napoleon had given the Jews the same rights and duties as all other citizens of his empire. Clearly this intellectual and spiritual freedom was a precondition for a responsible revaluation and rehabilitation of the Jew Jesus of Nazareth.[6]

A comparable development can be noted after the foundation of the State of Israel. Since 1948 Jewish scholars have written extensive books and articles on the life of Jesus of Nazareth.[7] He no longer needed to be ignored. He no longer formed a threat to Jewish identity. On the contrary, those who steeped themselves in his life and thought could discover that the man from Nazareth was a credit to Jewish tradition and Jewish history.

An un-Jewish Christianity

Who is Jesus? The degree to which Jews and Christians had taken different ways over the centuries emerged from the fact that New Testament scholars paid little attention to the Jewish revaluation of Jesus in the nineteenth and twentieth centuries. A great deal had to happen before Christians began to sense that they could learn something from Jews – also and even from Jesus of Nazareth.

Round about the turn of the century, certainly in Germany, we can see a tendency to trivialize or even to deny the Jewishness of Jesus. This development was not completely new, since the Jewishness of Jesus played only a subordinate role in classical christology also. But it did represent a new course, because the age-old and traditional theological anti-Judaism was now connected with nineteenth-century antisemitism, which was fed by nationalistic and racist sentiments.

It would take us too far afield to go too deeply into this question, but it is not without importance for discussion in the twentieth century. I might mention Houston Stewart Chamberlain (1855–1927), a many-sided and erudite man, son of an English admiral, who was largely brought up in France. He thought that he had found in Germany what he missed in English and French culture. He cherished a great admiration bordering on veneration for everything German. Chamberlain did not find it very difficult to move in prominent circles and he was a welcome guest in the homes of scientists and artists. He maintained friendly relations with no less a figure than Adolf von Harnack and was a son-in-law of Richard Wagner. The mention of these two names alone should make it clear that Chamberlain was not an isolated figure, but can be seen as an exponent of the spirit of the time. Already since the middle of the nineteenth century the composer Richard Wagner (1813–1883) had advocated a purging of Christian faith to such a degree that in fact it inevitably had to be regarded as a totally new religion, not only through 'his' statements and writings, but also through his imposing music dramas based on Germanic myths. The ideals of Wagner and kindred spirits found an echo among broad circles of the intellectual elite. The time seemed ripe for a new spirituality. Thanks to a series of spectacular successes in the diplomatic sphere and on the battlefield, in the second half of the nineteenth-century Germany had developed into an empire which was deliberately striving for hegemony in Europe.

In this sphere, the need grew for a form of religious experience which took account of awakening German nationalism. It was thought that traditional Christianity had little or nothing to offer here. That was inevitably the case, since its roots did not lie in the German past, but in the world of the ancient Near East and the history of the Jewish people. This meant that from the very beginning Christian belief had been alien to Germans. In this situation Richard Wagner and his supporters tried to bring about a change. They argued for a new religion – an authentic German, Aryan religion – no longer based on the Old Testament but composed of the valuable non-Jewish elements in Christianity combined with age-old Aryan and Germanic myths. Jesus was declared not to be a Jew and identified with Parsifal, a redeemer figure in Germanic mythology.[8]

Chamberlain trod in the footsteps of Richard Wagner. The Englishman proved to be an eloquent advocate of the ideas of his famous father-in-law. His great erudition and an excellent command of the language enabled him to write a book which was read by hundreds and thousands of Germans with enthusiasm as a new Bible. This work, with the pretentious title *The Foundations of the Twentieth Century*, also influenced for example, the thought of the later Nazi ideologist Alfred Rosenberg. Chamberlain thought that he could develop a total view of reality on the basis of Aryan myths stemming from the ancient Germans. Everything, even Christian belief, needed to be subjected to it. So Chamberlain called on the church to liberate itself from all Jewish influences and bid a final farewell to the Old Testament. He set an example with hundreds of pages of argument that Jesus could not be of Jewish descent. At the beginning of the twentieth century Chamberlain seems to have had plans even to compose an Aryan Gospel, but as far as is known that never came to anything.[9]

A surprising development

At the end of the Second World War it could hardly have been predicted that Jewish authors would begin to write books about Jesus of Nazareth, far less that Christians would take the trouble to read these books and that some would even be ready to revise their christology critically. Up to this time the gulf had seemed unbridgable. Conversation between Jews and Christians was sparse and even an exchange of ideas based on scholarly principles was still merely the dream of a few. This led to strange developments and situations. One example could be called almost tragi-comic. At the beginning of the 1920s, the Jewish scholar Joseph Klausner (1874–1960) in Jerusalem was the first to produce a study of Jesus of Nazareth in modern Hebrew.[10] His book was translated not only into English, but in the 1930s also into German. Klausner wrote respectfully about Jesus and gave him a prominent place in Jewish history. In the meantime antisemitism had assumed terrible forms in Germany. Some theologians could not escape the seductions of this 'new' thought. In Jerusalem, Jesus was rehabilitated and his Jewishness was recognized; in Germany Christian theologians strove to free Jesus from 'Jewish taints'.[11] There were hardly any reasoned arguments. Once again Jesus was a plaything in the hands of ideologists who saw themselves called to 'de-Judaize' Christian faith. They had no respect for the Old Testament. They regarded it as a book which was culturally and ethically inferior and morally reprehensible, and which should be excluded from the Christian Bible. It was impossible for Jesus to have been a Jew. Only a few Jews lived in Galilee in those days. There was much alien blood, perhaps even 'Aryan' blood, in this mixed Galilean population.

I wrote the above sentences with bewilderment and perplexity. How far can and may theologians go? When do they cross a frontier which cannot and must not be crossed? Evidently some New Testament scholars in Germany in the 1930s and 1940s were so bewitched by the successes of the Nazis that they had completely forgotten the warnings of Albert Schweitzer. They created a picture of Jesus which totally corresponded to the wishes and desires of the dominant ideology. Nothing was left of the alien, unassimilated, apocalyptic Jesus whom Schweitzer had portrayed so aptly.

Theology is a complicated science. It is concerned with the Word of God, but it also knows that this Word can be heard only in human words – and these are words which have to be weighed carefully, words which can provoke misunderstandings and even lead to wrong notions and concepts. Albert Schweitzer wrote that Jesus was a strange apocalyptic prophet. Many New Testament scholars in the past and present have written that Jesus was different. The influential theologian Adolf von Harnack asserted that Jesus' preaching was on a higher spiritual level than the theological ideas in the Old Testament and in the early Jewish tradition. Jesus created his liberal theology in conflict with the legalism of the Pharisees.[12] After the Second World War there was no longer any dispute over Jesus' Jewishness, but it was emphasized that he had spoken very critically about the foundation of the Jewish tradition. His death on the cross had ultimately not been the consequence of his political position, but of his critical attitude to the Torah and the Jewish tradition.[13]

The Jew Jesus among his people

It was indeed surprising that after the Second World War Jesus returned to his people. The lost son finally returned home. In Jewish literature the well-known parable from the New Testament (Luke 15.11–32) was now applied to Jesus, with a certain irony, but also with deep seriousness.[14] The Christian church had alienated him from his Jewish roots, had sketched a picture of him which Jews felt to be offensive. But after centuries, Jewish authors discovered that Jesus was not the instigator of the tragic parting of the ways of Judaism and Christianity, but had become the victim of a Christian theology which despised and rejected the Jewish tradition.

Jesus of Nazareth lived as a Jewish man in the midst of his people. He was not a strange outsider, but 'a child of his time'. Anyone who wants to have a reliable picture of him must necessarily become familiar with the time in which he lived. The Jewish world at the beginning of our era was very colourful. The fact that the age-old land of Israel was occupied territory led to division. Was armed opposition possible or necessary? Did the commandments of the Torah call for heroism and martyrdom? Or did they admonish patience and caution? The Romans were powerful, and it seemed improbable that the small Jewish people could fight against them. Which side did Jesus take in this debate? Did he join the ranks of the religious fanatics and take up arms without hesitation? Or did he propagate an attitude of non-violence? Jewish authors do not give unanimous answers to these questions. Anyone who reads their books and articles sometimes meets a revolutionary Jesus, a supporter of the Zealots, but sometimes a man with mystic gifts and interests who as a kindred spirit to the Essenes removed himself into the wilderness, far from the political turmoil of his time. Usually there is no mention of possible sympathies with the Sadducees, but Jesus is all the more connected with the Pharisaic movement.

Did Jesus in fact take sides? There is no unanimity in Jewish circles over the answer to this question. In a colourful Jewish society, complicated to the extreme by religious and political tensions, like everyone else Jesus sought his own way. From his youth upwards he was confronted with violence. Galilee was a disturbed part of Jewish territory, a hotbed of opposition to the Roman forces of occupation. At the beginning of our era there were some bloody clashes between Jewish freedom fighters and Roman legions in the region. For Jesus, 'hatred of the enemy' (Matt.5.43) was not an abstract concept. Ruined and plundered towns and villages reminded him that he lived in an occupied land. Reprisals, public executions, crucifixions and martyrdoms did not quench the Jewish love of freedom in Galilee. Even in Jerusalem a 'Galilean' was recognized and treated with mistrust (Matt.21.10; 26.69). He was a potential troublemaker, and in the view of the Jewish authorities was a real danger to the fragile *status quo* which they were cautiously trying to maintain (John 11.50). Jesus grew up in Nazareth, an insignificant small place in the north (John 1.47). Despite the risks involved in living in this part of Jewish territory, he did not seek his salvation elsewhere. He went round the villages and towns of Galilee (Mark 1.39). There was some interest in his appearances. He had success. Large crowds followed him (Luke 14.25). His healings and his words attracted attention. He did not mince his words, but spoke his mind honestly. In sharp contrast to this openness he seems to have been remarkably silent about himself. Who was he and what did he want? He proclaimed the approach of the kingdom of God. Was he therefore a messianic figure? Perhaps the Messiah himself? He rarely gave a clear and unambiguous answer to this kind of question (Mark 8.27–30). His decision to travel to Jerusalem did not arise out of a desire to flee a disturbed Galilee. His obedience to the commandments of God made it necessary for him to make this long journey as a pilgrim.

He 'went up to Jerusalem' (Mark 10.32) to celebrate the Jewish Passover, the age-old feast of liberation and redemption, in the midst of thousands of other pilgrims who had come there from near and far. He was aware that he was running risks. His words and actions attracted attention and recalled many messianic prophecies. Jesus was not to be the first – nor the last – who was consequently arrested by tense and nervous authorities in the festal throng of the Passover, as a precautionary measure against serious disturbances. Some Pharisees had warned him (Luke 13.31–33), but he disregarded their advice and went on his way to Jerusalem, a pilgrim in the midst of numerous other pilgrims, a Jew in the midst of his Jewish contemporaries. One of many . . . and yet different from others? Who was he, this Jesus from distant Nazareth?

Birth and youth

The Gospels differ over the place where Jesus was born. Matthew and Luke point unambiguously to the small town of Bethlehem in Judaea (Matt.2.1; Luke 2.4–7); Mark says nothing about the birth of Jesus and contents himself with reporting that the adult Jesus came from Nazareth (Mark 1.9); this small town in Galilee is also mentioned in the Fourth Gospel (John 1.47), but John presents it in a negative light, leaving open the possibility that Jesus was born in Bethlehem (John 7.40–44). Are Matthew and Luke right, or do their reports have to be read with reserve and even scepticism? Biblical critics in general tend not to attach too much importance to the historical reliability of the birth stories in the Gospels of Matthew and Luke. Neither evangelist is writing 'history', but 'theology'. Each in his own way hoped to be able to show that Jesus was the expected Messiah from the house of David.[15]

Jewish writers have little to add to this. They do not think the question whether Jesus was really a 'son of David' to be of any importance. He did not cherish royal pretensions and he did not behave like a prince incognito. He tended to reject the spontaneous efforts of the crowds to proclaim him their leader or king (John.6.15). Anyone who called him Messiah was told to keep quiet (Mark 8.30). Jesus did not enthrone himself high above ordinary people like an Eastern despot. In his ancestral city of Nazareth he was known as 'the carpenter' (Mark 6.3), who as was usual at this time had learned his father's trade (Matt.13.55). We can be brief here about the Christian dogma of the 'virgin birth of Jesus' (cf. Matt.1.18–25; Luke 1.26–38): Jews reject such a notion as unhistorical and completely un-Jewish. It is a notion which does not occur anywhere in the Old Testament or in Jewish tradition. Jesus was not a 'son of God' but an ordinary person of flesh and blood.

More attention is paid to the story told only by the evangelist Luke about the appearance of the twelve-year-old Jesus in the temple in Jerusalem (Luke 2.40–52). Is this episode to be attributed to pious fantasy or is it a historically reliable account? This question is answered in different ways. Schalom Ben-Chorin thinks that the aim of the story is to show that Jesus was already fully adult in religious matters before his thirteenth year – the age at which a Jew becomes *barmitzvah* – and was thus even more at home in the Torah than the scribes of his time. David Flusser does not interpret this story as an attempt to set Jesus against the scribes at an early stage and to play him off against them. In his view this is a quite innocent anecdote about a precocious Talmudic pupil: a remarkable 'wonder child' indeed, but nothing special or unique. Miracle children appear in every generation.[16]

A 'scholar'

Some statements can be found in rabbinical literature about 'learned' carpenters, men who were held in respect because they seemed to have a thorough knowledge of Torah and tradition. One can guess why carpenters in particular were thought to be learned. Their work required accuracy and attention to detail. The same characteristics were needed for careful study and interpretation of the commandments in the Torah. It may be said to be significant that Joseph, the husband of Mary, the carpenter of Nazareth, is described as a 'just' man (Matt.1.19): he lived in accord with the commandments of the Torah.

It seems legitimate to conclude that Jesus came from a pious milieu. He grew up in a home in which the commandments were taken seriously. David Flusser thinks that Jesus was given good teaching. Indeed the Jewish scholar does not hesitate to rate Jesus' education considerably higher than that of Paul.[17] In this positive evaluation of Jesus we can unmistakably detect a critical attitude towards the way in which the apostle to the Gentiles seems to have sacrificed the law for his ideals. Recent scholarly research has confirmed Flusser's view of the quality of Jesus' upbringing and education. He was no illiterate provincial, but thanks to his parents' home belonged to the circles of the experts in scripture and tradition (John 7.15).[18]

A father who worked as a carpenter and was regarded as 'just' was certainly known in the town where he lived. So too was a son who trod in his father's footsteps and similarly practised the trade of a carpenter (Mark 6.3). A religious education at a high level and familiarity with scripture and tradition made him capable of discussing as a young adult on an equal footing with the scribes. Anyone who has gained some knowledge of the Jewish world at the time of Jesus will immediately think of the Pharisaic movement on reading these descriptions. It is known that Pharisees usually engaged in manual work. They lived serious lives, steeped themselves in the study of scripture and tradition, and tried to put the commandments of the Torah into practice in everyday life. They formed groups of like-minded people to support one another. In these 'brotherhoods', among other things they used to have meals together. The number of Pharisees remained relatively small, but nevertheless in the time of Jesus their influence grew. Did Jesus also form part of such a brotherhood?

Jesus and the Pharisees[19]

All the Gospels contain pericopes from which it can be inferred that Jesus was repeatedly criticized by Pharisees. In their view he had insufficient or no respect for the commandments of the Torah: he performed certain actions on the sabbath (Mark 2.23–3.6; Luke 13.10–17; 14.1–6; John 5.10–18) and he did not speak positively about regulations on clean and unclean food (Mark 7.1–23). The evangelists emphasize that Jesus interpreted the commandments in a new way – the 'antitheses' in the Sermon on the Mount (Matt.5.21–48). Briefly, the evangelists' view of Jesus' interpretation of the Torah could be described as follows: Jesus did not abolish the Torah (Matt.5.17); however, unlike the Pharisees he was not concerned with the 'letter' but with the spirit of the Torah. He was no casuist but saw love of God and the neighbour as the purpose of the commandments (Mark 12.28–34). That is the *new* feature in

Jesus' activity, and that is the reason why he came into conflict with the Pharisees.

However, Jewish scholars think that the evangelists, consciously or unconsciously, give an unfair account of things. According to David Flusser Jesus never distanced himself from the the Torah piety of his day. Like other Jews who were faithful to the Torah, he respected the sabbath commandment. On that day he, too, went to the synagogue (Mark 1.21) and read from the scriptures there (Luke 4.16) – a notorious transgressor of the commandments would never have been allowed to do that. Usually he healed the sick only after the sun had gone down, at the end of the sabbath (Mark.1.32; Luke 4.40). During his trial in Jerusalem his accusers tried in vain to get testimony on the basis of which he could be condemned (Mark 14.55). Didn't people know about his conflicts with the Pharisees over the sanctification of the sabbath? The Torah, after all, says that 'he who desecrates the sabbath shall indeed be put to death' (Exod.31.14). Or must this lack of testimony be interpreted afresh as an indication of the fact that Jesus was not at all known as a man who did not want to take the commandments of the Torah seriously? He could not be accused in the Sanhedrin of any transgression of the Torah. Moreover, he was not killed by stoning – the punishment prescribed by scripture (Num.15.32–36); Roman soldiers carried out his execution.

Jesus did not transgress the Torah. He did not diametrically oppose the Judaism of his day. These are conclusions which raise new questions, since all the Gospels report fierce discussion between Jesus and the Pharisees. They even suggest that the hostility was so great that already at an early stage plans were made to kill Jesus (Mark 3.6). Which view corresponds to historical events? Did the four evangelists not know more, or did they deliberately distort history to some degree?

Thanks to historical criticism of the Bible, exegetes have also come to see the distinctive character of the Gospels. Compared with the writings of his fellow-evangelists, Luke is still relatively positive about the Pharisees (Luke 13.31–35). As a non-Jew was he least affected by rancour and was he therefore in a position to paint an objective picture? A careful analysis of the other Gospels shows clearly that the authors have a tendency to sharpen the conflict with the Pharisees and even to bring it to a head. Right at the beginning of his Gospel Mark mentions objections to Jesus and even serious plans to do away with him (Mark 2.1–3.6). In a long chapter Matthew criticizes the alleged hypocrisy of the Pharisees (Matt.23.10–39). In the Fourth Gospel the Pharisees are introduced as the opponents of Jesus (John 7.45–47; 10.40; 18.3). This development of the portrayal of the Pharisees reflects the schism between Judaism and Christianity in the years after 70 CE. The more the gulf widened, the more the number of texts increase in which the conduct of Pharisees is depicted in dark colours.

Were there never conflicts between Jesus and supporters of the Pharisaic movement? Jewish authors point out the complexity of this question and warn exegetes to be careful and not pass judgment lightly. Thus we need to take account of the fact that in the time of Jesus Pharisaism did not form a closed front. The movement had different trends, 'schools', within it which disputed with one another over the interpretation of the Torah. The sabbath was central in these discussions. The texts from the Scriptures leave no doubt that it was not permissible to work on the day of rest (Exod.20.8–11; Deut.5.12–15). The commandment made it necessary to give a clear definition of what was 'work on the sabbath'. Was it permissible during a walk on the sabbath to pick some ears of corn in a field or fruit from a tree? Was this 'work', or did it fall outside the commandment (Mark 2.23–28)?

No less difficult to answer was the question whether performing healings profaned the sabbath. There was no unanimity in Pharisaic circles over this problem either. The evangelists mention four healings that Jesus did on the sabbath (Matt.12.9–13; Luke 13.10–17; 14.1–6; John 5.1–16). The Gospels do not conceal the fact that Jesus came into conflict with the Pharisees over all of them. But a modern Jewish author like Pinchas Lapide writes that Jesus did not transgress the Torah even on these occasions. The saving of a human life was thought to be more important than the sabbath commandment. The Torah was not meant to make human existence unbearable but liveable, humane (Lev.18.5). So Jesus did not go outside Jewish tradition when he said that 'The sabbath is made for man and not man for the sabbath' (Mark 2.27). Of course there could be differences of opinion over precisely when a situation could be said to be life-threatening. Jesus healed a man with 'a withered hand' (Mark 3.1–6), a woman who 'had already been bent over for eighteen years with a spirit of weakness' (Luke 13.10–17), a 'man with dropsy' (Luke 14.1–6) and finally, as a tragic climax, a man 'who had been sick for thirty-eight years' (John 5.5). Were these in danger of death? Or did Jesus' view of the quality of life allow no further postponement? Now, on this particular sabbath day, the sick and the handicapped had to be liberated from their torments. So he did not desecrate the sabbath but emphasized an aspect that risked getting lost in the discussions: as a day of rest the sabbath was also a day of liberation, a weekly recollection of the Exodus from Egypt (Deut.5.12–15), and for that reason the sabbath day was particularly suitable for performing unusual acts of healing (Luke 13.16).

From what has been said, the conclusion may be drawn that the majority of present-day Jewish authors give Jesus a place *within* the Judaism of his days. His interpretation of the Torah did not make him an outsider, and his summary of all the rules and regulations in the commandment to love God and one's neighbour was not unknown or unusual in the Jewish tradition of the time. So was Jesus a supporter of the Pharisaic movement? Different answers are given to this question in Jewish circles. Jesus is seen by some as a kindred spirit of Hillel and as one who disputed the insights of Shammai. Others regard his interpretation of the commandments more as a 'third way': in other words, Jesus went his own way independently of the normative Pharisaic schools of Hillel and Shammai. This could be an explanation of the fact that the four evangelists have preserved the recollection of his critical attitude to the Pharisees. He was a kindred spirit, but a critical one. Moreover he was not alone in his criticism. Critical voices can also be heard in rabbinic literature about the conduct of the Pharisees, and the same is true of the Qumran writings: 'they speak fair words, but their teaching is deceptive' and 'they withheld the drink of knowledge from the thirsty and made them drink vinegar for their thirst, so that they should pay attention to their false teaching, so that they should make them senseless during their festivals and catch them in their nets' (cf. Matt.23.13; Luke 11.52).

Despite all the agreements, David Flusser thinks that Jesus was not a 'real' Pharisee. Nowhere is there evidence or any indication that he identified with them. They represented the official, institutional Judaism, whereas the activity of Jesus as a charismatic miracle worker who proclaimed the kingdom of God inevitably came into tension and even conflict with this. However, this opposition did not degenerate into hostility. Even the evangelists – at least the three Synoptists; the Fourth Gospel is a case apart – make the Pharisees disappear into the background during the trial of Jesus. It is the Jerusalem aristocracy – the high priest at the head of the priestly hierarchy, with the support of prominent Sadducean scribes and the heads of priestly families – who have him arrested. In the first confrontations between the early Christian community and the official Jewish authorities the Pharisees even appear as its defenders. The wise counsel of the Pharisee Gamaliel saves the lives of the apostles (Acts 5.17–42). Paul appeals to the Pharisees before the same Sanhedrin (Acts 22.30–23.10).

The search for the lost

It is possible that Jesus felt an affinity to the movement of the Pharisees. But he did not always behave like a 'real' Pharisee. He was pious and loyal to the commandments of the Torah, but his piety did not prevent him from moving outside the circles of the like-minded. At the beginning of this century the famous Jewish scholar Claude G.Montefiore (1858–1938) drew attention to three striking aspects of the activity of Jesus:[20] he sought the company of prostitutes and tax collectors; he drew upon himself the fate of the poor, the sick and the persecuted; and he saw it as his task to 'serve', to devote his life to the salvation of others. Montefiore did not hesitate to use the world 'original' in this context, but he refused to describe Jesus' attitude as un-Jewish: he preferred to say that it was hyper-Jewish. Jesus put into practice the commandment to love contained in the Torah, radically and consistently.

Jesus did not allow himself to be forced into the straitjacket of a particular group or party. He deliberately crossed dividing lines and regarded it as his task 'to seek out the lost' (Matt.9.11–12) and to restore 'the lost sheep of the house of Israel' to the fold (Matt.15.24). This attitude brought him into conflict with kindred spirits in Pharisaic circles, but his effort to save sinners did not lead to a definitive break with the Jewish tradition: in his love for the powerless, those without rights and the outcast, and in his courageous resolve not to rule but to serve, Jesus showed his true aims. These were neither un-Jewish or anti-Jewish, but primally Jewish and in accord with the deepest significance of the commandments of the Torah.

Why was this Jew who was loyal to the Torah arrested in Jerusalem and condemned to death?

The trial of Jesus[21]

After the Second World War the question of the reason for Jesus' arrest and violent death took on an extra dimension for many Jewish authors. For centuries Jews had been blamed by their Christian fellow-citizens for the death of Jesus on the cross. This accusation was a constant source of anti-Jewish feelings and expressions of antisemitism. Again this background it was understandable that Paul Winter should dedicate his extensive and detailed study of the trial of Jesus to the victims of the 'Holocaust' in Nazi Germany.

Alarmed by the atrocities of antisemitism in the Second World War, among the survivors there was a desire to reckon with the past once and for all and to clear the memory of the victims. They were not murderers. They had not put Jesus to death. It was impossible to make the Jewish people as a whole responsible for this execution of 'a man of good will'. Jesus was arrested on the orders of a small but influential group within the Judaism of his day: the Jewish leaders belonged to the party of the Sadducees and were opponents of both the Pharisees and the Zealots and of all those groups which were inspired by apocalyptic expectations of the future or had pinned their hopes on the coming of the Messiah.

Jesus knew that his life was in danger in Jerusalem. He was warned not to go there by Pharisees. Nevertheless, faithful to his prophetic calling, he went (Luke 13.33). On the way to the city he abandoned all caution. Face to face with the danger he even challenged the authorities. Surrounded by pilgrims, he entered the city as a true claimant to the throne (Mark 11.1–10) and provoked the spiritual leaders by not concealing his criticism of their conduct in the temple (Mark 11.15–17). Ordinary people were deeply impressed by his words and actions. Initially there was uncertainty among those in power (Mark 11.27–33), but gradually people thought it necessary to take action against this charismatic prophet who came from a Galilee which was always troubled and rebellious (Mark 12.12; 14.1–2).

On Passover night Jesus was arrested in Gethsemane. Presumably this was a combined operation by the Jewish temple police and the Roman forces of occupation (John 18.2, 12). Who took the initiative for this action is uncertain. Was it Pontius Pilate? Or did the Jewish leaders resolve to intervene and did they find Pilate ready to collaborate? The latter seems most probable, because the Gospels say that Jesus had first to answer before the Sanhedrin, and only after that was handed over to the Roman procurator Pontius Pilate (Mark 15.1–5).

It is impossible here to present all the details of the trial of Jesus. I shall limit myself to a few aspects. Jewish authors emphasize that Jesus was not condemned to death by the *whole* Jewish people. Some texts in the Gospels which seem to suggest that (like Matt.27.25) do not do justice to the historical course of events and need to be presented as evidence that violence was done to historical truth at a very early stage in church history: there was an interest in acquitting Pilate – Christianity was gaining increasing support in the Roman empire – and accusing the Jewish people as a whole.

However, Jesus was not stoned by the Jewish authorities and their minions, but mocked and crucified by Roman soldiers. He did not die as one who had transgressed the commandments of the Torah, but was executed as a *political* troublemaker. The Jewish leaders and the Roman occupation authorities entered into a monstrous alliance because they both thought it necessary that this wonderful charismatic prophet who was admired by ordinary people should be arrested as unobtrusively as possible and done away with. Recent history had taught them that 'messianic' emotions could run high among the people in the days of the Jewish Passover. Therefore Jesus was a danger to public order (John 11.50).

After his nocturnal arrest Jesus was interrogated by the high priest and finally accused of blasphemy: a religious concept (Mark 14.64). Nevertheless, the Jewish leaders handed him over to the Romans. Clearly for them the political aspects of the affair were the most important. As supporters of the Sadducean trend within the Judaism of this time they were not interested in messianic expectations. For them a messianic pretender was not very different from a man with dangerous *political* aspirations. This was a view which was shared by the Roman forces of occupation, as is witnessed by the fact that Pilate had the words 'king of the Jews' inscribed on the cross (Mark 15.26).

From Passover to Easter[22]

Jesus of Nazareth died on the cross. Was this the tragic end of a good man, the undeserved martyr death of a man full of ideals and good intentions? The Christian tradition points to Easter and speaks not of an 'end' but of a striking new beginning: God raised the crucified Jesus from death (Mark 16.6; I Cor.15.3–4).

There is a fundamental difference between Jewish views of Jesus of Nazareth and Christian *faith* in the risen Lord. As an illustration, here are some lines from the work of Schalom Ben-Chorin: 'Thus according to the Jewish view of history Jesus' life ends as a tragic failure. This does not detract from his greatness, even for the Jewish view of history. That is certainly not the case. Rabbi Akiba, who regarded Bar Kochba as the Messiah, also perished tragically and died a martyr for his faith. In the eyes of the Jewish people his tragic error does not detract from his greatness. Rather, the Jewish tradition explains such a mistake with the argument: "God sometimes blinds the eyes of the wise out of love for Israel." Jesus of Nazareth, too, made a tragic mistake: his eyes too were blinded out of love for Israel.'[23]

At the end of the first century the ways of Judaism and Christianity parted. In the Christian community it was confessed that Jesus is the Christ, whereas the Jewish tradition could not recognize him as the Messiah. In the course of history the gulf grew deeper and deeper and seemed to have become unbridgable. In our century the well-known Jewish philosopher Martin Buber expressed the difference between the Christian and Jewish view of the 'messiahship of Jesus' in an impressive way. He did so with reference to the Gospel story about Peter's confession in Mark 8.27–30: 'I believe that in Caesarea Philippi a word was spoken which was meant honestly and yet is not true; and the fact that it has been repeated down the centuries does not make it true. I believe that God does not reveal himself in men, but only through men. I believe that Meshiach did not come at a particular moment in history; his coming can only be the end of history. I believe that the redemption of the world did not become a fact nineteen centuries ago: we still live in a world which has not been redeemed; we still look for redemption, and each of us is called to collaborate in the redemption of the world. Anyone who exalts Jesus so highly no longer belongs among us; and if he wants to reject our belief that redemption lies in the future, then our ways part.' For Martin Buber Jesus is not *the* Messiah; he was one of the servants of God. These servants were forerunners of the end, people equipped with messianic power, but for that reason they need not be identified with the Messiah. Not even Jesus need be. However, Buber calls Jesus his brother. Schalom Ben-Chorim also speaks of Jesus of Nazareth in this spirit: 'I feel his brotherly hand grasping me and drawing me to follow him. This hand marked with wounds is *not* the hand of the Messiah. It is definitely not a *divine* hand but a *human* one, and the deepest suffering is etched in its lines. This distinguishes me, a Jew, from Christians. And yet we know that we are touched by the same hand. It is the hand of a great witness to the faith in Israel.'

Paul to blame?

Who is Jesus? A Jewish man who lived in the land of Israel at the beginning of our era. Despite his violent death on the cross he had no intention of going outside the limits of the Jewish tradition.

Jesus did not found a new religion. But after his crucifixion Christianity came into being, and the Christian church began its triumphal progress through the Gentile world. Since the rise of Enlightenment thought in the eighteenth century this development has become an issue in Christian theology, and the Jewish contribution to the discussion gives it an extra dimension. New Testament scholars trained in historical criticism often say that the rise of Christianity does not go back to Jesus of Nazareth but to the apostle Paul. And usually in Jewish literature an accusing finger is pointed in the direction of the apostle to the Gentiles.[24] Whether this accusation is correct depends on the interpretation of the apostle's letters. Did he deliberately create a distance from the Jewish tradition and did he trivialize the meaning of the Torah, or did he not do that in principle, but was simply concerned also to give Gentiles a share in Christ's salvation? To win the Gentiles he played for high stakes – were they perhaps too high?

9

Nag Hammadi and Qumran

New sources?

Historical investigation takes place on the basis of sources, oral and written: archives, chronicles, accounts and narratives of eye-witnesses. There is great delight and high expectation when new sources are discovered. Sometimes a musicologist finds a hitherto unknown work of a famous composer in the dusty corner of an old library. After countless fruitless attempts archaeologists come upon the remains of an age-old city. Unexpectedly letters are found among the papers left behind at the death of a famous writer or an influential politician.

Perhaps the thought has occurred to many readers of the previous chapters that investigation into the historical Jesus has got bogged down and that therefore the discovery of new documents is needed. In the debate, for a long time there was agreement that there were no sources outside the New Testament writings which could withstand the test of historical criticism. In such a situation new sources which could give powerful impetus to the investigation would of course be very welcome. However, in the recent past no direct new sources have yet to come to light. So far no writings which could have been written by Jesus himself have been found.[1] No picture of him has ever been discovered. Archaeologists have not been able to lay their hands on Jewish or Roman archives which give an account of the trial of Jesus.

When it comes to indirect sources, however, the situation is much better. Since the second half of the eighteenth century more and more has gradually become known about the world in which Jesus lived. The rediscovery of early Jewish writings led to the insight that the intertestamental period is of the utmost importance for the exegesis of the Gospels. Thus as early as 1773 the complete text of the Apocalypse of Enoch, an intertestamental writing consisting of more than 100 chapters, turned up; in it ideas appear – like the 'Son of Man' – which are associated with Jesus in the Gospels.[2] During the nineteenth century scholarly studies appeared of Jewish apocalyptic in the period around the beginning of our era.[3] On the basis of this research Albert Schweitzer developed his thoroughgoing eschatological interpretation of Jesus' preaching. Nor did things stop there. In the nineteenth and twentieth century knowledge of the Jewish world at the time of Jesus increased further. Freed from dogmatic presuppositions, exegetes ventured to go beyond the limits of their discipline and seemed prepared to learn from rabbis.[4] Honesty compels one to say that of course the problem of the historical Jesus cannot be solved definitively in this way. Things are not as simple as that. Knowledge of the world in which Jesus lived does not immediately create a new direct approach to him. But it does not seem rash to suggest that it is now possible, in a roundabout way, to sketch a fairly accurate profile of him, because the 'context' in which he lived has become so much clearer. Jesus did not exist in isolation, but formed part of early Jewish society at the beginning of the first century of our era. It may be expected that with this newly acquired knowledge the quest of the historical Jesus can form a better 'picture' of him than was possible in the past.

Apocryphal Gospels[5]

To this point it could have been concluded from my account of the discussion of the historical Jesus that the quest was exclusively concerned with the New Testament in general and the four canonical Gospels in particular. And in fact non-canonical writings have played no role in the debate. That is not strange. Under the impact of the confession that scripture has to stand at the centre – *sola scriptura* – Protestant exegetes have usually showed little interest in early Christian writings which claim to be of equal value to a canonical Gospel, letter or apocalypse. Although these books bear the name of apostles, they have not found a place in the canon of the Bible and therefore they have no authority. The verdict of historical criticism was no less negative. Of course the law can no longer be laid down on the sole basis of Scripture, but biblical critics have been just as unenthusiastic as others about the value of such early Christian writings.

For centuries it has been customary to call these writings *apocryphal*. The term is evocative but unhelpful. 'Apocrypha' originally means 'hidden'. However, apocryphal books are not called apocryphal because they remained unknown or hidden, but because they were not accepted into the canon. The consequence is that the term 'apocrypha' has taken on another meaning: obscure, dark and above all inferior. The conclusion must still be that apocryphal Gospels contain no information relevant to the quest of the historical Jesus. Even today such a negative judgment can be made without difficulty. However, that does not mean that these books are uninteresting; apocryphal Gospels provide information about theological developments in the first centuries of church history. Their authors seem to have been surprisingly creative. Stories from the canonical Gospels are worked over, new facts added and gaps filled in. The apocryphal Gospels have considerably more to say about those episodes from the life of Jesus about which the canonical writings are silent. Pious fantasy created all kinds of new stories. That applies in particular to Jesus' birth and his early years. A well-known and influential apocryphal Gospel written in the second half of the second century goes even further back and gives a lengthy account of events before the birth of Jesus.

This apocryphal Gospel is known by the name *Protevangelium Jacobi*, literally 'Pre-Gospel of James'.[6] It deserves attention because it contains the foundations of the dogma of the virgin birth and the veneration of Mary the mother of Jesus.[7] In this 'Pre-Gospel', attributed to the James who is known in the New Testament as 'the brother of the Lord' (Gal.1.19), the past is deliberately re-written to disarm for good attacks by the opponents of early Christianity. Mary is not an ignorant young woman from a poor milieu who was made pregnant by a Roman soldier. The apocryphal writing emphasizes the great wealth of her parents, Joachim and Anna. Inspired by well-known stories in the Bible about barren parents – Abraham and Sarah in Genesis, Elkanah and Hannah in I Samuel 1, Zechariah and Elisabeth in Luke 1 – it tells of Anna's barrenness. Just as the miraculous conception and birth of Isaac and Samuel can be described, so too can that of Mary, the mother of Jesus. From her youth up, Mary too, like Samuel, spends her time in the temple. So she can be cleared of any suspicion of ever having had a love affair. Mary lives as a nun, a holy virgin who has the task of weaving curtains for the temple. She marries Joseph, an old man who poses no threat to her virginity. He has children by an earlier marriage. When the Gospels speak of brothers and sisters of Jesus (Mark 6.3), these are children of the earlier marriage of Joseph. Mary was not simply virgin before the birth of Jesus but also remained virgin during and after his birth.

Unknown Gospels[8]

In the introduction to his Gospel, Luke says that he is not the first to have tried to set down recollections of Jesus' words and actions in writing. Others have preceded him. Luke even speaks of many who have done so (Luke 1.1). Evidently a number of Gospels were in circulation in the first Christian century. In all probability the evangelist completed his book in the 80s. At that moment he could not have known of the existence of any of the apocryphal Gospels that we have. They are unmistakably of a later date. That Luke nevertheless writes that 'many have tried to set down an account' must mean that he knew Gospels which have since disappeared.

We can also infer from writings of the church fathers that they knew not only of the existence but also of the content of yet other non-canonical Gospels than those apocryphal Gospels which have been known for some time. They refer to them and sometimes quote from them. Usually they do so, not to give their approval but to warn their readers against the heretical character of these non-canonical Gospels. For that reason, in the long run such Gospels were to disappear from circulation.

A number of these non-canonical Gospels unmistakably have a Jewish-Christian character.[9] The best known in the early church was the Gospel of the Hebrews. It is mentioned in the works of both Clement of Alexandria and Origen, who also lived in Alexandria. That could indicate that this Gospel was mainly in circulation in Egypt. It was presumably written in the first half of the second century. Fragments also of the Gospel of the Nazareans can be found in the writings of the church fathers Jerome and Epiphanius. This work seems to have been a revision of the canonical Gospel of Matthew. It was written in Western Syria in a Jewish Christian community which called itself the Nazareans, because they wanted to be followers of Jesus the Nazarean (Matt.2.3; 26.71; Acts 24.5). This non-canonical Gospel, too, in all probability comes from the first half of the second century. The same also applies to the third writing which deserves mention in this connection: the Gospel of the Ebionites. The name 'Ebionites' is derived from a Hebrew word meaning 'poor'. Probably a group of Jewish followers of Jesus were inspired by the Beatitudes of the Sermon on the Mount to give themselves the honorific title 'the poor': poor in spirit, or poor before God (Matt.5.3). The church father Irenaeus, bishop of Lyons in the second half of the second century, already seems to know the Gospel, if only from hearsay. He thinks that it was composed east of the Jordan.

At the end of the first century the position of Jewish Christians became increasingly more difficult.[10] As followers of Jesus they were no longer welcome in the synagogue; and they were increasingly becoming 'strangers' in the Christian church. They were aware of their Jewishness and attached great importance to observing the commandments of the Torah. Thanks to the successful preaching of the Gospel by Paul and other apostles, however, this Torah was fading into the background in the Christian community. It is evident from the letters of Paul – in particular his letter to the Galatians – that the apostle felt compelled to make a sacrifice: for Gentiles the way to Christ does not go through circumcision – and thus the Torah – but directly through faith. This development meant that Jewish Christians who wanted to remain faithful to the Torah were isolated. Their isolation was heightened by their inability to subscribe to the high christology which was gaining increasing influence in the church. With an appeal to Scripture, they saw Jesus primarily as the 'eschatological' prophet after the pattern of Moses (Deut.18.15–18). The consequences were inevitable. In the long run the official church no longer accepted their 'low' christology. The church fathers challenged their ideas. Finally the Jewish Christians were condemned as heretics. Their writings, including the Gospels mentioned above, vanished from the scene.[11]

In the winter of 1886–7 a team of French archaeologists made a surprising discovery. In a cemetery in the small place of Akhmim in southern Egypt they found in the grave of a monk a small book consisting of thirty-four parchment leaves from the eighth or ninth century. Among other things, the book contained Greek fragments of the Gospel of Peter[12] and the Apocalypse of Peter. The first of these writings is particularly interesting for us. The Gospel of Peter is mentioned once in the patristic literature of the second century, but exclusively in a negative sense. That will be why it disappeared from circulation and only re-emerged by chance in Egypt after many centuries. Can a satisfactory explanation be found as to why a work which had already had aspersions cast on it in the second century could have been put in the grave of a monk as late as the eighth or ninth century? It is difficult to give an answer. Perhaps the discovery shows that even the authority of famous church fathers had its limits and that their orders were not followed slavishly by everyone.

The fragment of the Gospel of Peter that was found in Egypt comprises around sixteen verses which relate the passion, death and resurrection of Jesus. Generally speaking, there are many agreements with the account in the four canonical Gospels. However, there are also differences. Pilate is acquitted, and the Jews are made responsible for the crucifixion. The silence of Jesus is explained as a consequence of the fact that he felt no pain. The author of the apocryphal Gospel unmistakably intended to emphasize Jesus' divinity. Jesus was not completely human. His humanity was only 'semblance'.

What is the value of such a work? After its publication, for a long time it was a focus of interest and was intensively studied. Finally, some degree of consensus developed among scholars that the Gospel of Peter could have no significance for the question of the historical Jesus. However, the writing is interesting as a notable voice from the early church. Moreover later in the present book it will emerge that the Gospel of Peter has not wholly disappeared from discussion of the historical Jesus.

Some years after the publication of the Gospel of Peter, archaeologists at work in Egypt could announce a notable new find.

In 1897, English researchers in the middle of Egypt, around ancient Oxyrhynchus, discovered a papyrus leaf which seemed to contain eight sayings of Jesus. Each saying was introduced with the words 'Jesus said'. Some sayings showed a good deal of agreement with sayings of Jesus known from the Gospels, but others were completely new. In 1903 and 1905 this discovery was followed by further discoveries in Oxyrhynchus of papyri containing sayings of Jesus. Unfortunately some texts were so badly damaged that it was impossible to make a reliable translation. We shall see later that the investigation has even more surprises in store, and the new discoveries made it possible to fill some of the gaps in the Oxyrhynchus papyri. At that point it will also make sense to consider the value of these discoveries for the debate on the historical Jesus.

In the course of time it proved that the discoveries mentioned above did not exhaust the potential of the Middle East. The greatest surprises were still hidden in the sand of the desert and in caves.

Nag Hammadi[13]

In December 1945, peasants digging graves in a cemetery near Nag Hammadi, a village in the south of Egypt, came upon a large jar. It was completely filled with ancient manuscripts on papyrus leaves. Unfortunately it is impossible to say precisely how many manuscripts the peasants found. Leaves have disappeared, but no one knows how many. The finders did not realize that they had a treasure of great value in their hands. They sold the contents of the jar for a small sum to the son of a Coptic priest. In the course of time the manuscripts found a place in the Coptic Museum in Cairo.

Thus fifty years ago an age-old 'library' was rediscovered in Nag Hammadi. The jar contained around 1,000 papyrus leaves, of which almost 800 remained intact. From the good state in which by far the majority of the manuscripts were preserved, we should probably infer that in the distant past they were not thrown away heedlessly because they were no longer read and no one had any interest in them. They were carefully hidden in thirteen codices bound in leather – not scrolls, but bundles of papyrus leaves in book form.

The Nag Hammadi 'library' consists of around fifty works in Coptic.[14] It seems certain that the manuscripts date from the fourth century and that they were written by Gnostics. We know from writings of the church fathers that in the first centuries of church history 'gnosis'[15] (= literally 'knowledge': redemption through knowledge) found a considerable following in Christian circles. After a long dispute, Gnosticism was branded a heresy in the course of the third and fourth centuries. Gnostic writings disappeared or were destroyed, and after that were known only from quotations in the books of church fathers who vigorously disputed them. It is conceivable that in the fourth century Egyptian monks in the immediate vicinity of Nag Hammadi felt compelled to hide their library temporarily, perhaps with sore feelings and in the hope of better times.

The New Testament and Nag Hammadi

What has just been said could lead to the simple conclusion that the discoveries in Nag Hammadi are particularly interesting, but have no importance for the quest of the historical Jesus. The manuscripts which were found in Nag Hammadi date from the fourth century, whereas Jesus lived and died in the first decade of the first century. But the Dutch scholar Gilles Quispel, who played an important role in the publication of the first writings from Nag Hammadi, wrote in 1971: 'We live in a great time. On all sides discoveries are being made which put the earliest history of Christianity in a new and unexpected light.' These words raise questions: how can writings from the fourth century shed new and surprising light on the earliest history of Christianity?

A large number of manuscripts were found in the Gnostic library of Nag Hammadi which bear the name of apostles known from the New Testament: Paul, John, James, Thomas, Peter and Philip. Were all these Gospels, letters and apocalypses really written by Christians of the first generation? This seems hardly likely. Moreover it is not true. There is sufficient reason to suppose that we can rule out the possibility that any of the writings found in Egypt had an apostolic origin.

The Nag Hammadi library gives a fascinating picture of a 'trend' which was not unusual in the first centuries of Christianity. New Gospels and letters, new acts of apostles and new 'revelations', were modelled on writings which had attained canonical status. New Testament scholars are largely agreed on the historical value of such writings. They cannot be used as sources for a reconstruction of the life of Jesus. Apocryphal Gospels do not give us any new facts about the past, but they show how Christianity was thought out and believed in during the first centuries.

All this also applies to the Gnostic library of Nag Hammadi. The manuscripts which were found there are extremely important, because they give modern readers a picture of an early Christian movement which was strongly influenced by Gnostic ideas. Such notions were to some degree known from quotations in the works of influential church fathers, but the Nag Hammadi discovery made it possible to read the actual writings and get a more complete insight into Gnostic thought.[16]

The Gospel of Thomas[17]

Without changing the conclusions arrived at above, an exception needs to be made for one manuscript from Nag Hammadi. In the context of the quest for the historical Jesus we now need to look at this writing more closely. Its importance only gradually became clear. So it was a while before a complete edition of the text was produced. Other manuscripts were given preference.

The publication of very old manuscripts is always a time-consuming affair. That is the case with the Qumran scrolls, and it also applied to the Nag Hammadi Library. Scholars need time and tranquillity to set to work and present their findings in a responsible way. Thanks to the efforts of Gilles Quispel, who has already been mentioned, in 1956 the first complete manuscript was published. This was The Gospel of Truth, a Gnostic work from the second century which had been known previously (but not very well) from quotations and comments in the church fathers. The word 'Gospel' can easily arouse misunderstandings, since this is not a Gospel in the usual sense of the word, but rather a homily in which the truth of the gospel of Christ is revealed. This 'Gospel', too, does not offer researchers new access to the historical Jesus.

According to present-day insights, such a conclusion can no longer be drawn about the Gospel of Thomas. The complete Coptic text of this work was only published in 1959,[18] but immediately it attracted a great deal of attention world-wide. References could be found in the patristic literature to a Gospel by the apostle Thomas, but it seemed to have disappeared for ever. Centuries later it turned up in Egypt. At present there is agreement that this 'Gospel' should be seen as the most important discovery of Nag Hammadi. That is certainly the case if we look at the relationship between the Nag Hammadi manuscripts and the New Testament in general and the Gospels in particular.[19]

It is customary to speak of the 'Gospel of Thomas', but even this name can lead to misunderstandings and give the impression that the work is comparable to the four known canonical Gospels. That is certainly not the case. The Gospel of Thomas is not a consecutive account which begins with the birth of Jesus in Bethlehem, goes on to his activity in Galilee and ends with his death on the cross in Jerusalem. We look in vain in the Gospel of Thomas for anything like a birth narrative, far less for a passion narrative. This 'Gospel' consists of 114 sayings of Jesus. The length of these sayings differs greatly. Some comprise only a few words, others are a few lines long. Rarely does Jesus discuss with anyone, and usually he engages in a monologue. Since there are no stories, it is hard to speak of a chronology. Moreover, so far it has not been possible to demonstrate convincingly anything like a development of thought in the sayings.

From Egypt to Syria

The description of the Gospel of Thomas presented above will presumably give little confidence that the content of this Gospel could be a new way to the historical Jesus. Moreover, honesty compels us to recognize that here we are treading on very controversial ground. It will not be possible to discuss all the details at length here. I shall limit myself to those questions and points for discussion which are important for my theme.

Research into the Gospel of Thomas sometimes seems like a detective story. Slowly insight into the complex problem began to grow, and pieces of the jig-saw puzzle fell into place. The first question which needed to be answered was, 'Where and when was this work written?' Shortly after the publication of the Coptic text, scholars made a surprising discovery. Some sayings from the Gospel of Thomas showed a close affinity to the Greek texts which were found on the Oxyrhynchus papyri mentioned above. Thus there must have been a Greek version of the Gospel of Thomas as well as a Coptic one. It does not seem improbable that the origin of the Gospel of Thomas is to be sought in the south of Egypt.

A second discovery focussed attention on Syria. The Syrian church played an important role in the first centuries of Christianity. Above all Antioch in the west and Edessa in the east were important centres of theological reflection.[20] The most important literary 'products' of this time may be said to include the *Diatessaron* (= a Gospel harmony) by the Syrian theologian Tatian.[21] Unfortunately the complete work has been lost, and only parts can be reconstructed from references and quotations in writing of the church fathers.

Little can be said with certainty about the way in which Tatian worked and the literary sources which he used in compiling his Gospel harmony. Sometimes his text shows striking divergences from the four canonical Gospels. It is not easy to explain this. It is possible that he had access to a textual variant which already contained these differences. However, it seems more probable that in addition to the four canonical Gospels he made use of a non-canonical tradition of the sayings and actions of Jesus. Is it too much to suppose that the Syrian Tatian may have been in possession of one or more of the above-mentioned Jewish-Christian Gospels?

The discovery of the Gospel of Thomas in Nag Hammadi disclosed new elements within the early Christian tradition.[22] A careful comparison between the Gospel of Thomas and Tatian's *Diatessaron* disclosed a certain affinity between the two writings. That focussed the investigation on Syria, and after that it was quite natural to direct attention towards Edessa. Tatian had spent some time in this city and had perhaps written his *Diatessaron* there. Moreover the apostle Thomas was held in high repute there. In Edessa the title of the Gospel of Thomas will have been read with satisfaction: 'These are the secret sayings which Jesus the living one spoke and which Didymos Judas Thomas wrote down.' Little can be said with certainty about this period. The *Diatessaron* was written around 170; perhaps we can assume that the Gospel of Thomas was earlier. The year 140 is usually given as a date.

This conclusion may disappoint some people. To all appearances, the Gospel of Thomas does not make us any wiser about the historical Jesus. The middle of the second century is still around a century away from the period in which Jesus lived. In that case the Gospel of Thomas can hardly be regarded as a historically reliable source of the life of Jesus. That is, unless traditions can be found in it which seem to be considerably older.

Authentic sayings of Jesus

How far back can we go? My attempt to answer to this question must be a very cautious one. There is absolutely no consensus in scholarly literature. One might almost say that there are 'as many opinions as there are heads'. However, there is no escaping the problem in the short term, because it will prove that at present the Gospel is playing an important role in discussion of the historical Jesus.

Scholars gradually realized that the Gospel of Thomas can hardly be regarded as a historical unity. Initially emphasis was mainly put on the Gnostic character of the work. That was not so surprising, since the Gospel had long had a place in a Gnostic library and it contained quite a number of sayings which had to be interpreted as Gnostic. The title speaks of 'secret sayings'. Moreover it remains significant that the 'Gospel' limits itself to the sayings of Jesus and has little or no interest in his actions. At the centre are words which give people the possibility of gaining knowledge (*gnosis*). Only through this gnosis can believers be redeemed. There is not a word about the suffering of Jesus on the cross. This is not mentioned, nor does it seem to have any soteriological significance.

Must the conclusion then be that the Gospel of Thomas is a typically Gnostic writing – attractive, but of no significance for the quest of the historical Jesus? The problem seems to be more complex. Initially the view prevailed that the whole of the Gospel of Thomas was Gnostic. At the same time, though, researchers recognized that it was less Gnostic than the other writings in the Nag Hammadi library. The Gospel occupied a separate position in that it also contained writings which were influenced by other theological traditions. Thus in Saying 12 Jesus gives his disciples remarkable advice. They ask him who will be their leader when he has gone away. Jesus' answer is surprising: 'Wherever you are, you are to go to James the righteous, for whose sake heaven and earth came into being' (Logion 12). Gilles Quispel in particular repeatedly pointed to this sort of passage at a very early stage of the investigation. He challenged the idea that the Gospel of Thomas was Gnostic and believed that it was influenced by a Jewish-Christian tradition.[23] This 'James the brother of the Lord' is mentioned in the New Testament (Gal.1.19). He emerged as leader and spokesman of the early Christian community in Jerusalem (Gal.2.9; Acts 15.13). The facts are sparse and so it is not easy to get a clear picture of James and his position within earliest Christianity. In the New Testament, he emerges above all as a wise mediator and arbitrator between on the one hand those who want to impose the law even on Gentile Christians, and on the other Paul and those like him who reject such a rigorous view. In the non-canonical writings James is called 'the Just' or 'the Righteous' because he opted for a Christianity in which the Torah continued to apply undiminished and without exception.[24]

Clearly the Gospel of Thomas has different 'layers': a late layer with a Gnostic character, but also earlier layers which are not (yet) influenced by Gnostic ideas. Anyone who has detected this can look for the earliest layer in the Gospel of Thomas, like an archaeologist. In this way the researcher comes upon a number of sayings which are related to sayings of Jesus in the canonical Gospels. Here is a well-known example as an illustration:

There was a good man who owned a vineyard. He leased it to tenant farmers so that they might work it and he might collect the produce from them. He sent his servant so that the tenants might give him the produce of the vineyard. They seized his servant and beat him, all but killing him. The servant went back and told his master.

The master said, 'Perhaps he did not recognize them.'

He sent another servant. The tenants beat this one as well.

Then the owner sent his son and said, 'Perhaps they will show respect to my son.' Because the tenants knew that it was he who was the heir to the vineyard, they seized him and killed him.

Let him who has ears hear (*Logion* 65).

Those who are at home in the New Testament will have heard many familiar echoes in this story. But it will presumably not have escaped them that it sometimes differs from the more familiar, canonical, version. A comparison with the parable of the wicked husbandmen in the three synoptic Gospels (Mark 12.1–12; Matt.21.33–46; Luke 20.9–19) brings out the fact that the version in the Gospel of Thomas is brief and simple. Already long before the Nag Hammadi discovery, exegetes pointed out the possibility that the parable in the canonical Gospels was strongly influenced by the christological reflection in the early Christian community. Thus Joachim Jeremias once reconstructed an 'original' parable of Jesus which shows striking similarities to the logion of the Gospel of Thomas quoted above.[25]

Does this 'Gospel', which was hidden in a jar in Egypt in the midst of a collection of Gnostic writings, finally bring us close to the historical Jesus? Does this 'Gospel', with the complex history of its origin, contain elements which can be evaluated as authentic sayings of Jesus? That seems almost too good to be true. However, there are exegetes who defend such a thesis and reckon that the earliest 'layers' in the Gospel of Thomas could be old, perhaps even older than the canonical Gospels. It will prove later that this has significant consequences for the quest of the historical Jesus. However, things had not yet got that far in the first years after the Second World War.

Qumran: the discovery

At the end of 1945, Egyptian peasants in Nag Hammadi had found a Gnostic library. A short time later, in the spring of 1947, some Bedouins caused new excitement. In a remote cave in the hills on the north-western shore of the Dead Sea they found jars which proved to contain scrolls. This time too there were enough ingredients for an exciting thriller: mysterious writings from centuries long past; the fascinating surroundings of the Dead Sea; Bedouins who kept the place where they had found the scrolls secret; scholars who contradicted and even worked against one another; church leaders who looked on the publication of the writings with anxiety; and all this taking place in the turbulent period around the foundation of the state of Israel in 1948.[26]

Since 1947, over the course of time writings have been found in eleven caves – sometimes reasonably to well-preserved scrolls, often fragments hardly bigger than a postage stamp. Archaeologists investigated a ruined hill in the immediate neighbourhood of the caves – called Hirbet Qumran – and uncovered the remains of a complex of buildings. Clearly this was the domicile of the writers and readers of these mysterious writings. Who were they and why had they chosen this strange place, on the edge of the wilderness, to live and work in?

Excitement increased when it became clear that the writings and buildings dated from the period around the beginning of our era. In other words, Qumran was inhabited in the time of Jesus. Not far away – around six miles as the crow flies – John the Baptist was baptizing in the Jordan. Could John have been acquainted with the existence of Qumran? According to the evangelist Luke, some time beforehand he had retreated into the wilderness (Luke 1.80). Is it too much to suppose that he spent those days in the complex of buildings on the shore of the Dead Sea?

Essenes

Often one question leads to another. Soon after the first discoveries in 1947, scholars and journalists began to speculate on possible relations not only between John the Baptist and Qumran, but also between Jesus of Nazareth and Qumran. After his baptism in the Jordan, Jesus too went into the wilderness. In the synoptic Gospels it is emphasized that the Spirit of God led him into the wilderness and that there he was tempted by the devil (Mark 1.9–11; Matt.4.1–11; Luke 4.1–13). That means that it is not impossible that at one stage Jesus could have spent some time in the Qumran community.

The discussion is made more difficult by the simple fact that the New Testament contains no references to a community on the shores of the Dead Sea. There is no satisfactory explanation for this silence on the part of evangelists and apostles. In some contemporary extra-biblical sources we find mention of pious groups who are called Essenes. Descriptions of their way of life can be found in two places in early Jewish literature: (*a*) in the work of Philo, the Jewish philosopher and scriptural scholar, who lived in Alexandria in Egypt;

he lived from around 15 BCE to 50 CE and thus can be regarded as a contemporary of Jesus;[27] (b) in writings of the Jewish historian Flavius Josephus (37/38 – after 100).[28] Both authors make no secret of their admiration for the life-style of the Essenes, pious Jews who strictly observed the commandments of the Torah. When members entered the community they parted with their possessions and lived a celibate life. Was Qumran the place where the Essenes had lived? At present this question is answered in the affirmative by most scholars.[29]

Origin and destruction

Little can be said with certainty about the origin of Qumran. There are indications that the community formed shortly after the Maccabean victory in 164 BCE and as a consequence of a serious conflict between priests in Jerusalem. Under the leadership of the man who is called the 'Teacher of Righteousness' in the Qumran writings, a group of priests definitively turned their backs on the temple. Inspired by Isa.40.3 – 'In the wilderness prepare the way of the Lord' – they went into the desert area on the shores of the Dead Sea. There they formed a closed community which had a hierarchical structure, with strict rules and regulations.

After the discoveries in 1947, words like 'sect' and 'conventicle' quickly became established in both popular and scholarly literature. This is understandable, since in their writings the members of the community described themselves as 'the elect'. They termed themselves the 'sons of light' and called on one another to hate 'the sons of darkness' – i.e. all outsiders and thus also those Jews who did not sympathize with their ideals.

The Qumran community existed for quite some time and was certainly no flash in the pan. Traces have been found in the ruins of damage which was the result of an earthquake around 30 BCE. Probably the then inhabitants abandoned the complex of buildings at that time, but in due course Essenes returned to the age-old community centre and restored it so that it could be inhabited again.

The end came during the Jewish war which broke out in 66. Archaeological investigation indicates that a Roman garrison was camped in Qumran already before the destruction of Judaea. Before the members of the community tried to save themselves, they hid their writings in the caves high above their settlement. Perhaps they hoped that they would return again one day when God had defeated their enemies in an apocalyptic battle.

Jesus and Qumran[30]

Since 1947 it has constantly been asked whether Jesus possibly spent any time in Qumran. Because there are no lists of members, such a question can never be answered with certainty, and we are necessarily in the realm of conjectures and presuppositions. In the first instance people are inclined to deny the existence of any relationship between Jesus and Qumran. It can be deduced from the writings of the Qumran community that its members had opted for a 'sectarian' existence. They sought power in the isolation of their own group. John the Baptist and Jesus of Nazareth were active in the outside world, attracted much attention, and deliberately did not limit their activities to a group of like-minded people. The evangelists report that Jesus even moved in the society of the unclean and the sinners, people who were looked down on by the pious. He saw it as his task to restore 'the lost sheep of the house of Israel' to the fold (Matt.15.24). In contrast to Qumran, Jesus emphasized that the love of neighbour may not be limited to those of like mind (Matt.5.43–48).

So there are differences but also agreements. Already at an early stage, the Teacher of Righteousness attracted attention. Did he have the same role in his community as Jesus was later to have in the circle of his disciples? Behind this question lies another question: does the comparison between Jesus and the Teacher of Righteousness lead to the conclusion that Jesus is less unique than the church has always claimed? There were more parallels: the ritual purity of the community suggested the baptism by John the Baptist; the communal meals could be regarded as forerunners of the Christian eucharist; the voluntary poverty recalled the ideals of the early Christian community in Jerusalem; the dualism of light and darkness in the Qumran writings could indicate an affinity to the Gospel according to John.

In newspapers and magazines, in programmes on radio and television, it is regularly suggested that there is a 'secret of Qumran'. It is said that the uncovering of this secret would have dramatic consequences for the Christian church. For this reason, the Vatican was said to be opposing the publication of the 'dangerous' writings of Qumran with every possible means. Some also point an accusing finger in the direction of scholars who are burdened with the deciphering of the writings. They are said to be going slow because they do not want to put their jobs at risk and because they are involved in academic disputes.

Would the Christian church really be shaken to its foundations if all the Qumran writings were published?[31] Would almost two thousand years of Christian theology prove to be based on a fiction and would the traditional picture of Jesus Christ need to be radically revised?

Anyone who ventures to ask such sensational questions can be guaranteed an audience, and recently the publications of the American Robert Eisenman have been attracting a great deal of attention. Briefly, he argues that early Christianity – inspired by Jesus – had a revolutionary character and found a following among the Zealots who between 66 and 70 unleashed the Jewish War against the Romans. According to Eisenman, the Teacher of Righteousness in the Qumran writings is none other than James 'the brother of the Lord' (Gal.1.19), the influential leader of the early Christian community in Jerusalem.[32] Those who take that line have little difficulty in concluding that the community of Qumran can very well be identified with the early Christian community in Jerusalem.

It is hardly surprising to find that in this view, too, the apostle Paul is given a negative role. The Jewish Sanhedrin, dominated by opponents of the Zealot movement, sent him against the Qumran community. Paul realized that making victims does not weaken a revolutionary movement, but in fact strengthens it, so he chose another way. In modern terms, he acted as an undercover agent. He presented himself as a sympathizer and became a member of the community. He then slowly but surely began to undermine the dominant points of view from the outside. With references to scripture and tradition Paul argued that Jesus did not die as a martyr for the ideals of the Zealots, but as the crucified Christ who has brought about reconciliation between God and humankind.

Barbara Thiering, Professor of New Testament in Sydney, has also caused a sensation.[33] Her view is that all the important events in the life of Jesus took place principally in and around Qumran. Jesus belonged to this community from his youth. At the time when he became an adult and a full member, Qumran was led by John the Baptist. John was called the Teacher of Righteousness. However, the demands which he made of his disciples were so strict that tensions arose within the community. Jesus took the side of the opponents of John. In the Qumran writings – manifestly from the hand of supporters of John – the controversy between John and Jesus is described as the conflict between the Teacher of Righteousness and the Wicked Priest.

As a descendant of David Jesus thought it his duty to continue the line, so he entered into marriage with Mary Magdalene. Moreover, he joined the Zealots and made his royal entrance in the area of Qumran. Pilate felt compelled to oppose this and advanced with his troops to the Dead Sea. Jesus was arrested and crucified in the immediate vicinity of Qumran.

Barbara Thiering seems to have a lively imagination. Thus she claims that Jesus did not die on the cross. His supporters succeeded in freeing him in time and after loving care he recovered from his wounds. After these dramatic events his life moved into a tranquil backwater. He had children, was abandoned by Mary Magdalene, remarried Lydia the purple merchant, visited Jerusalem and Rome, and disappears permanently from our view at the age of seventy.

New light on Jesus

I am often asked, 'Did Jesus belong to the Qumran community? Was he an Essene?' I answer, 'If only that could be true!' And after a short pause I continue, 'What I think important is that all events he did not stay in Qumran. The Gospels report his travels through Galilee and Judaea. Evidently he shared the fortunes of those very people who in the Qumran writings are regarded as the "sons of darkness".'

Do we know more about Jesus after 1947 than in the previous

centuries? Different answers are possible to this question, too. It can be argued that we are none the wiser, since nothing is said about a certain Jesus of Nazareth in the Qumran writings. However, such a reaction fails to do justice to the great value of the Qumran discoveries for both theology and the church. We know a little more about the colourful Jewish world in which Jesus lived and in which the New Testament was written. Those who want to give free rein to their imagination may do so. And those who prefer to keep their feet on the ground will find much to think about. Words and concepts in the New Testament like the Beatitudes, the expectation of the coming of messianic figures, the hope of a final apocalyptic conflict between God and evil, seem to have parallels in the Qumran writings. The community is led by a teacher; it held communal meals and attached little value, if any, to personal possessions.

After the Qumran discoveries theology knows better than before that at the beginning of our era the Jewish world was very complex and that Jesus was part of this world. Does this conclusion deprive him of his 'uniqueness'? There is no room here to dwell at length on precisely what is meant by this term 'uniqueness'. However, it is certain that thanks also to Qumran, certain aspects of Jesus' words and actions stand out more clearly. I think it possible that he spent some time in the Qumran community, but at a particular moment he left the 'sect'. He did not seek isolation, but went into the world in search of people who risked being lost.

10

New Pictures of Jesus

An 'unacademic' intermezzo[1]

Who is Jesus? So far, with one exception – the famous book by the Romantic Ernest Renan in the nineteenth century – I have mainly given an account of the academic debate about the historical Jesus. In the next chapter I shall continue my account, but I shall interrupt my survey of New Testament scholarship here and venture outside this area, so as also to give others a say. I can imagine that readers interested in scholarship will regard the following pages with some caution. Have Albert Schweitzer's warning words been uttered to no avail? Have the hermeneutical questions of Rudolf Bultmann now been forgotten? Are we returning to the nineteenth century apparently without having learned anything from history? These questions can indeed be raised with some justification, and I will make no secret of the fact that they are also my own. But I wanted to write this 'unacademic intermezzo', and have done so with great pleasure.

Theologians have no right to claim Jesus for themselves. Historians and exegetes look at the past with a particular interest. Those who think that scholarship has the last and decisive word are imposing unnecessary limitations on themselves. The words and actions of Jesus have to be put on the dissecting table of historical criticism, but they are also heard in churches where the Christian community is assembled. I can make an extensive exegetical investigation of the Gospel of Matthew, but I hear the same words in quite a different way when they are presented in the setting of Bach's *St Matthew Passion*.

The significance of Jesus extends further than the limits which scholarly investigation can and indeed must impose. Jesus inspires men and women of all times. His words make them think, and his actions are also experienced as liberating by people of the present-day; his suffering on the cross can still make an impact in our time, to move us and to encourage us. The historian is in search of historical truth: what happened in that last passion week in Jerusalem? Who were responsible for the death of Jesus? The exegete explains and makes connections; poets, painters and composers are in a position to add new facets and experiences to whatever the historical reality was.

New biographical interest

Has the tide turned? As a result of its experiences, theological scholarship radically dismissed any idea that the four Gospels could form a biography of Jesus. Exegetes have become careful and keep quiet, or limit themselves to responsible scholarly conclusions full of 'perhaps', 'possibly' or 'probably'.

Some time ago the appearance of a real biography of Jesus caused such a stir that reviews of it even appeared in magazines and journals which usually show little interest in biblical subjects.[2] The author, A.N.Wilson, had made a name for himself by writing a dozen novels and five widely-read biographies.[3] He knew what he was doing, since he had studied theology in Oxford for a couple of years. He had dropped his studies because he could not find a way of integrating his traditionalist point of view – based on a classical dogmatic christology – with the insights which are the consequence of scholarly critical investigation of the Bible as a whole and the New Testament in particular.

In an interview, he said something about the sphere in which he had studied. To his amazement there was very little interest in the theological faculty in historical facts about the life of Jesus. 'The discipline was dominated by Germans who were exclusively interested in faith and how that had developed. At that time it was better for a theologian to know German than to know Greek.' He quoted a lecturer who even claimed that it did not matter for Christianity whether or not Jesus had really existed. Wilson continues, 'And that's a strange thing.' He also thought that he could explain the lack of interest in history. Theologians are afraid of a bad conscience and therefore make a virtue out of necessity and retreat to the safe ground of faith.

One of the lecturers in Oxford inspired Wilson. It is no chance that this was the Hungarian Jewish biblical scholar Geza Vermes, the author among other things of an interesting historical study of the life of Jesus.[4] After leaving the theological faculty Wilson wrote a great deal, but that did not prevent him from investigating the historical Jesus. He read everything that he could lay his hands on and in the meantime abandoned the last remnants of his Christian faith. The contradictions had become too great, and the tension had broken: Christian faith does not go back to Jesus, but to Paul and the other apostles of the first days. They founded the Christian church. This had not been Jesus' aim at all. He was a prophet, to some degree a worldly figure with special powers of healing. He did not regard himself as the Son of God. On the cross he died the martyr death of a Jewish rebel. This was not his wish, but the Romans could only translate his preaching of the approaching kingdom of God into political terms.

It is certainly true that anyone who knows something about the discussions which were begun by Hermann Samuel Reimarus, David Friedrich Strauss, Ernest Renan and others in the eighteenth and nineteenth centuries will not be surprised in this biography by new arguments, but to say that is not a satisfactory answer to Wilson's questions about theology and the church.

An un-churchly Christ

The Christian church and Jesus Christ seem to be inseparably linked. What would Christianity be without belief in the crucified and risen Lord? Yet since the eighteenth century – under the influence of Enlightenment thought – there have been critical voices. A clear distinction needs to be made between Jesus' proclamation of the kingdom of God on the one hand and the preaching – the kerygma – of the early Christian community in which Jesus Christ was central on the other. Jewish authors have emphasized the Jewishness of Jesus and claimed their right to him. He is returning to the history of the Jewish people as a lost son.

The Christian church comes under sharp criticism, but Jesus is admired. Whereas age-old dogma and traditional ideas are losing their value, Jesus remains a source of inspiration. This was already the case in the last century, as is evident from a passage from a work by Multatuli (1820–1887): 'There are few people mentioned in history – indeed I would venture to say that there are none – whom I love as I love Jesus. I would so love to get to know him with his faults. It is impossible that anyone who thinks Jesus sinless could love him as much as I do. There is a strange confusion in the view that I am an enemy of Jesus. Of the thousand and one Christianities, yes. And I assert that Jesus would be my ally in this hostility.' The same voices are heard in the twentieth century. Usually in attractive, well thought out sentences, sometimes even said quite simply, the message is 'No to the church but yes to Jesus'.

Does Jesus no longer feel at home within the walls of the traditional church? Has it become too narrow for him? Even within the church, many people find that the classical dogma is a constricting straitjacket. They are discovering a new Jesus. Jesus was evidently different from what the church and theology had always asserted. Views are strongly divided over the 'otherness' of Jesus. Some see him as a fierce revolutionary, but others are inspired by him for having only been interested in spiritual things. Jesus was not someone who was content with taking well-trodden paths. He behaved in an unconventional way. Anyone who liked that felt attracted to him, but others were provoked by his strange conduct. He did not sanction the traditional patriarchal authority. His behaviour was anti-authoritarian, and he was a friend of women. Jesus was not a son of God but an ordinary man with human characteristics, and it is precisely these which make him an attractive and inspiring personality.

A human being among human beings

The Son of God has become a man of flesh and blood. That was already happening in the last century, and since then this tendency has only been reinforced. In 1926, the surrealist Max Ernst (1891–1976) painted a picture with a curious title, 'The Virgin chastizes the child Jesus before three witnesses'. A small window allows three men – the painter and two of his colleagues who are portrayed as modern three kings – to see a scene which would have been quite unthinkable in mediaeval paintings: the mother Mary has put the child Jesus over her knee and is giving her son a sharp smack on his naked buttocks – obviously he has been naughty.[5]

Who is Jesus? He was a child among children, sometimes loving and tender, sometimes naughty and even a burden. He grew up in Nazareth and for a time worked as a carpenter in his father's workshop. That is what the Gospels tell us, though they do not all do so in precisely the same way (cf. Mark 6.3, 'the carpenter', with Matt.13.6, 'the son of the carpenter'). The evangelists give us strikingly little information about Jesus' emotions. On one occasion he reacts crossly or with irritation (Mark 1.43). After a long journey he seems to be tired (John 4.6). On seeing Mary's sorrow after the death of her brother Lazarus, Jesus is said to be 'deeply moved in spirit and troubled' (John 11.34). After that he weeps over the loss of a beloved friend (John 11.35). According to the evangelist John there was a special friendship between Jesus and Lazarus and his sisters: 'Now Jesus loved Martha and her sister and Lazarus' (John 11.5). In this connection, finally we can note the appearance of a special disciple of Jesus in the Fourth Gospel. He is mentioned as a key witness on a number of occasions and is described as 'the disciple whom Jesus loved' (John 13.23; 19.26; 20.2; 21.15–23).

As a human being among other human beings Jesus knew human feelings and emotions like joy and happiness, but also hunger and thirst, pain, anxiety and sorrow (cf. Heb.5.7–8). He was no monk who preferred a secluded life. He sought the company of others. He had disciples; women followed him. He was particularly concerned for the anxieties of others, their physical and spiritual pains. He was full of love for other people. Does that also mean that Jesus could have been in love, could have had 'butterflies in the stomach'? Did he kiss, touch and caress the body of another? Did he lie in the arms of a woman and love her?

I know that I am now treading on dangerous territory. Emotion can run very high in circles of orthodox believers. Such people even reject the notion that Jesus could be described as a human being among other human beings – he is also and in first place the Son of God who knew no sin – and there are doubts whether he could ever have been associated with human feelings like sexual feelings, which even now are surrounded by so many tabus. In the second half of the 1980s there was a great controversy when the American director Martin Scorcese made a film entitled *The Last Temptation of Christ*. This was based on a book by the Greek author Nikos Kazantzakis (1883–1957) with the same title which had appeared some twenty-five years earlier.

In the novel Jesus is portrayed as a human being with human experiences and emotions, and also as a man who knew erotic feelings: 'Jesus went pale, closed his eyes and saw the exuberant Mary Magdalene running along the shores of the Sea of Galilee . . .' The book did not attract a great deal of attention, but the film certainly did – all over the world. The writer was restrained in his descriptions of Jesus' love for the seductive woman from Magdala; the film director lived in another time and showed much less restraint over scenes with an erotic character. And of course it is also true that images on film are much more direct than written texts. At all events, the film confronted church and theology with a troublesome problem: anyone who takes the humanity of Jesus seriously will sooner or later have to take his sexuality into account. And anyone who claims that this cannot be done, or that it is theologically irrelevant, may expect to be asked whether adopting that line over the humanity of Jesus does not eventually lead to docetism.

A rebel Jesus

Who is Jesus? If he really lived as a human being among human beings and nothing human was alien to him, he must also have felt the burden of oppression under which the Jewish people suffered around the beginning of our era. Certainly his 'ancestral' town was not very highly regarded at this time (John 1.47). It was quite close to a much larger city, Sepphoris,[6] an important centre of trade, industry and commerce in Galilee. During the revolts which were the consequence of the Roman decision in 6 CE to hold a census in Jewish territory, this city had grown into a hotbed of opposition and the Romans destroyed it in revenge. At around the age of twelve Jesus must have witnessed battles and the consequences of the destruction of the city: pursuing soldiers and destitute refugees. The Gospels make no reference to this event at all. According to the evangelist Luke, the twelve-year-old Jesus went with his parents to the temple in Jerusalem to 'be about his father's business there' (Luke 2.49). At that moment political reality seems far away. The fact that the evangelists paid so little attention to the social and political circumstances of the time of Jesus already prompted mistrust in Reimarus in the second half of the eighteenth century. He caused quite a stir with his challenging thesis that Jesus had striven for very political aims, in contrast to what the later early Christian community had said about him. Jesus was said to have seen himself as a political Messiah, and his preaching of the imminent kingdom of God had also to be understood in this context. After Jesus' death on the cross his disciples resolved on an unpolitical reinterpretation of his original message. It took a long time for Reimarus to find any followers, but that happened at the end of the 1920s. At that time a great two-volume work appeared which has been well described as Reimarus *redivivus*. This book with a long and unique title – it was in Greek and means 'Jesus a king who did not become a king'[7] – was written by Robert Eisler (1882–1949), a Jewish scholar from Vienna. He had a great deal of knowledge, but his love of rash theories meant that he found little of a hearing in academic circles. In his study of the 'historical Jesus', Eisler thought that on the basis of a passage in an Old Slavonic translation of the works of Flavius Josephus (which in all probability is in fact corrupt), combined with some texts from the Gospels (including Luke 12.49,53; Luke 22.36–28), he could prove that Jesus was a revolutionary and that at the head of a group of rebels he had made an attempt to occupy the Jerusalem temple by force (cf. the story of the cleansing of the temple in Mark 11.15–19). With this action Jesus intended to spur on his Jewish contemporaries to a general rebellion against the Roman occupying forces. His plan failed miserably. He was taken prisoner by the Romans and condemned to death.

Eisler's view provoked much opposition. However, the storm of protest quickly faded and his book was forgotten. At a time when the Nazis were seizing power in Germany, the picture of Jesus as a failed pretender to a crown had little or no power of conviction for the champions of the Nazi ideology and even less for the opposition. Moreover Eisler's thesis was largely based on sources which almost all scholars regarded as historically unreliable.

However, Eisler's book again attracted interest some decades later, in the 1960s, thanks to the appearance in 1963 of a new study of the historical background of the death of Jesus. The author was an American Jew, Joel Carmichael,[8] who in fact offered a popularized version of Eisler's ideas. This book became a best-seller and also attracted attention in Christian circles. Clearly the time was now ripe for the creation of a picture of Jesus as a revolutionary. In a number of studies the English historian of religion S.G.F.Brandon defended the thesis that Jesus had sought links with the revolutionary movement of the Zealots.[9] Of course Brandon was challenged,[10] but he was more influential than Eisler and Carmichael, because his scholarship was of a higher quality.[11]

Jesus had become a rebel, an inspiring picture for all the oppressed in the world of the 1960s, who had joined the opposition. Jesus assumed the features of people like the Cuban revolutionary Che Guevara or Camillo Torres, a South American priest who had taken sides with the poor and exploited peasants. Torres' sympathy for the rebels was so great that he joined the rebels. He was tracked down and killed by special anti-guerilla units.

In this revolutionary guise, Jesus once again entered the church. To the terror of all good citizens and members of the congregation he ascended the pulpit, and in his sermon called for a fight against all exploiters and capitalists. Not only the church but also theological scholarship was in an uproar. Publications appeared on 'the theology of revolution'. Theologians made positive statements about revolutionary changes. They thought it necessary to achieve a just society. Jesus' proclamation of the approaching kingdom of God was interpreted as a summons to revolutionary changes in society.

Politics and social involvement

The statue of Jesus as a revolutionary did not stand on its pedestal long. It was too challenging, too scandalous and too extreme. Many found it very difficult to imagine Jesus as an armed rebel, a charismatic leader of a group of guerrilla fighters in the hill of Galilee. The Gospels present a different picture of Jesus: riding on an ass, as a by no means militant but gentle king he enters Jerusalem (Matt.21.5); he does not oppose his arrest in Gethsemane (Mark

14.43–52); he does not insist on the use of power, but calls the peacemakers blessed (Matt.5.9) and even requires love of the enemy (Matt.5.44). Anyone who adopts such an attitude will not choose armed struggle and will quickly be pushed aside as a collaborator.

Jesus was not a revolutionary who took up weapons. However, that does not mean that he had no eye for injustice and the social abuses under which the people of his time had to live. In 1964 the famous Italian film director, Pier Paolo Pasolini, controversial for his Communist sympathies and mistrusted by the church, made his film *The Gospel according to Matthew*. As the title indicates, the script of this film about Jesus is based on the Gospel of Matthew. It is certainly no chance that Paolini opted for that Gospel. Only Matthew has an extended version of Jesus' Sermon on the Mount (Matt.5–7); this Gospel puts great emphasis on doing the commandments and loving one's neighbour (Matt.25.31–46). In Pasolini's film Jesus appears as a man alert to social abuses.

Anyone who has learned to look at Jesus in this way will no longer find it strange that the man from Nazareth was welcomed even in Marxist circles.[12] The Christian church was rejected, but there was respect for Jesus. He was regarded as an early forerunner of Marxism. It evident that here, too, a clear discrepancy is seen between the preaching of the historical Jesus and the power politics of the institutionalized Christian church. This was expressed very clearly in the title of an article in a collection in which Marxists express their view of Jesus: 'Jesus the Incendiary – Christ the Fire-Extinguisher'.

Jesus was no unworldly prophet, uninterested in the specific needs of men and women. His message of the kingdom of God had unmistakably political implications. In a discussion with Rudolf Bultmann and his like-minded pupils, Dorothee Sölle argued for a 'political theology'. She saw such a 'politicization' of the biblical message not so much as a far-reaching corrective but rather as a continuation of hermeneutical perspectives which had been developed by the influential New Testament scholar, whom she also respected as her teacher. Sölle saw a danger that a one-sided emphasis on the Christian kerygma could lead to a 'depoliticization of the gospel'. She thought that the historical Jesus was of abiding significance because only in this way could it also become clear what political choices he made. Anyone who no longer has any interest in the historical Jesus no longer has anything to say about the political Jesus either, and in the end proclaims an apolitical and unworldly gospel.

Jesus takes sides

Politicians have to make choices. They cannot sit on the fence indefinitely; the time comes when they have to speak out for or against something. A 'political' Jesus, too, cannot limit himself to manoeuvring between social groups and social classes with opposed interests. Such a Jesus cannot be everyone's friend, but must take sides, deliberately and unambiguously. He has to become a 'supporter' and choose radically for one and against another.

This 'political' picture of Jesus came up against a good deal of opposition. That was not surprising. For centuries preachers in the traditional churches had proclaimed from the pulpit that Jesus made no distinction between people of different rank and status. He fought against sin, but opted for the sinner. On the cross he died for sinners, and all human beings were sinners: rich and poor, powerful and powerless, masters and slaves, the haves and the have-nots, men and women, white and black.

In the 1970s there was a widespread conviction that Jesus did take sides. He was the champion of the poor. He was the Messiah of the crowds who did not know the law, of oppressed provincials, of sinners and beggars. He was a slave among slaves. In South America Jesus opted unambiguously for the numerous exploited farmers in the countryside and for the millions of pariahs living in shanty towns on the periphery of great cities. This gave rise to 'a theology of liberation' in which Jesus filled the role of liberator.[13]

In the United States he left the white areas, to share the fate of the blacks in their ghettos. He did not feel out of place, since he himself was a black man. It was felt to be a misconception that Jesus corresponded to the well-known romantic picture which was particularly popular in the world of white people: an attractive, friendly young man looking like a Western European, often with long blond hair. The falashas from Ethiopia and the Israelis from countries like Yemen and Morocco showed that Jews were not necessarily always white. It did not seem impossible that Jesus and his contemporaries had much darker skin than is usually assumed in the Western world. In Black Africa, too, Jesus came to be recognized as a brother, as a liberator of white people. The time was past when whites could force their picture of the Messiah on other peoples and races as the only correct one. In the 'Black' world of North America and Africa Jesus became a *black Messiah*.[14]

A friend of women

Who is Jesus? He comes to us from the distant past, a human being among others. The Son of God leaves christological dogma behind and proves to be a man of flesh and blood. He knows sexual desires and seductions. Women attract him, he falls in love and perhaps even entered into marriage with Mary Magdalene.[15] He was a human being among other human beings, a man among men: a white man or a black man, but a *man*! What can Jesus mean for women? In classical christology this question was answered only by saying what Jesus could mean for men. He died for sinners and in so doing removed many differences of rank and status, differences between races and families. The apostle Paul states this briefly and tersely (Gal.3.28). However, in the feminist theology which developed in the second half of the twentieth century this question was felt to be a problem. The consequence of the emphasis on Jesus' humanity was a discovery of his masculinity.[16] After the unmasking of the classical male image of God as a time-conditioned, patriarchal notion, confrontation with the historical Jesus had to follow. God is other, more than a man or a woman. Those who use a male or a female image of God know that they are only making a modest attempt to express in pictures what in fact cannot be put into human pictures. God goes far beyond our capacity to imagine. But Jesus is a historical reality. He is the 'image of God' (John 1.18). However, he is unmistakably a *male* image. He is called 'son' of God and not daughter.

Can christology be reinterpreted in a way which is friendly to women? It proved possible to bring out the role of Mary more strongly along the lines of Roman Catholic mariology.[17] Alongside that, initially the idea that Jesus was a man who was particularly friendly towards women enjoyed a great deal of popularity. Feminist theologians tried in every possible way to show from the canonical Gospels that Jesus did not discriminate against women but got completely involved with them in a way different from that customary in his time.[18] This way of thinking in terms of contrasts, typical of Christian theology and difficult to eradicate, provoked fierce criticism in Jewish feminist circles. Jewish feminists accused their Christian sisters of trying to prove that Jesus was friendly to women by depicting the Old Testament Jewish tradition as blackly as possible – in this context as patriarchal and hostile to women.[19] For centuries Christian theologians had spoken without qualifications in this negative way about the Jewish tradition. Only in recent decades has the awareness grown that this view does not correspond with reality, but is the consequence of anti-Jewish ideas. The criticism of their Jewish conversation-partners was an unpleasant experience for Christian feminists.

How can women speak positively about Jesus without hurting other women in the process? That seems to be possible only if the person or Jesus occupies a less central position than is customary in church or theology. The issue is ultimately not Jesus, but inter-personal relations. In a 'relational' christology, salvation is no longer brought only through Jesus Christ, but takes place in specific human inter-personal dealings. Gradually, however, it is also becoming increasingly clear that it cannot be right to strive for something like the feminist christology. That would become a new dogma. Women are not equal; they live in different lands and in different cultures. What 'salvation' means for women ultimately seems to depend on the context in which they live and work.

Neo-romantic

Who is Jesus? In many modern pictures of Jesus the term 'liberation' plays a central role. He is a liberator. Thanks to his message, people have the courage to struggle against oppression and discrimination. In the process of emancipation he functions as a source of inspiration. However, the picture of the political Jesus also raises questions. What significance can his message have if the process has come to an end and liberation has been achieved? With due respect to the good aspect of a political interpretation of the gospel, must it not be asked whether such an interpretation is not too limited? The American theologian Harvey Cox put another emphasis at the end of the 1960s. Jesus did not enter Jerusalem as the leader of a band of rebels. He knew all too well that any attempt at a coup was doomed to failure. So he refused to involve others in a hopeless bloodbath. Jesus was not a militant leader but rather a tragic clown. In his masquerade before the gates of Jerusalem he mocked those who held power in their palaces.[20]

In the well-known film *Jesus Christ Superstar* (1971), Jesus has become a hippie-like figure. He seems to be a carefree character, fluttering gaily through life. He is also an anti-hero who is used and abused by everyone. Mary Magdalene, who sings a love song, and perhaps Judas, an obsessed figure who makes a sympathetic impression, are the exceptions. Despite all the fine effects, the death of Jesus on the cross is not the dramatic apotheosis of his life. But the film does not leave those who see it unmoved. I was particularly affected by a short scene which portrays Jesus almost literally submerged under a mass of hopeless, wretched people. They cry out from cracks in the rocks, holes and caves. The black-clad unfortunates – lepers, handicapped, blind, maimed and poor – shout and scream. They advance on Jesus and bury him under the burden of their suffering and symbolically that of all humankind.

Jesus and suffering – that is a theme which constantly recurs not only in theology but also in art. Jesus is the 'man of sorrows'. However, suffering is not only physical suffering but also mental suffering. Eugen Drewermann, the eloquent theologian and psychotherapist, whose powerful writings have spread beyond Germany all over the European continent, writes that modern men and women are sick, psychologically sick. He is opposed to the historical criticism of the Bible which has led to the gulf between the stories of the Bible and the world in which we live becoming unbridgable. Just as Bultmann went in search of a bridge between the past and the present and thought that he had found it in the human 'existentialia' – typically human things which determine existence in all times, like care, anxiety, sorrow and joy – so Drewermann makes a similar connection by psychotherapy. He reads the Gospel stories in this light and shows how Jesus appeared as a liberator above all in a psychological sense: he redeemed people – like the man who was possessed by a legion of evil spirits (Mark 5.1–20) – from their psychological anguish.[21]

Jesus in India

To conclude this 'unacademic intermezzo' I want to draw attention to some writers who think that they can make connections between Jesus and the wisdom of ancient India. Jesus was a 'searcher' after knowledge and insight. At the age of twelve he already proved capable of discussing with the scribes in Jerusalem on equal terms (Luke 2.40–52). After this, he is said to have gone East as a young adult. He travelled around in Kashmir, in the region of the Himalayas, and in Tibet. In this way he came into contact with Buddhism. He returned to Palestine around his thirtieth year.[22]

Thus Jesus drew his knowledge and experiential wisdom not only from the Old Testament and early Jewish tradition but also and above all from the teaching of Buddha and other mystical views of human nature and the world in the ancient Near East. He could even be regarded as a reincarnation of Buddha. Again the apostle Paul is the great criminal here. He not only revised the original message of Jesus but also falsified it. The result was the rise of a religion called Christianity – which in fact did not understand Jesus. Paul put belief in the crucified Christ at the centre. But anyone who is inspired by a possible connection between Jesus and Buddhism will trivialize or wholly deny the significance of the cross. Jesus was indeed crucified, but he survived his execution. He only seemed dead, and recovered from his wounds thanks to the medical knowledge of Joseph of Arimathea – a prominent member of the Essene community, which was also influenced by Buddhism. Together with his mother, Jesus finally went to India.[23]

Readers of what I have just written may have been amazed. What is the value of such ideas? But much seems possible in the realm of legends and speculations. In the north of Japan is a place called Shingo which has been given a remarkable nickname: 'Kirisuto no Sato', 'the village of Christ'. Jesus is said to have lived in Japan between the ages of twenty and thirty and to have steeped himself the wisdom of monks there. After his return to Palestine he laid the foundations of Christian faith. He did not die on the cross in Jerusalem, but his brother Iskiri (perhaps a distortion of Judas Iskariot?) did. Taking the body of his crucified brother with him, Jesus escaped to Japan. In Shingo he married, had children and died at a great old age. He found his last resting place beside the tomb of his brother.

Again the question which is so difficult to answer arises: truth or fiction? India or Japan? Did Jesus really live for a shorter or longer period far away from Palestine? It cannot be demonstrated that he did – there are legends, but he left no visible traces. However, it cannot be proved that he did not go to India or Japan either. Still, there are no indications in the four canonical Gospels that Jesus ventured far outside the limits of Jewish territory. He preferred to remain in the area of the Sea of Galilee.[24]

11

Back to Jesus?

A unique person

Who is Jesus? The quantity of literature about him is enormous and the answers are legion: he is one human being among others, a source of hope, an image of God's love; he is a black man, a rebel, the liberator of the marginalized in society; he is a friend of women, an unconventional figure who was little affected by prevailing morals and customs; he is an unworldly 1960s-type hippie, a clown who told the truth to the authorities with a grin on his face, a master dreamer who faced the future with optimism; he is the symbol of suffering humankind; he took the consequences of his love of humankind to the bitter end; he is the kind of human being God had always intended, his humanity and being for others, his liberating life, his death on the cross not the definitive end, and his resurrection by God the confirmation that it is worth living as he did.

That is how we might briefly describe the previous chapter – 'the unacademic intermezzo'. That is how Jesus 'lives' today for people. His meaning for today can still be presented through these varied pictures in contemporary terms. But how do academic theologians judge such pictures of Jesus?

Systematic theologians on Jesus

By far the vast majority of New Testament scholars are hesitant about the new biographical interest in Jesus and are even suspicious or negative. The conclusions drawn by Albert Schweitzer – now almost a century ago – have not yet been forgotten. Jesus is not a contemporary. He seems a stranger in the modern world, in the culture of the twentieth century and in the church and theology of our day. The academic scepticism of Rudolf Bultmann is still very much alive. The four Gospels are not biographical sketches of the life of Jesus. They were not written with that aim. The 'message', not the reconstruction of the past, is central. Therefore the evangelists differ from the authors of biographies in classical antiquity – like e.g. Plutarch – and cannot be compared with historians of our day. Mark and his three colleagues were believers and they could write about the historical Jesus simply on the basis of their belief in the risen Lord.

In general, systematic theologians are less restrained in what they say. Moreover they have to be, because they see it as their task to connect past and present and to make the basic structures of Christian faith clear to people of our day. Influential systematic theologians like Jürgen Moltmann,[1] Johann Baptist Metz[2] and Friedrich Wilhelm Marquardt[3] have, each in his own way, sought as far as possible to react in their christological reflection to such divergent trends as 'theology after Auschwitz', 'theology of liberation' and 'political theology'. The scepticism of New Testament scholars can make systematic theologians themselves decide to go in search of the historical Jesus. This is the way taken by Henk Berkhof[4] cautiously and carefully, as if he was afraid of critical reactions from New Testament scholars.

In the first half of the 1970s, both Edward Schillebeeckx[5] and Hans Küng[6] entered this field. Both wrote studies which can be described as 'Jesus books'. After an introductory chapter giving a survey of modern pictures of Jesus, each thought it necessary to go back, and on the basis of the Gospels arrive at a historically reliable description of the life of Jesus. Hans Küng calls the chapter in which he presents his picture 'The Real Christ'. He explains his choice by pointing out that the Christ of the Christian tradition is not a timeless myth or a profound idea but a concrete human figure, Jesus of Nazareth, who lived among Jews almost two thousand years ago. For this reason Küng sets historical reality over against all kinds of modern wishful thinking.[7] Schillebeeckx too emphasizes the importance of historical research into the time of Jesus. He recognizes that this research cannot prove Christian faith, but it does give concrete 'content' to that faith.[8]

In search of criteria

As we know (see Chapter 7 above), during the 1950s Ernst Käsemann caused a stir among New Testament scholars. Despite the scepticism which was familiar to him as a pupil of Bultmann, he gave new impetus to the quest of the historical Jesus. Käsemann did not write a 'life of Jesus'. He himself remained a fervent opponent of attempts in this direction, but he did point to the shadow side of a theology which played off the kerygmatic Christ against the historical Jesus. He warned that the difference could be so great that there is no longer any continuity.[9]

There is a broad consensus that the four Gospels are unsuited to serve as sources for writing a biography of Jesus. Many scholars are agreed that theologically speaking this need not be a catastrophe. However, it is also true that Christian faith has its roots in the past: the Christ who is proclaimed is none other than Jesus of Nazareth. The New Testament scholar, too, will ultimately have to investigate the words and actions of the historical Jesus in a way which is 'academically responsible'. How can this way be taken without the results of the investigation being decisively influenced by dogmatic presuppositions or by contemporary daydreams and longings?

Learning from the mistakes that had been made in the past, exegetes pinned their hopes on finding objective criteria. The name of Joachim Jeremias was mentioned often earlier in this book. He did not share Bultmann's scepticism and thought that he had found a reliable method of detecting *authentic sayings* of Jesus.[10] His thorough knowledge of Aramaic, the vernacular in Palestine in the period around the beginning of our era, enabled him to translate the Greek vocabulary of the synoptic Gospels back into Aramaic idiom. Thus Jeremias hoped that he could build a bridge and hear the voice of Jesus himself – *ipsissima vox Jesu* – behind the words in the Gospels. He heard this voice in the parables;[11] in a series of sayings with an enigmatic character (Mark 4.11); in texts which speak of the imminent coming of the kingdom of God (Mark 1.14–15); and in the specific use of the words 'amen' and 'abba' (Mark 14.36).

Initially this 'linguistic' approach seemed very attractive – at least it did to me at the beginning of the 1970s! In the midst of all the scepticism and uncertainty it seemed a way which created a historically reliable basis for faith in Jesus. However, I know from my own experience that this attraction can only be relatively short-lived. Doubts slowly creep in. How certainly can we know that the voice of Jesus himself can be heard in the texts mentioned above? He certainly told parables, but so too did others at that time.[12]

Who can guarantee to me that all the enigmatic statements in the Gospels can be attributed to Jesus? And how shall I ever be certain that even in the texts which mention the kingdom of God or in which the words 'amen' and 'abba' occur the voice of someone else is not being heard? Because no satisfactory answers can be given to these questions, Jeremias finally found little following.

Minimal or maximal?

Rudolf Bultmann had already argued earlier for the use of another criterion. He himself defined it as a 'minimal criterion'. Only those sayings could be attributed with certainty to Jesus which cannot in any way be derived or explained from the Jewish tradition or from the situation of the early Christian community.[13] Bultmann still spoke cautiously here, but in the course of time this criterion took on a more 'maximal' significance.[14] The consequence was that above all the 'underivable' texts began to determine the picture of the historical Jesus.

In the investigation, attention was directed in the first place to the differences between Jesus and the Jewish tradition. Thus he became a stranger in the Jewish society of his days. He lived differently, reacted differently and defended other views from those of his contemporaries. He deliberately distanced himself from the Torah and opposed the 'legalism' of the Pharisees. He refused to call himself Messiah, because he did not want to arouse any false expectations. Nor did he wish to correspond to the Jewish messianic expectation with its nationalistic colouring. Gradually he distanced himself so much from Judaism that his following visibly shrank and he became increasingly isolated. His death on the cross illustrated the deep gulf between him and the Jewish tradition which had opened up.[15]

Opposition to such a view developed in particular among exegetes who attached great importance to the Jewishness of Jesus and believed that the knowledge of the early Jewish tradition is of essential importance for the interpretation of the New Testament. They feared that the 'minimal criteria' could easily lead once again to a radical de-Judaizing of the Gospel. This development was in flagrant contradiction to the recent rehabilitation of Jesus by Jewish authors. It was pointed out that Jesus completely respected the commandments of the Torah. He did not break with Judaism. He was not condemned and killed because he was said to have transgressed the Torah. Jewish leaders and the Roman occupation authorities made a monstrous alliance because they were agreed that Jesus' appearance in Jerusalem posed a real danger to the *status quo*, which was being maintained with difficulty.

The dilemma in which research into the life of Jesus sees itself placed can be summed up in a few sentences. As for a 'minimal criterion', the group of New Testament scholars first mentioned above think that a responsible scholarly picture of the historical Jesus can be painted only if the difference from the Jewish tradition is accentuated; by contrast, the second group mentioned above defends the view that it is precisely the recognition of the Jewishness of Jesus which needs to be the concrete starting point for any investigation of the historical Jesus.

Faced with this dilemma, no exegete can avoid making a choice. In my view, here the developments of the last decades cannot be left out of account, and it is necessary to opt for the latter alternative. The modern Jewish rehabilitation of Jesus has left no doubt about the extent to which his roots lie in the early Jewish tradition. A historically responsible picture of Jesus can be sketched out only if the starting point is consistently and in principle his Jewishness.

Valid and invalid criteria[16]

However, the 'minimal criterion' does not seem to be completely unusable. If it functions within a theological framework which presupposes the continuity between Jesus and the Jewish tradition, it offers the exegete the possibility of arriving at a balanced judgment. Without putting Jesus' loyalty to the Torah in question, one cannot deny that he regularly came into conflict with Pharisees and scribes (Mark 2.1–3.6). Sometimes his interpretation of the commandments raised questions, and his unconventional behaviour caused both amazement and scandal (Matt.11.18–19; Luke 15.1–2). Thanks to the 'minimal criteria', attention has been focussed on those facets of the conduct of Jesus which make him a special, original figure. He lived wholly within the bounds of the law but he interpreted the commandments in a creative way. He was a pious man, but he did not limit himself to a circle of like-minded people. To the bewilderment of other pious men he sought the society of sinners and tax collectors. The 'minimal criteria' shed clear light on the 'otherness of Jesus'. In this sense it may be said to be a meaningful criterion. Anyone who uses it, however, needs to be aware that it registers only the differences, and cannot take into account the agreements between Jesus and the Jewish tradition.

The 'minimal criterion' draws lines. That is important, but it is not enough for arriving at a reliable picture of the historical Jesus. Therefore New Testament scholars went in search of other criteria.[17] So far the debate over this problem is still continuing. Meanwhile experience has taught that it is a fiction to think that there are any objective criteria. Those who go in search of the historical Jesus have no sources at their disposal other than writings coming from people who believed in Jesus as the Christ. Although they had been eye-witnesses, they now looked on the time before the cross and resurrection with different eyes. They did not intend to write an objective account of the past. While they were looking towards the past, they were expressing their belief in Jesus, the Risen Lord.

While well aware that criteria have only limited value, I would draw attention to two which – applied cautiously and with under-standing – can withstand the test of criticism. First is a criterion based on respect for tradition – it is discussed in the next section entitled 'conservative evangelists'. Then comes a criterion which takes account of the fact that certain words of Jesus can be found in different traditions – see the section I have entitled 'different traditions'.

'Conservative' evangelists

Four evangelists give accounts of Jesus' words and actions, his life and death. Sometimes their stories agree in a surprising way, but often they show notable differences, and in some cases they even seem to be contradictory. In the middle of the nineteenth century exegetes came to the conclusion that the short work by Mark is the earliest of the four canonical Gospels. After about a century of intensive investigation, however, it has to be concluded that the earliest Gospel is not by definition historically more reliable than the two other synoptic Gospels. All the evangelists are writing some time after Easter, and their description of the past is influenced by their faith in the risen Lord.

The authors of the four Gospels made use of both oral and written sources. They went to work creatively. They did not copy their sources, but 'composed' a new Gospel. However, on the basis of redaction criticism – careful and detailed comparisons of passages especially from the three synoptic Gospels – we must conclude that the evangelists could not or would not allow themselves too great a freedom. They edited and brought up to date, revised and corrected, added some stories and omitted others, but nevertheless at the same time remained astonishingly faithful to the tradition. For these reasons the authors of the synoptic Gospels may be called 'conservative'. They tried to preserve the essence of the tradition, to 'conserve' it.

Evangelists are not chroniclers or biographers, but theologians.[18] Their theology plays an unmistakable role in their description of the past. But they also tell stories which fit less well into their overall views. It seems legitimate to conclude that they preserved texts out of respect for the tradition. Here are a couple of examples by way of illustration.

In christological reflection within the early Christian community there was a tendency to minimize and relativize the difference between God and Jesus. Whereas the evangelists themselves encouraged this development, at the same time they include statements by Jesus in which the difference is emphasized (Matt.19.17; 24.36). It does not seem rash to suppose that such texts present a picture of Jesus which may be regarded as historically reliable.

From the first two chapters of the Gospel of Matthew it emerges that Matthew – in contrast to his most important source, the Gospel of Mark – attaches great value to the fact that Jesus is of the house of

David (cf. Matt.1.1–17 – the genealogy; Matt.1.23 – the name Immanuel and the fulfilment of the prophecy in Isa.7.14; Matt.2.5–6 – Jesus' birth in Bethlehem). Anyone who is aware of this 'theology' of Matthew's will read with amazement in the same Gospel the passage in which Jesus puts critical question marks against the expectation that the Messiah will be a son of David (Matt.22.41–45). A comparison shows that the evangelist has taken this text over from his 'source', the Gospel of Mark, without making far-reaching changes (Mark 12.35–37). This critical distancing fits the theological view of the writer of the earliest Gospel amazingly well, but in the Gospel of Matthew it leads to a notable tension with the theological trend that is developed, in the opening chapters in particular. It emerges from all this that Matthew was a consistent thinker and theologian. So he must have been aware of the tension that he created. However, certainly out of respect for the tradition, he took over this part from his source. From all this it may be concluded that the critical attitude towards the current messianic expectations of this time did not arise in the early Christian community but can be attributed to Jesus himself.

Creative evangelists

Anyone who goes in search of the 'authentic' Jesus cannot avoid answering the question of the *historical* value of the various Gospels. Matthew and Luke say that Jesus was born in Bethlehem (Matt.2.1–12; Luke 2.4–20); Mark says nothing about this (Mark 1.9), whereas John even seem to deny it (John 7.40–44). Is the story of Jesus' birth in Bethlehem of essential significance for Christian faith? Matthew and Luke answer this question in the affirmative. Matthew above all also sees this event as proof that Jesus' 'roots' are in scripture (Matt.2.5–6). Was Jesus really born in Bethlehem? The two other evangelists, Mark and John, seem to know nothing about this. Did Matthew and Luke have additional information? Or must their stories of Jesus' birth in Bethlehem be read as theological treatises and not as accounts of historical events?

Mark took pleasure in telling stories about healings by Jesus (Mark 2.1–12; 5.1–20, 21–43). Sometimes, however, the earliest evangelist is strikingly sober in his account. So he says no more about the 'temptations' of Jesus in the wilderness than that Jesus was tempted by Satan (Mark 1.12–13). Matthew and Luke say a great deal more (Matt.4.1–11; Luke 4.1–13). Evidently they took their details from the Q source. But of course this statement does not solve the problem how we are to explain why the Q source has more information than the Gospel of Mark.

A long list of differences between the four Gospels can be added to these two examples without difficulty. However, that is not the aim of this book, so I shall end by giving just one more – characteristic! – example. Almost anyone will feel a profile of the historical Jesus incomplete in which hardly any attention is paid to the 'Sermon on the Mount' (Matt.5–7). Over the course of the centuries this impressive discourse of Jesus has inspired people to oppose oppression and violence, to protest against injustice and humanity, and to stand up for all those who are tormented by poverty and hunger. However, we must seriously consider whether Jesus ever uttered the whole discourse. We seek the Sermon on the Mount in vain in the Gospels of Mark and John. The Third Gospel has only an abbreviated version (Luke 6.17–49). It is thanks to Matthew that the term 'Sermon on the Mount' has become established in the church and theology: 'When he saw the crowds, he went up the mountain' (Matt.5.1). Matthew is again referring to scripture. He does not want his readers to look for the 'Mount of the Beatitudes' on a map. He thinks that a hint is enough for anyone who knows the Bible: just as Moses once ascended Mount Sinai to receive the Torah from God (Exod.19), now Jesus climbs the mountain to make public for the first time his interpretation of the commandments. Matthew is not a historian; he is a scribe (Matt.13.52). He creates the Sermon on the Mount from words of Jesus. So when do we hear the voice of Jesus and when do we have Matthew's interpretation?

Jesus lived among Jews in the first decades of the first century. At the beginning of the 30s he died on the cross in Jerusalem. Forty to fifty years later the canonical Gospels were written. In this relatively short time a good deal had happened and many changes had taken place. After the cross and resurrection the very first followers began to reflect on – in modern terms, to come to terms with – the past. The apostle Paul saw himself called (Gal.1.15–16) to enter the Gentile world with the gospel of Christ. The way in which he crossed frontiers made a theological reorientation urgently desirable. The dramatic events in Judaea in the 60s and 70s – revolt against the Romans, conquest of Jerusalem and destruction of the temple, the increasing influence of the Pharisees – intensified the opposition between the early Christian community and the Jewish tradition and ultimately led to the schism between Judaism and Christianity. This was the complicated situation in which the evangelists were writing. They called the past to mind, but they did not do so primarily out of historical interest. They looked back in the hope of finding answers to questions and problems of their own time.

Different traditions

The evangelists respected tradition, but they were not afraid to deal with words and traditions from the past in a creative way. They were 'conservative', but they also renewed and brought up to date. According to a saying in Matthew the evangelists are to be compared with 'a householder who brings from his store things new and old' (Matt.13.52). This combination of continuity and discontinuity is the reason why it is difficult to describe the life of Jesus in detail. Thanks to 150 years of intensive historical criticism of the four Gospels much has come to be known about how they were composed, but it also has to be recognized that for lack of reliable sources, a great deal remains hidden in the darkness of the past.

The evangelists were not writing fiction. They were no novelists. They hoped to keep alive the recollection of the words and actions of Jesus. They did not create a new reality but based themselves on their oral and written sources. Different 'streams of tradition' can be distinguished in early Christianity: one stream issued in the Gospel according to Mark; alongside it there was a stream corresponding to a greater or lesser degree with Q. The first tradition comprised mainly – but not exclusively! – stories about Jesus, while in the second tradition the emphasis fell on sayings of Jesus. Matthew and Luke made use of both traditions, each in his own way. Moreover, a comparison shows that independently of each other they also had other oral and/or written traditions at their disposal.

Different streams of tradition underlie the four Gospels. Some stories and or words of Jesus occur in a number of streams, whereas others remain limited to a single stream. In investigating the historical Jesus, there is the possibility here of formulating a criterion based on the number of traditions: the greater the number of streams of tradition in which texts occur, the greater the chance that they are authentic and can be attributed to Jesus himself. I deliberately use the term 'chance'; certainty can never be attained in this way. Moreover a warning must be issued against the temptation to use the criterion in a negative sense. If words of Jesus occur in one tradition, that does not 'automatically' mean that they could not be authentic. That is even true of the Gospel of John. The author made wide use of traditions which the synoptic Gospels do not seem to know. But account must be taken of the possibility that John has worked authentic traditions into his Gospel.[19]

Eye-witnesses and immediate audience

Two apparently contradictory words can be used to characterize the work of the evangelists: creative and conservative. The authors of the Gospels interpreted the material available to them and brought it up to date, but they did not do so without great respect for tradition.

What has been said above raises the question of the *origin* of the tradition. Because of the views of Rudolf Bultmann, for a long time hardly any attention was paid to the role of Jesus' disciples. Doubtless this aspect of his view of the history of the origin of the Gospels needs to be evaluated critically. Bultmann emphasized the significance of the cross and resurrection, For this reason he was more interested in the discontinuity between the time before and the time after Easter than in the continuity. In his view faith was not about the historical Jesus but about the kergymatic Christ. If the disciples of Jesus were led to speak of Jesus, this was not as bearers of the tradition, the eye-witnesses and immediate audience of his words and actions, but as apostles who put into words the 'kerygma' of the early Christian community.

During his lifetime Jesus gathered a group of followers – men but also women (Mark 15.40–41; Luke 8.1–3). Why he did so is difficult to say with certainty. Matthew suggests that Jesus envisaged the founding of the church and that he commissioned Peter to lead and guide it (Matt.16.17–19). However, it seems certain that these words convey not so much the voice of Jesus as that of the evangelist. Jesus did not lay the foundation for the Christian community, but proclaimed the imminent coming of the kingdom of God (Mark 1.14–15). He saw himself above all as a prophet of the approaching kingdom of God and not as the founder of a new religion. The question proves complicated. At any rate, this eschatological prophet gathered disciples around him and they saw him as their teacher. Did Jesus in fact seem like a rabbi? Exegetes do not agree over this. In a popular book, the well-known Dutch New Testament scholar Lukas Grollenberg writes: 'Jesus was not a priest or anything like that: he was an ordinary layman. He had not been taught by rabbis, and he had no official authority to speak about God and his will.'[20] Thus the question whether Jesus was a scribe must be answered in the negative. He was not a rabbi, and he cannot be regarded as a professional exegete.

It seems to me that Grollenberg presses things too far. In his zeal to preserve Jesus from the influence of scribes and other experts in scripture and tradition, he creates a picture which does not do justice to the situation in the time of Jesus. It may well be true that Jesus was a layman and not a 'professional exegete', but that can also be said of the vast majority of Pharisees. They had a good deal of influence and were well known for their great knowledge of scripture and tradition. To me there seems no doubt that Jesus came from these circles. This view was also defended in a study by the American Jew Philip Sigal (1927–1985), who on the basis of expert knowledge can show that Jesus certainly deserves a place in the company of the scribes of his time.[21] Thus he went through the Jewish countryside, a teacher accompanied by his disciples.[22] Cross and resurrection separate the times before and after Easter, but the origin of the tradition may be said to lie in the the words and actions of Jesus. His disciples functioned as the first bearers of the tradition.

Continuity

Did Jesus himself aim at continuity? Those who see him mainly or exclusively as the prophet of the approaching kingdom of God will conclude that he attached little importance to any extensive instruction of his disciples. In a 'thoroughgoing eschatological' view the time is short and the kingdom will soon bring about a radical change. But how 'thoroughgoing' was Jesus himself in his eschatology? It is possible to describe him as a prophet, but he also appeared as a 'teacher'. He deliberately gathered disciples around him (Mark 1.16–20; 2.13–14) and instructed them. He prepared them for the tasks which they were to fulfil and instructed them in how they had to proclaim the gospel (Matt.10.5–42). Thus the image of Jesus can take on other features. He was not an apocalyptist who was exclusively interested in the end of the world. During his lifetime he also looked to the near future. After his death it would be possible for his work to be carried on by his disciples. They form the 'bridge' between the time before and the time after the cross and resurrection.

12

The Return of the Historical Jesus

World-wide

Who is Jesus? The discussion continues unabated. The stream of literature swells by the year and no one can completely keep up with it. In a bibliography which appeared at the end of the 1980s, no less than 1,300 relevant books and articles were mentioned.[1] Nowadays the debate has become world-wide. For a long time New Testament scholarship was dominated by German-speaking theologians. One need only mention the names of Samuel Reimarus, David Friedrich Strauss, Albert Schweitzer, Adolf von Harnack, Rudolf Bultmann, Ernst Käsemann, Joachim Jeremias and others.

The world changes quickly, and that time is now behind us for good. Above all since the Second World War, Christians in other continents and cultures have gone in search of their 'own' image of Jesus. In Africa Christ is given a different face from the one he has in Asia or South America.[2] Even in New Testament scholarship the warnings of Schweitzer and the relativizing of Bultmann have no longer had the influence they once had. The historical Jesus is again the focal point of interest.

As will become evident shortly, at present this is the case above all in the United States.[3] That is not completely new. In the past, too, New Testament scholars in the Anglo-Saxon world followed the discussion in Germany with some restraint and even with suspicion.[4] They were less critical about the historical reliability of the Gospels and therefore attached more importance to the reconstruction of the life of Jesus. Exegetes in Scandinavian countries arrived at similar insights. They, too, regard the Gospels as sources which in general may be taken to be historically reliable. Here the Scandinavians emphasize the importance of oral tradition. They think that there is a reliable link between the Gospels on the one hand and the life of Jesus on the other. The evangelists were not fantasizing, but in the first place based themselves on oral tradition. The origin of the Gospels shows parallels with similar processes of tradition in the early Jewish tradition.[5]

Closer to the historical Jesus?

As I have already indicated, I shall now concentrate on the Anglo-Saxon countries, where surprising developments are taking place. The scepticism about the historical Jesus which slowly became traditional is gradually giving place to a much more optimistic view of the reliability of the Gospels. Here are three examples. In the middle of the 1970s John Robinson – who a decade earlier had become world famous as the author of *Honest to God*,[6] a book which did not leave either the church or theology untouched – produced a notable study in which he advanced arguments for the daring position that all the New Testament writings had already been completed before the crucial year 70 (the destruction of the temple).[7] That meant that the Gospels would have been written hardly more than thirty years after the cross and resurrection, a period which can be said to be relatively short. Furthermore, in 1972 the Spanish papyrologist José O'Callaghan, a Jesuit and at that time dean of the Pontifical Biblical Institute in Rome, published a surprising article. In the spring of 1955 Greek texts had been found in one of the Qumran caves – Cave 7. However, the fragments were so small that it seemed impossible to establish what writings they came from. In his article, O'Callaghan revealed that he had been able to identify three fragments as parts of the New Testament. The largest fragment was said to agree with the text of Mark 6.52–53. O'Callaghan was less certain of the two other fragments, supposed to be parts of Mark 4.28 and James 1.23–24.[8] Could it be concluded on the basis of this discovery that there were connections between the early Christian community and the Essenes in Qumran? O'Callaghan's thesis commanded assent from some scholars,[9] but also encountered a good deal of criticism. Is the argument really convincing? If it is, though, further inferences can be made. If the Gospel according to Mark was already known in Qumran, the work must have been written some time before the flight of the Essene community in 68.[10] Some exegetes even suggest the year 50. In that case it can again be concluded that the gulf between the life of Jesus and the composition of the Gospels was relatively short.

Finally the third most recent and most curious example. In 1994 the front page of the Christmas number of *The Times* carried a striking headline: 'Papyrus in Oxford Contains an Eyewitness Account of the Life of Jesus'. The article claimed that this was the greatest breakthrough in New Testament scholarship since the Qumran discoveries. In the next issue of *The Times* an extended interview appeared with the man who had made the discovery and who thought that the time had come to publish the striking news, a German scholar, Carsten Peter Thiede, who was working in England – he is also a defender of the thesis mentioned in the previous example. A month later, on 23 January 1995, *Time* magazine came out with a new article on this question with the challenging headline, 'A Step Closer to Jesus?' Is all this publicity right?

There are fragments of a Greek text of the Gospel of Matthew in Magdalen College, Oxford. They were discovered in Luxor in Egypt in 1901 and for a long time little attention was paid to them. Initially there was hardly any disagreement between experts over their date: the fragments came from the second half of the second century. On the authority of Thiede, *The Times* now broke the great news that the fragments in Oxford were around a century earlier. The consequence was that the Gospel of Matthew would have been written as early as the middle of the first century. However, disappointment awaited sensation-seeking readers. In a scholarly article which Thiede wrote on the same question a short time later,[11] he expressed himself far more cautiously and suggested a date of composition in the years after 70 CE. In that case the discovery is considerably less spectacular, and certainly no completely new light is shed on the origin of the Gospels. In a recent publication Graham Stanton, Professor of New Testament at King's College, London, even thinks that he can prove Thiede wrong. Failing other arguments, it seems most likely that the Oxford papyrus comes from the second half of the second century. According to Stanton the papyrus certainly reflects the fact that in this period the Christian church deliberately departed from the scrolls which had hitherto been in use. It opted for the codex – i.e. the book form – because this way the four Gospels could be kept together, in one volume.[12]

Is the tide turning?

The examples given above, especially the last two, are not convincing. But they are interesting and even revealing. They show that serious scholars, too, feel the need to make the gulf between the origin of the Gospels and the life of Jesus as narrow as possible. Granted, the evangelists are not writing eye-witness accounts of the actions of Jesus, but they are drawing on reminiscences which, given the short span of time that they bridge, should be regarded as reliable. By contrast, Rudolf Bultmann and his colleagues and pupils thought that the Gospels gave more information about the life of the early Christian community than about the life of Jesus. Anyone who wants to describe the beginning of church history could use the Gospels as sources, but they offer insufficient material for the reconstruction of the historical Jesus.

Many other New Testament scholars agreed with Bultmann, but recently the tide seems to be turning. Especially in the United States, this negative view of the historical reliability of the four Gospels has declined. The same can also be said of the view that the biblical narrative needs to be demythologized, as Bultmann argued. The New Testament proclamation was said to have been clad in a mythological garb. Stories were told about the meaning of Jesus' life and death, the future and also miracles, in the form of myths. These myths were time-conditioned, but they contained a nucleus – the message – which is relevant before all time. In order to get on the track of this message – the kerygma – the narratives needed to be demythologized.

Did Jesus perform miracles? For Bultmann and others this was an irrelevant question. The stories were not told to inform readers about the past, but to call on them to change their lives in such a way that they and others experienced their conversion as a miracle. At present there are exegetes who ask themselves why the miracle stories should immediately be banished to the realm of fable. Why couldn't Jesus have performed miracles?[13] He unmistakably possessed special gifts. He healed the sick, he rescued people from the spirits that tormented them, he appeared as an exorcist and in addition performed numerous other signs and wonders.[14]

Since the rise of Enlightenment thought in the eighteenth and nineteenth centuries this aspect of Jesus' life has perplexed many people. Is belief in miracles essential? Before this time such a question was rarely, if ever, asked. Mediaeval men and women took it for granted that they lived in a 'miraculous' world. So did the authors of the apocryphal Gospels. They had no hesitations about adding new miracle stories to those which already existed. Jesus could perform miracles even as a child and a baby. Pious fantasy proved particularly creative, and met the need to emphasize the miraculous power of Jesus. That was also necessary because he had rivals. In the ancient Near East and the Hellenistic world miracles were clearly not exceptional. Thus at the beginning of the second century CE the Greek author Philostrates, who lived between 170 and 245, wrote an imposing eight-volume biography of a miracle worker, *The Life of Apollonius of Tyana*. Philostrates was not the only person to be interested in this man. Apollonius is also mentioned by other writers.

Who was this Apollonius? He lived in the first century of our era and can be regarded as a contemporary of Jesus. In all probability Apollonius lived to a ripe old age. He was born at the beginning of the first century – precisely when we do not know – and died at the beginning of the 90s. He was a philosopher, a disciple of Pythagoras, who had lived 500 years earlier. Apollonius performed many miracles and was already venerated as a saint during his lifetime. He led a sober life and was held in high respect. It is not too rash to suggest that in his day Apollonius was far better known than the crucified Christ.

'We know a great deal'

Since the last century interest in the humanity of Jesus has increased. The Second World War was followed by the (re)discovery of his Jewishness. Anyone who takes Jesus' humanity seriously will want to give him a place in history and will go in search of the historical Jesus. Those who have become aware of his Jewishness can form a better picture than before of the Jewish world in which he lived. Thanks to this knowledge it is possible to test the historical reliability of the Gospel stories. That is also the view of E.P.Sanders, an influential New Testament scholar in the 1980s and 1990s. He comes from Texas, but also spent some time as a professor in Oxford. His publications reflect the development in his thought. In 1977 he produced a monumental study in which he described the theological views of the apostle Paul against the background of the early Jewish tradition.[15] In the 1980s he published books and articles on New Testament themes, but also about Judaism around the beginning of our era.[16] In this way he created the foundations for his next studies: he argued that starting from the Jewishness of Jesus, and thanks to a thorough knowledge of Jewish tradition from this period, it is possible to arrive at a reliable description of the historical Jesus. A book appeared in 1993 which was given the eloquent title *The Historical Figure of Jesus*.[17]

Sanders seems to be surprisingly optimistic about the problem which has now occupied us for many pages. His view is that a great deal can be said about the historical Jesus: 'We know a great deal'.[18] In his view, sources for the life of Jesus are considerably more reliable than, for example, those about Alexander the Great.[19] Sanders recognizes that the evangelists were not objective about the subject that they describe. But he concludes that – even from a historical perspective – they did their work well.[20]

One assertion at the end of the book seems to contradict this optimism: there is some mystery about the figure of the historical Jesus.[21] This is a sober statement for readers who have come to the end of a fascinating quest and have perhaps concluded that all the problems have now been solved. Historical investigation cannot explain everything, so Sanders remains modest in his conclusions.

Jesus made a public appearance when the preaching of John the Baptist was attracting attention. We know that Jesus had disciples and that he lived in expectation of the imminent coming of the kingdom of God. It is also certain that he healed the sick and rescued the possessed from the spirits that were tormenting them. As a pilgrim he travelled from Galilee to Jerusalem and attracted attention there by his royal entry and his critical remarks about the temple. He was arrested, condemned to death and crucified. After his death his disciples had experiences which led them to the conclusion that he had been raised.[22] On the basis of these experiences they formed a community which removed itself increasingly further from the original message of Jesus.[23]

Sanders' book ends with this crucial conclusion. After the cross and resurrection the preacher himself becomes the content of Christian preaching. Anyone who goes in search of the historical Jesus does not find the Christ of church dogma but encounters a Jew from Nazareth, an inspired man, sometimes mysterious but always full of life. He claims to act in the name of God, a God whom he had come to know as a God of love and grace. In Christian theology – under the influence of Paul – the cross is central, but Sanders insists on paying little attention to the suffering of Jesus. He puts the spotlight on the life of Jesus, his liberating words and actions.

Was Jesus the Messiah? What are we saying when we call him the son of God? Sanders relativizes the age-old debate about this title. The term 'messianic' seems to have many colourings and the title 'son of God' in the context of this time does not indicate the uniqueness of Jesus. All those people who had been chosen by God were called 'sons of God' in the Old Testament and in the early Jewish tradition: the people of Israel (Exod.4.20; Hos.11.1) and the king as representative of that people (II Sam.7.14; Ps.2.7).[24] Sanders does not need these titles to identify what was special about Jesus. The evangelists give us better information because they tell us about the words and actions of Jesus. He saw himself as the last prophet of the approaching kingdom of God. Therefore he rode into Jerusalem as a 'king', certainly on an ass, but with royal pretensions. Because Jesus himself seems to speak consistently about God's kingdom, he should be given the title 'viceroy'.

Jesus' interpretation of the Torah was not discussed in the trial in Jerusalem. He was not stoned but crucified. He remained within the limits of the Jewish tradition, but caused a scandal because of his friendly dealings with men and women who did not seem prepared to live according to the Torah (Mark 2.13–17). Moreover Sanders does not portray Jesus as a radical 'reformer' or a strict prophet of repentance. The Gospels have preserved the recollection that Jesus was different from John the Baptist. Jesus did not threaten anyone with 'hell and damnation' (Matt.3.7–12; 11.16–19). He ate with sinners and tax-collectors and told of God's love, even for people who risked being lost (Luke 15). He laid down no prior conditions and did not call for conversion. Clearly he was convinced that people should change through the discovery of God's love.

This is what is new and surprising in Jesus' preaching. In his words and deeds he wanted to give expression to this picture of God. For that reason, sometimes he did not obey the rules, came into conflict with the pious, and put old commandments and traditions in a new light. The early church shrank from the consequences of this attitude of Jesus. It can already be inferred from the Gospels that the church began to make demands, and in contrast to Jesus emphasized the need for conversion.

Jesus' claim to act on behalf of God finally also explains why the Jewish leaders gave orders for his arrest. They felt responsible for the well-being of the Jewish people and feared that the appearance of Jesus at the approaching Passover would lead to disturbances. So he had to be removed from the scene as unobtrusively as possible. According to Sanders, the direct occasion seems to have been Jesus' criticism of the temple. At least that is how the Jewish leaders interpreted his warning that the temple would be razed to the ground. That was a misunderstanding, since Jesus did not attack the temple. As a prophet inspired by an apocalyptic expectation of the future he hoped for the break-up of the existing order and the coming of a new temple.[25]

Sanders' book ends where christological discussion begins. How did Jesus, the one who proclaimed the kingdom of God, become the centre of the Christian preaching? Sanders indicates only that the community distanced itself from the original preaching of Jesus. This is a statement which raises questions. One could speak of a logical development: after Easter the Christian community knows more about Jesus than before Easter. But has a boundary to be drawn which may not be crossed? Are there dogmas, pictures of Christ which have removed themselves too far from Jesus of Nazareth? The quest of the historical Jesus goes back to the beginning and reminds the church of its origin: Jesus' preaching, as simple as it is surprising, about God's love for men and women.

Let's vote

In the 1960s I studied at the Theological College of the Reformed Churches in Kampen. One of the professors who made an impression on me was the New Testament scholar Herman N.Ridderbos, a theologian with an international reputation. He was a skilled exegete and a man with a sense of humour. I recall that sometimes he jokingly suggested that we should vote on a complicated exegetical problem for which there were different more or less acceptable solutions. I was reminded of this when I was told about the Jesus Seminar in the United States.

Marcus J. Borg gives us an impression of what happens at the meetings of the seminar.[26] He is one of its regular members. Moreover we shall be coming back to him later, because his own contribution to the discussion deserves attention. Borg begins by noting that the Gospels contain not only recollections of the disciples of the time before the cross and resurrection, but also experiences of the early Christian community from the time after Easter. Thus there are at least two levels of tradition or two sorts of material in the Gospels. There is material that goes back to Jesus before Easter and there is material which comes from the early Christian movement. In other words, the Gospel contains at least two voices: the voice of the historical Jesus and the voice of the post-Easter community. In order to sketch out a picture of the pre-Easter Jesus one must therefore separate these two layers, these two voices.

The work of the group of scholars who form the Jesus Seminar gives a good indication of how this must be done. Since 1985 it has met twice a year to vote on the historical reliability of sayings of Jesus. Many people may find this idea of voting about Jesus bizarre, some even blasphemous. But the vote has a simple aim: to measure the degree of scholarly assent on the question how much of the Gospel material goes back to Jesus himself. Scholars vote on every saying by putting one of four coloured balls in a box. The different colours – red, pink, grey and black – stand for a decreasing spectrum of historical probability. A red vote means, 'I am quite certain that Jesus said this'; a pink vote indicates somewhere between 'probable' and 'more likely than not'; a grey one, less likely rather than more, and probably not; and a black one, 'I am quite certain that Jesus did not say this'.

What picture of the pre-Easter Jesus emerges from this procedure? Two main written sources are examined. The first and most important consists of the earliest levels of Matthew, Mark and Luke (the synoptic Gospels), which contain sayings, characteristic actions and a framework for Jesus' adult life-work. The second source consists of the earliest layer of the Gospel of Thomas.

The Gospel of John does not appear in the list of sources. It is thought not to give an accurate picture of Jesus before Easter, although it is a powerful and truthful witness to the experiences of the community with Jesus after the Easter event. In terms of the colour code of the Jesus Seminar, John has almost exclusively been given black votes.

What does all this mean for the question 'Who is Jesus?'? Berg is quite clear about this. Jesus was Jewish through and through. He was not only a Jew by birth and upbringing but he remained a Jew all his life. He did not intend to found a new religion, but saw his task within Judaism. He spoke as a Jew to other Jews. His first followers were Jews. All the New Testament authors (except perhaps the author of Luke–Acts) were Jewish.[27]

Borg gives a fascinating account of the method of working in the Jesus seminar, but his account also prormpts questions. Can the problem of the historical Jesus be resolved by voting? Is the 'red' Jesus really most like the Jesus who lived among Jews two thousand years ago?[28]

Non-canonical sources

The first extended publication of the results of the Jesus Seminar appeared in 1994. It was given an evocative title, *The Five Gospels*.[29] Borg's account tells us that members of the seminar think that the Gospel of Thomas is important for the quest of the historical Jesus.[30] So far such importance had not been attached to non-canonical texts in the discussion.[31]

In Chapter 9 I went more closely into the importance of the Gospel of Thomas which was found in 1945 in the 'Gnostic library' of Nag Hammadi. After its publication at the end of the 1950s its date of composition was steadily pushed backwards. To begin with it was seen as a Gnostic Gospel of the third or fourth century. However, quickly the suggestion arose that it must be earlier, and that the influence of Gnosticism is less great than was presupposed in the first instance. So there was some consensus over a date in the first half of the second century, around 140. Meanwhile it had also become clear that the Gospel of Thomas is composed of different 'layers': it contains Gnostic sayings, but also sayings which are certainly not influenced by Gnosticism. The conjecture that they are early is legitimate. How much earlier is difficult to say. Some exegetes regard the Gospel of Thomas as a fifth independent source which can take its place alongside the four canonical Gospels in the New Testament.[32] In that case an early dating is necessary, and the nucleus of the Gospel can be put as early as between 50 and 60.[33]

The results of the Jesus Seminar reflect the above development in the evaluation of the Gospel of Thomas. The 'picture' of Jesus is changing. This emerges above all in discussions of the significance of the cross. As we have seen, the Gospel of Thomas contains only sayings of Jesus. It has no miracle stories, nor any stories about his passion and death. There is not a word about Jesus' death on the cross in any of its 114 sayings. If recent statements about the Gospel of Thomas are right and it contains old independent traditions, that is an indication that at an early stage of church history a form of christological reflection was already beginning to develop in which, in contrast to the letters of the apostle Paul, the cross did not have a central place. According to this tradition, Jesus' significance coincides with his words and is no different from these words.[34]

In the framework of this discussion exegetes have again called attention to the apocryphal Gospel of Peter. In Chapter 9 above I referred to the discovery of this work at the end of the last century. The publication caused a sensation in some areas for a while, but in academic circles the conviction soon became established that this work could have no significance for the quest of the historical Jesus. In the 1980s the rise of the Gospel of Thomas seemed to have consequences for the evaluation of the Gospel of Peter. The issue here was above all the place and significance of the passion.

So as not to make things too complicated, I shall limit myself here to a short account of the most widely divergent viewpoints.

Some scholars argue that a short time after the cross and resurrection, in Jerusalem an unknown figure – one might perhaps even imagine one of the apostles – set down his recollections of the passion and death of Jesus in writing. His description is doubtless coloured by belief in the risen Lord, but the dramatic event was still fresh in his memory and his account may therefore be regarded as a valuable historical document. This account of Jesus' passion and death is the basis for the canonical Gospels. Mark knew it, revised it to some degree and introduced it with stories about Jesus: his activity in Galilee.[35] This is how we could imagine the origin of the earliest Gospel. I have gratefully made use of this thesis in a book of my own on 'The Messianic Way'. It seems to be an important link in christological reflection in the early Christian community.[36]

However, nowadays an opposite position is also being defended. It is a result of the discovery of the Gospel of Thomas – as we have seen, a Gospel without a passion narrative. The reputation of this work is growing among New Testament scholars, with the consequence that developments in early Christianity are being looked on with new eyes.[37] Attention is shifting. The cross is slowly moving from the centre and interest is being directed toward the sayings of Jesus. This far-reaching reorientation is leading to a revaluation of the canonical Gospels. Their basis is said not to have been a story about the suffering and death of Jesus but collections of sayings and parables. The historicity of the passion narratives in the New Testament Gospels is no less problematical than that of the stories of the birth of Jesus in Bethlehem. In the early Christian community these stories were created with the aim of making theological statements about Jesus' descent and origin: son of David, son of Abraham, son of God.[38]

The evangelists are now also said to have gone to work on the passion narrative in a comparable way. They probably did not have many historical facts, but they were creative, and they wanted to see this dramatic event from Jesus' life in the perspective of scripture and tradition. Jesus had been condemned to death by Pontius Pilate, and subsequently Roman soldiers crucified him. The historicity of these events may be taken as assured. However, all the other episodes in the Gospel passion narratives were created by the authors.[39] This also includes the pericopes about the last supper of Jesus with his disciples, his prayer in Gethsemane, the hearing before members of the Sanhedrin and the interrogation by the high priest, Peter's denial and the words on the cross.

At this point in the discussion the apocryphal Gospel of Peter suddenly crops up again. As we have heard, only a fragment of it has been preserved, but that contains a description of the passion and death of Jesus. In this fragment we can see clearly that the description of the event is totally governed by the need to interpret Jesus' death on the cross in the light of scripture and tradition. According to some exegetes, the apocryphal Gospel of Peter is independent of the canonical Gospels in this 'scriptural' reworking of the passion narrative and may even have been the basis for the passion narratives in the Gospels.[40] Unfortunately there is not enough space to discuss this aspect here. But it is certainly remarkable that so much value is attached to an apocryphal writing.[41]

Christological titles occur rarely, if ever, in the Gospel of Thomas. Nowhere is Jesus called Messiah or Christ, nor is his name connected with the titles Lord or Son of man. Nor does he appear as a prophet of the approaching kingdom of God. The New Testament has a tension between texts in which the future is central – the synoptic apocalypse in Mark 13, passages in the letters of Paul (e.g. Rom.8.18–30; I Thess.4.13–18; 5.1–11; II Thess.2.1–17; the last book in the Bible) and others which concentrate on the present – this is true above all of the Gospel of John and to a lesser degree of the letter to the Colossians. A flood of literature has appeared in the twentieth century about the eschatological expectation in the New Testament. In the Gospel of Thomas Jesus is primarily a wisdom teacher with his gaze on the present. The kingdom of God does not lie hidden in the future, but can already be perceived by believers now:

His disciples said to him,
'When will the kingdom come?'
Jesus said,
'It will not come by waiting for it.

154

It will not be a matter of saying "Here it is" or "There it is".
Rather, the kingdom of the Father
is spread out upon the earth
and men do not see it' (Saying 113).

A Cynic wisdom teacher

At the beginning of the 1990s, John Dominic Crossan, one of the most important representatives of the American quest for the historical Jesus, wrote an extended study which became a best-seller in the United States: within a short time 50,000 copies had been sold. Crossan gave his book a title which could hardly have been clearer, *The Historical Jesus*, with the intriguing sub-title *The Life of a Mediterranean Jewish Peasant*.[42] The great success of his book inspired Crossan to write a popular summary, *Jesus. A Revolutionary Biography*.[43] No less striking is the book by another eloquent member of the Jesus seminar in the United States whose name has been mentioned earlier: Marcus J.Borg, *Meeting Jesus Again for the First Time. The Historical Jesus and the Heart of Contemporary Faith*.[44]

These studies give an original description of the life of Jesus – Borg speaks of 'Jesus before Easter'. By contrast, they pay little attention to the christological reflection within the early Christian community – Jesus after Easter. Borg and Crossan also make the distinction customary in New Testament scholarship between the time before and the time after Easter. However, they differ from the circle around Rudolf Bultmann and others of like mind in where they put the emphasis. Both American exegetes concentrate on the quest of the historical Jesus and attach little importance to the discussion of the kerygmatic Christ. The reconstruction of the life of Jesus is not an exegetical hobby but is of essential importance for belief today.

A century ago, Albert Schweitzer demonstrated that on closer examination the nineteenth-century portraits of Jesus were no more than projections of the authors' own wishes and desires. Jesus was adapted to the ideals of 'enlightened' Europeans of this time. Schweitzer thought that he had discovered the 'authentic' Jesus: an alien apocalyptic prophet who lived in the expectation of the speedy coming of the kingdom of God. Marcus Borg sketches a completely different picture: Jesus was not an apocalyptist and did not see himself as the Messiah or as a messianic prophet.[45] Crossan's book also asserts that the kingdom of God in Jesus' preaching must not be seen as an eschatological/apocalyptic concept but as the kingdom of God here and now.[46] This kingdom does not lie hidden in the future, but is a reality in the present. It is a 'process' which is dominated by love, solidarity and radical openness: there is no longer any discrimination in the kingdom; the boundaries between human beings disappear and conflicts between social groups and classes are bridged.[47]

Marcus Borg sees Jesus primarily as a wisdom teacher. He even calls him a 'teacher of alternative wisdom'.[48] This term clearly presents the dilemma: apocalyptic or wisdom, two views of faith and life which seem to be mutually exclusive.[49] As I have already indicated, for both Borg and Crossan the Gospel of Thomas plays an important role in forming a picture of Jesus. This Gospel no longer speaks of apocalyptic or eschatology, and the way to a non-eschatological, Gnostic interpretation of Jesus' words is open.

Neither exegete is sufficiently clear about the relation between Jesus and the Jewish tradition. Borg certainly emphasizes the Jewishness of Jesus in a short paragraph,[50] but after that he pays no attention to his attack on the system of purity prevailing in his days which was based on Old Testament Jewish regulations.

Here lies the source of Jesus' conflict with the Jewish leaders. Both parties read scripture. They paid special attention to the texts which called for purity; he concentrated on mercy. The early Christian community after the cross and resurrection ventured to take the same line. Borg writes attractively, but he runs the risk of constructing a sweeping contrast between Jesus and the Jewish tradition of his days. Moreover he suggest that this opposition could also have characterized the relationship between Judaism and Christianity. Perhaps unwittingly, as a result he again gives the impression that the Jewish tradition had a legalistic character, whereas mercy was central to Christianity.

Crossan, too, seems to be prejudiced about the Jewish background to the New Testament – in both religious and social terms. He concludes from the fact that both Joseph and Jesus are said to have been carpenters (Mark 6.3; Matt.13.55) that Jesus' family belonged to the lower class of peasants and manual workers in society. In general these were uneducated people. Jesus, too, must be presupposed to have been uneducated and even illiterate. However, because Jesus lived in a world in which oral tradition was the norm, he knew a large number of biblical stories, fragments of psalms and prophetic sayings. Because he was illiterate, he never cited texts literally and completely.[51]

This description of Jesus is very much open to attack. In his richly documented study *Jesus as Teacher*,[52] Rainer Riesner showed that there was great concern for the instruction of young people and parents especially in Pharisaic circles. There is every reason to suppose that Joseph and Mary belonged to these circles, in which case it seems legitimate to conclude that Jesus was not uneducated, but received a thorough orthodox education in scripture and tradition.

Like Borg, Crossan also depicts Jesus as an itinerant wisdom teacher. He does so in a chapter with a surprising title: 'No Staff, No Sandals, And No Knapsack'. In the light of what has been said above, it is perhaps no longer surprising that Crossan does not explain the words and actions of Jesus exclusively from the Jewish tradition, but makes a comparison with Greek philosophers, especially the Cynics. Crossan concedes that it is quite possible that Jesus had never met a Cynic philosopher and perhaps had never even heard of Cynicism as a philosophical school. However, he seems to think that this does not invalidate his thesis. Even if Jesus did not derive his wisdom directly from Greek philosophy, that does not mean that there may not be agreements. Crossan calls both Jesus and the Cynic philosophers 'populists'. Both address ordinary people; both emphasize that not only words but also actions are important, that practice is as important as theory; the dress of both dramatically symbolized their message. However, Jesus lived in the country, while the cynics lived and worked in the towns; Jesus founded a community, whereas they addressed individuals. Perhaps we may describe Jesus as the representative of a Jewish Cynicism which had taken roots above all in the countryside.[53] Now that Cynicism is attracting so much attention, of course it is important to know something more about this philosophical trend. According to Crossan, it first presupposes a critical attitude towards society.

157

Cynics deny values which are usually regarded as essential, and create new values which threaten to turn existing social relations upside down. There is some agreement with the ideals of the Old Testament prophets and the apocalyptists who turn their backs on the world. The difference is that their view is directed hopefully towards the future, whereas the Cynics concentrate on the present. In a sense we have here ideas here which appear at all times. Where culture comes into being, a counter-culture develops; where social values exist, some seek their salvation in a fundamental criticism of this society.[54]

The answer to the question why this Jesus, a teacher of alternative wisdom, finally died a violent death on the cross, must also be sought in this attitude of opposition in principle. During his time in Jerusalem Jesus increasingly provoked resistance among the Jewish authorities. Above all his sharp criticism of the temple was a stumbling block to the priests and the like (Mark 12.10–12). Jesus was radical. He saw himself as one who translated God's radical love for human beings.[55]

13

Jesus Has Many Faces

Jeshua from Nazareth

In the first half of the first century there lived in Galilee a Jew who made history. He answered to the name Jeshua, but later became known all over the world as Jesus Christ. He came from Nazareth, which at that time was a small unimportant town without traditions or pretensions. Virtually nothing can be said for certain about Jeshua's youth. He grew up as the oldest son of the carpenter Joseph and his wife Miriam/Mary. The family consisted of five sons and an unknown number of daughters. Presumably both parents were sympathetic to the ideal of the Pharisees and brought up their children to be familiar with the scriptures and to respect the commandments of the Torah. Joseph practised the trade of a carpenter and, as was usual at that time, Jeshua as the oldest son followed in his father's footsteps. He learned the trade of a carpenter from Joseph.

Marriage and a family were held in high regard in the early Jewish tradition. By present-day standards, the age of marriage was particularly low: for girls around their thirteenth or fourteenth year, for young men a few years later. Anyone who was not married by the age of twenty was regarded as rather odd. Parents on both sides played an important role in the arrangement of a marriage. Joseph and Mary, too, will have looked in and around Nazareth for a bride for their oldest son. We do not know whether a marriage ever took place.

But something different did happen. At a given moment the life of Jeshua changed decisively. It is not clear precisely when this change took place. Probably it happened somewhere between his twentieth and thirtieth birthday. Then Jeshua left Nazareth and began to lead an itinerant existence. However, he remained in the north of Jewish territory. He preferred to limit himself to the area around the Sea of Galilee. He was regularly seen in some small towns set attractively on the shores of this sea, Magdala and above all Capernaum, and he seems to have had friends and acquaintances who offered him hospitality.

Jeshua very soon attracted public attention. The former carpenter from Nazareth gathered a group of disciples around him, men and women who had come under his spell and were fascinated by his words and the things that he did. Quite often his interpretation of the commandments was surprisingly creative. Moreover he had special powers. He healed the sick and cleansed lepers, and after his intervention evil spirits left their victims in peace. Jeshua was an inspired man, a real charismatic. He also seems to have been a mystic. For him the God of Israel was not far away. He experienced this God as a reality in his own life. Jeshua felt a deep spiritual bond with the God who had made himself known to the people of Israel in scripture and tradition and was also now revealing himself to him.

Jeshua lived an exemplary life. But he did not just spread joy and happiness. He also caused offence. His piety and loyalty to the commandments of the Torah did not prevent him from seeking the society of people with a less scrupulous life-style. He entered into friendships with sinners and publicans. He even ate with them. When asked for an explanation of what in the eyes of the pious was offensive behaviour he said that he had come to seek the lost. Just as a shepherd makes an effort to restore to the flock a sheep that has gone astray, so he was drawn by the lot of people who risked the same fate. Jeshua's conduct aroused curiosity. Who was he? What could be expected of him? Almost a century earlier, Judaea had become part of the Roman empire. This situation left deep marks on society and divided the Jewish population into parties which threatened, hated, and even fought with one another. There was considerable conflict, and there were those who even encouraged their supporters to engage in armed resistance to the Romans. They were firmly convinced that God was their ally and would not leave them in the lurch. Others were afraid that rebellion would end in a blood-bath and thought it better to renounce weapons and wait for divine intervention. There were also Jews who collaborated with the

Roman forces of occupation. The fanatics regarded them as collaborators, and when they gained the upper hand they took their revenge on them.

Jeshua lived in this sharply divided Jewish society. Which side did he take? It is not easy to give a clear answer to this question. He does not seem to have been a hothead, far less a fanatic. Jeshua made it quite clear that he opposed the use of force. He refused to write people off or to vilify them because they adopted different standpoints. He even seems to have been notably forgiving towards tax collectors, who became rich as a result of the unfair Roman system of taxation. In the view of fanatical Zealots, Jeshua was far too gentle. He was attracted by people's fate, but he showed little or no interest in political questions.

Jeshua was cautious and restrained. He seldom if ever used big words. He usually rejected the term Messiah. Sometimes he spoke about the coming of the Son of Man, but what he meant by this was vague: himself or someone else? On numerous occasions he pointed to the nearness of the kingdom of God. But even then, his view has an ambiguous character. In general he gives the impression that the kingdom still lies hidden in the (imminent) future. However, on one occasion he seems to suggest that in principle the kingdom of God is already present in this world.

In accord with the commandments, when the annual Passover approached he went to Jerusalem as a pilgrim. When he arrived in the city, the situation became dangerous for him. Remarkably, though a gentle and peaceable man, he now no longer avoided conflict. On the contrary, he deliberately created tensions. He organized an entry into the city, with the result that he invited suspicions of having pretensions to be king. In the temple he perplexed friend and foe by his unexpected action against the traders present there. His criticism of how things were done recalls some Old Testament prophets.

What did Jesus of Nazareth want? On one point at any rate the authorities were clear: he was dangerous and so had to be done away with as quickly as possible. His strange behaviour could inspire others to take action and therefore formed a serious threat in a situation which at best could be described as an armed peace. Jewish leaders and Roman occupation authorities soon got together and entered into a monstrous alliance. In the darkness of night they arrested Jesus, and condemned him to death in a mock trial. The execution took place the very next day and Jeshua died on the cross.

Was that the tragic end of a good man? A short time later the mood of his followers changed dramatically. Despite the death of their teacher, their spiritual leader and source of inspiration, they took new courage. They told an amazing story. Some of them had seen Jeshua again alive. They believed that God had raised him from the dead. His followers reported this with so much conviction and joy that others also began to believe. Jeshua is not dead, but alive!

A consensus

In scholarly literature at present there is no longer any discussion about whether Jesus of Nazareth really lived. Things were different in the nineteenth century. And at the beginning of the twentieth century, too, theologians trained in historical criticism even went so far as to deny the existence of Jesus. In his survey of the history of the quest Albert Schweitzer also considers this denial of the historicity of Jesus at length.[1] That time is now behind us. At the foundation of Christianity stands Jesus of Nazareth, who according to by far the vast majority of exegetes really lived.

There is much difference of opinion between New Testament scholars. However, that does not mean that a certain consensus has not been reached. So it is not rash to suppose that at this moment the sketch of Jesus' life given above – a mini-biography – would be accepted in principle by the vast majority of exegetes. Of course all the aspects mentioned could be developed further, but that is neither possible nor necessary in this context.[2]

Theologically irrelevant

The life of Jeshua/Jesus began two thousand years ago. That is a long time. Despite this distance it seems possible after careful analysis and sifting of facts to sketch a reliable historical profile of him from the Gospels. The way to the past is not blocked. There is every reason to be pleased at this discovery. Historically speaking we are not groping in the dark.

Jesus did live. The main outlines of his life can be mapped out. But is such a historical investigation theologically relevant? As we read earlier,[3] in the 1920s Rudolf Bultmann wrote a book about Jesus which was included in a series of biographies of great figures from world history. This mini-biography, of course in a further revised edition, could still find a place today in a series about influential philosophers and founders of world religions: Moses, Confucius, Socrates, Buddha, Jesus, Muhammad and others.

After completing his Jesus book Bultmann consistently maintained that while biographical interest in Jesus can be historically interesting, it has little if any importance for Christian faith. Was Bultmann right? It has to be said that historical investigation has its limits. Since the last century New Testament scholars have passionately gone in search of the authentic Jesus, but the results of their efforts is no more than a brief biographical sketch of someone who lived long ago in the past. He seems to have been a special person, an attractive and creative personality, a man with an inspiring and liberating message. All that is true, but the reader perhaps gets a feeling of disappointment. Is that all that can be said? The historian will reply 'yes' to this question. By present-day scholarly standards, at present no more can be stated than the mini-biography given above.

Jesus Christ

Is all this labour ultimately vain? In the eighteenth and nineteenth centuries theologians thought that they could uproot the age-old Christ of dogma. In an optimistic mood they went in search of the *real* Jesus with the help of what they saw as *objective* historical methods. However, they found the *historical* Jesus. To begin with, they acted on the presupposition that they had achieved their aim: the historical Jesus and the real Jesus were one and the same. However, slowly disillusionment set in and they realized that they had not succeeded in their aim. Theologians began to see that the historical quest of the real Jesus was doomed to failure. Anyone who uses historical methods to look at the past can only map a bit of the past. It is possible to sketch a picture of the historical Jesus, but that does not mean that we have become much wiser about the real Jesus.

As we know, the Gospel of John is considerably less reliable than the three Synoptic Gospels, at least from a historical perspective. But does that mean that the Fourth Gospel no longer has anything to say to us? A priori we cannot rule out the possibilty that nevertheless it might provide more information about the real Jesus than a modern historian who has constructed a historically reliable picture of Jesus of Nazareth with methods which are accepted in today's society.

For this reason, even in circles of theologians who do not belong to the orthodox wing of Christianity there has been constant opposition to an approach which takes it for granted that the historical Jesus and the real Jesus are to be identified. Time and again such theologians have emphasized that Christian faith cannot be based on historical research. At the end of the nineteenth century Martin Kähler argued for a concentration on the biblical Christ.[4] Some decades later, Rudolf Bultmann gained a following with his call to concentrate on the kerygmatic Christ. Recently Rochus Zuurmond has written a book on this problem in which he argues that the preached Christ is much deeper and more profound than the historical Jesus. Moreover he calls for as little attention as possible to be paid to the quest for the life of Jesus and for priority to be given to the 'Jesus of the scriptures'.[5]

There seems to be no doubt that such critical voices will continue to be heard in the future. The views of theologians like Martin Kähler, Rudolf Bultmann and Rochus Zuurmond continue to convince readers. They do so because they illuminate an aspect that must not be negelected. Historical research can neither deny nor confirm Christian faith. The historian is in a position to write a mini-biography of Jesus; believers know themselves to be addressed by Jesus Christ and for this reason can say much more about his significance. However true all this may be, it cannot close our eyes to the following problem. Not only does the historical reality seem to be more complicated, but the reality which is evoked by faith cannot be expressed in a few words or sentences.

Multicoloured

To say that we should be concerned with the kerygmatic Christ, whom others called Jesus or the Christ of scripture, sounds attractive and is even seductive by virtue of its simplicity. But this difference in terminology casts a first shadow over the optimism. The history of the quest has taught us that the terms Jesus and Christ are not completely interchangeable. It therefore makes a difference whether we concentrate on the kerygmatic Christ or on the Jesus of scripture.

The New Testament seems to be multicoloured. In their descriptions and their interpretations of events in the past, each evangelist or apostle goes his own way. Here are some illustrations. As can be inferred from my mini-biography of Jesus, little or nothing can be said from a historical perspective about the 'origin' of Jesus. He comes from Nazareth and he knows that he has a mystical bond with God. The apostle Paul at one point says that Jesus is sent by God (Gal. 4.4). By contrast, Mark is very restrained on this point and in fact says nothing about Jesus' origin. His three fellow evangelists tell us much more. According to Matthew, Jesus' roots lie in the Old Testament: Jesus is son of Abraham, but also son of David (Matt. 1.1). Prophetic voices begin to sound when Matthew writes about Jesus' birth in Bethlehem (Matt. 1.23; 2.5–6). Luke agrees with Matthew. He too relates that Jesus came into the world in the town of Bethlehem (Luke 2.1–20). The Third Evangelist then sets other accents, because his context differs from that of his fellow evangelists. Luke is concerned to give Jesus a place in world history (Luke 2.1–13; 3.1–2). Moreover, he devotes more attention to the circumstances in which Jesus was born. Luke grew up in a culture in which it was thought normal for special people to come into the world in a special way. He felt compelled to relate the birth of Jesus in such a way. The Fourth Evangelist does not draw attention to the town of Bethlehem (John 7.40–44), but compels his reader to look upwards. In keeping with the picture of the world in this time, Jesus comes 'from above': his origin lies with God (John 3.31–36).

Anyone who wants to read about the life of Jesus is dependent on the four Gospels. Although Paul is writing his letters a comparatively short time after the cross and resurrection, he is almost completely silent about Jesus' words and actions. The apostle to the Gentiles emphasizes the significance of the cross. In their stories about Jesus the evangelists do not hesitate to express their choice. Mark sees Jesus above all as a miracle worker and exorcist. The earliest evangelist gives a vivid description of the hopeless situation of the sick and possessed who are healed by Jesus and freed from their pains and evil spirits (Mark 5.1–20; 5.21–43). Anyone who compares the texts of Mark and Matthew on this point will make surprising discoveries. Matthew usually follows Mark's text more or less exactly. However, at the precise moment when his fellow-evangelist pays attention to the seriousness of the disease or possession, he begins to shorten the story notably (Matt. 8.28–34; 9.8–26). Evidently Matthew was not very interested in the healing powers of Jesus. As a result his account of the event is matter-of-fact, and he contents himself with few words. His interest is above all in the interpretation of the commandments of the Torah. For him, Jesus is the scribe and teacher who teaches his disciples what they must do and how they need to live, with a view to the speedy coming of the kingdom of heaven (Matt. 5–7; 25.31–46).

The Third Evangelist has a different interest, and so he writes a different Gospel. Luke is addressing Theophilus, clearly an important man, a high official in the Roman empire (Luke 1.1–4). Luke leaves no doubt that the gospel of Jesus Christ is also intended for Gentiles. He emphasizes that the gospel contains a joyful message (Luke 2.10). There is a celebration in heaven when a sinner is converted and those who have gone astray are saved (Luke 2.10). Poor people get a free ticket for the kingdom of God (Luke 6.20–26). Immediately after his death the poor Lazarus is taken by angels to Abraham's bosom (Luke 16.19–31). Luke writes a Gospel for the well-to-do. He also wrestles with what for him is the existential question how a rich man can be saved and when he will be received into the eternal habitations (Luke 16.1–9).

The Fourth Evangelist goes his own way, and sketches out a picture of Jesus which those familiar with the synoptic Gospels will have difficulty in recognizing. The sentence from his prologue, 'The Word became flesh and dwelt among us and we have seen his glory, a glory as of the only-begotten of the Father, full of grace and truth' (John 1.14), can be regarded as the starting point: Jesus is one human being among others, but as such he also reveals the glory of God. This ambiguity recurs in all the stories in the Fourth Gospel. By Jacob's well sits someone who to all outward appearances is a tired Jewish man (John 4.6), but on closer inspection he proves to be the 'saviour of the world' (John 4.42). The work of God the Father is manifested in the work of Jesus (John 5.17–18). Father and Son are one. God and Jesus are completely of one spirit: in work, will and purpose.

The Gospels relate the passion and death of Jesus at length. That he is crucified is part of their account, but each of the four evangelists gives this fact a special, soteriological significance. In his account of the passion, Mark emphasizes that Jesus dies on the cross as a righteous sufferer (Mark 15.34). His death is the ultimate consequence of his life: he lived for others, and therefore his death on the cross can also be interpreted as suffering and dying 'for others'. His words and actions during the last supper with his disciples also need to be translated in that light (Mark 14.22–25).

In respect of this facet of Jesus' life, too, the Fourth Gospel goes its own way. In his passion story Jesus is not the victim; he is in control. He knows what awaits him and what has to be done. He does not hesitate, nor does he doubt. The Fourth Gospel says nothing about a spiritual wrestling in Gethsemane. Jesus has no difficulty in fulfilling his task. He goes and overcomes the darkness. His cross is not a defeat or a humiliation but a victory and a glorification (John 18–19). Paul looks at suffering in general and the crucifixion in particular in another way. This event has a central place in his view of the core of Christian faith. In his view the cross is primarily a symbol of humiliation, definitely not a symbol of glorification (Phil. 2.6–11). According to the Torah the crucified one is cursed by God (Gal. 3.13). His death on the cross is a scandal and a folly (I Cor. 1.23). After his encounter with the risen Lord in Damascus Paul knows that the curse has become a blessing and that what for human beings is folly can prove to be wisdom for God. From that moment he sees the crucified Christ as the source of life, freedom and reconciliation (II Cor. 5.16–21).

I shall restrict myself to what I have just said. Those who want to include yet further biblical writings – like the letter to the Hebrews, the letters of Peter and the last book of the Bible – in their reflections will find new factors in addition to those already mentioned. For this reason the exegete may never ultimately be content on concentrating on something like the Jesus or the Christ of the scriptures. Precisely which Jesus or which Christ of the scriptures is meant? Which picture of Jesus or Christ is preferred? The reader will recall that this discussion is not a new one.[6] In the 1950s Ernst Käsemann criticized his teacher Rudolf Bultmann, who claimed that Christian faith had to be based exclusively on the kerygmatic Christ.

Discussion begins in the New Testament

The Bible is a multicoloured book. The New Testament has a large number of pictures of Jesus. Perhaps I may be doing some scholars an injustice, but I cannot avoid the impression that anyone who argues for a concentration on the Jesus or the Christ of the scriptures is insufficiently aware of the danger of trivializing the differences between the various books of the New Testament. Such an approach presupposes and constructs a unity which simply is not there. Thus already in the first centuries of church history theologians developed christological dogma. Of course they also noted the various differences between the Gospels, but they felt called to seek agreements, and therefore tried patiently and carefully to fit the different elements together like bits of a jig-saw puzzle, so that finally one picture of Jesus resulted. Then attempts were made in confessional writings and dogmatic formulae to put that image of Jesus explicitly into words. This effort at unity had consequences for the church community. Anyone who had difficulty in agreeing with the current picture ran the risk of being expelled from the community as a heretic. The supposed unity of New Testament christology was to form the basis for church unity. Church history has shown that this ideal seldom if ever became a reality.

The New Testament does not know one clear, well-rounded picture of Jesus Christ. Every biblical author looks at the past in his own way, depending on his circumstances, interests and desires. A century ago Schweitzer demonstrated how in the nineteenth century those who wrote about the Jesus of history described him in their own image. A century later this remark seems to have lost little importance or relevance. It has become increasingly clear in the debate that the writers of the New Testament are in fact doing the same thing. They, too, are sketching their own pictures of Jesus. Again, here are a few examples – to enliven the discussion I shall assume here that the biblical writers know one another's works and can ask one another critical questions.

An attractive conversation could be arranged between the four evangelists and Paul about the value and meaning of stories about Jesus' conduct. It is not impossible that during this discussion Matthew and Paul would get into a fierce argument about the place and function of the commandments of the Torah. It seems impossible that the two would ever agree on this question. If they could be persuaded to quieten down a bit, then perhaps the voice of Mark would be heard. He would perhaps ask Paul in surprise why he consistently called Jesus the Christ in all his letters. To clarify matters Mark would remark here that he had heard that Jesus himself often told his disciples not to use this term. Since the resurrection, did that command for silence no longer hold?

The Fourth Evangelist would stand apart from this whole debate. His fellow-evangelists would want to know how he got hold of so many stories that they do not know: the wedding at Cana, the conversation with Nicodemus, the meeting with a Samaritan woman, the healing at Bethesda, the resurrection of Lazarus – where did he get them all from? Not to mention all those long discourses which, according to the Fourth Gospel, Jesus is said to have given. How did John come to know more than they did? Paul would impatiently wait for his turn and have difficulty in not interrupting. The discussion about the origin of these stories would not interest him very much. He would want to ask how so remarkably little could be said in the Gospel of John – at least to his mind – about the suffering of Jesus. Humiliation or glorification? Paul and John would find it hard to agree on this point.

Who would be the first to raise the question of the 'future'? It is certain that at that point the conversation would threaten to degenerate into a real cacophony of voices, sometimes in vigorous agreement but more often in contradiction. Would we also hear for the first time the voice of the author of the Gospel of Thomas? Would he join in the debate, because he thought all this attention to the future reprehensible? In his writing he concentrates wholly on the words of Jesus. How would his contribution to the discussion be received in a group of 'canonical' authors inclined to regard him as an 'apocryphal' outsider? Of course his voice, too, would have to be heard.

The debate which has already begun in the New Testament is continued in church history and has still not come to an end. It need not surprise us that the church is not a unity, since the New Testament is a multicoloured book. How can that be explained?

In the first place, all individuals – including the biblical authors – look at events in the present and the past in their own way. Precisely what happened? Experience tells us that even eye-witnesses contradict one another. That also applies to the picture that we have of others. People react to one another and change as a result. In encountering one person I am slightly different from the person I am in encountering someone else. The picture that I have of someone can never agree completely with the picture which someone else has of that same person. Thus evangelists and apostles each describe their views of Jesus in their own way. They were not objective, nor could they ever be.

Secondly, it can be inferred from the mini-biography of Jesus given above that he was a multicoloured personality. Words seem insufficient to do him justice, and traditional titles are inadequate. On what aspect of his appearance does emphasis need to be placed? On the cross? Of course there is much to be said for that. But why should we not pay at least as much attention to his life on earth? Does it make sense to emphasize that Jesus did miracles? A positive answer can also be given to that question. But why shouldn't we begin by emphasizing his radical interpretation of the Torah? And is his concern to seek out the lost as good as a 'miracle'?

Jesus has many faces. No single confessional writing or dogmatic formula can sketch out a picture of Jesus in which all these 'faces' have a full place. It is even impossible to achieve this aim, because some interpretations seem to contradict one another. Unlike Rochus Zuurmond, I do not think that 'the Jesus of the scriptures is richer than the historical Jesus'. Even the biblical Jesus or Christ is not, strictly speaking, the real Jesus, but is the result of a selection of facts. In my view the exegete cannot therefore ever avoid embarking once again on the quest of the historical Jesus. Here the mini-biography at the beginning of this chapter could function as a kind of conscience. It is always misleading to follow Paul and concentrate completely on the crucified Christ. The history of the church and theology show countless examples of how liberating Paul's *theologia crucis* has proved. At the same time, though, it needs to be recognized that this view of Jesus, too, is one-sided and needs correction. Those who base themselves exclusively on the crucified Christ forget all too easily to tell stories from which it emerges that Jesus' life has an 'exemplary' character: his conduct can shape the life of his disciples.

Jesus is always different

Jesus has many faces. We know a Jesus of Paul, of Mark, of Matthew, of Luke, of John, and also of Thomas. We know that Jesus hoped for the imminent coming of the kingdom of God, but we also know that he thought that he could perceive the same kingdom in his own life and world. Jesus could be called an apocalyptist, but he also seems to have been a source of inspiration for Gnostic thinkers. We know stories about Jesus' actions: liberating and healing, giving hope and showing love for men and women, creative and challenging. We also know that Jesus died on the cross, and we believe that God raised him from the dead. The New Testament is surprisingly open. Jesus was not set down in formulae and imprisoned in expressions which were to apply everywhere for all time. Anyone who attempts that gives the impression of having said the last and definitive word about Jesus. But the attractive thing about encountering Jesus is that clearly the last word about him has yet to be said and perhaps will never be said. Jesus is always different, surprising and confusing, known and familiar and yet again a stranger or unexpectedly new. That is how Jesus lived among the Jews, and that is how he lives today.

Notes

1. *Jesus of Nazareth, the Son of God*

1. Those interested should refer to W.Pannenberg, *Jesus God and Man*, Philadelphia and London 1968; A Grillmeier, *Christ in Christian Tradition*, Oxford and Atlanta, Ga. ²1975.
2. For the text of the Chalcedonian Definition and a commentary on it see T.H.Bindley, *The Oecumenical Documents of the Faith*, London 1950, 181–206; see also Frances Young, *From Nicaea to Chalcedon*, London 1983.

2. *Holy Scripture under Discussion*

1. See, for example, the discussion between Rome and the Reformed churches over the interpretation of Col.1.24, in which Paul writes, 'and in my flesh I complete what is lacking in Christ's afflictions'.
2. See especially G.S.Robbert, *Luther as Interpreter of Scripture*, St Louis 1982; T.H.L.Parker, *Calvin's New Testament Commentaries*, Edinburgh ²1993; id., *Calvin's Old Testament Commentaries*, Edinburgh 1993.
3. See now James M.Byrne, *Glory, Jest and Riddle. Religious Thought in the Enlightenment*, London 1996.
4. This term plays a central role in the well-known definition of the Enlightenment given by Immanuel Kant in 1784: 'Enlightenment is man's coming of age from his self-imposed tuelage. This tutelage was his inability to use his understanding without the guidance of another.'
5. K.Held, *Treffpunkt Platon*, Stuttgart 1990, 36f. gives a good definition: 'Only now did the greater or lesser chronological distance from the past become a problem for science, and consequently for men and women generally. People now became aware that they could not relate to the bearers of earlier culture as they could to contemporaries. People of antiquity had lived in another age, in quite different circumstances. They were separated from us like fish in an aquarium, and we could only look at them through a window.'

6. Angelus Silesius, 'Cherubinischer Wandermann', in *Sämtliche Poetische Werke* (ed.H.L.Held), 1949, III, 18.

7. In 1778 Lessing published a book with a programmatic title, *Neue Hypothese über die Evangelisten als bloss menschliche Geschichtsschreiber betrachtet*.

3. A 'Rational' Christology

1. For more detail see J.M.Robinson, *A New Quest of the Historical Jesus*, London 1959.

2. J.Jeremias, 'Der gegenwärtige Stand der Debatte um das Problem des historischen Jesus', in H.Ristow and K.Matthiae (eds.), *Der historische Jesus und der kerygmatische Christus*, Berlin 1961, 13.

3. For more information see G.Hornig, 'Lessing', *Theologische Realenzyklopädie* (henceforth = *TRE*) 21, Berlin 1991, 20–33.

4. Lessing worked for some time as a librarian in the city of Wolfenbüttel. Between 1774 and 1778 he published a selection of the writings of Reimarus under the title *Fragmente eines Ungenannten*. They quickly became known and notorious as the Wolfenbüttel Fragments (they are conveniently available in an English translation in *Reimarus: Fragments*, ed. Charles H.Talbert, Philadelphia 1970 and London 1971). In wide circles these 'Fragments of an Unknown' were regarded as an extremely sharp attck on Christian faith. The publication of Remarus' writings led to a stream of polemic.

5. The book was in two volumes and was published in Tübingen. An English translation was made by George Eliot, *The Life of Jesus Critically Examined* (reissued Phildelphia and London 1973, ed. Peter C.Hodgson). Years later a new version appeared, D.F.Strauss, *A New Life of Jesus*, London 1865.

6. Cf. *Ferdinand Christian Baur. On the Writing of Church History*, ed. Peter C.Hodgson, New York 1968.

7. In *De consensu evangelistarum* 12, Augustine writes: *Marcus eum (= Matthew) subsecutus tamquam pedisequus et breviator eius videtur.*

8. There is a tremendous amount of literature on this question. The basic issues can be seen clearly from B.H.Throckmorton, *Gospel Parallels*, London 1979, and E.P.Sanders and Margaret Davies, *Studying the Synoptic Gospels*, London and Philadelphia 1989.

9. H.J.Holtzmann, *Die synoptischen Evangelien. Ihr Ursprung und geschichtlicher Charakter*, Leipzig 1863.

10. For further information see O.Merk, 'Holtzmann', *TRE* 15, 519–22.

11. At the beginning of the 1970s, E.Lohse wrote in his *Die Entstehung*

des Neuen Testaments, Stuttgart 1972, 79: 'Rather, the complicated relationship between what the synoptic Gospels have in common and where they differ only found a satisfactory explanation with the so-called two-source theory, which now has gained almost universal recognition.' For more discussion see e.g K.F.Nickle, *The Synoptic Gospels*, Atlanta, Ga 1979 and London 1980. Meanwhile it has proved that the discussion is far from having come to a definitive conclusion. Cf. M.E.Boismard, 'The Two-Source Theory at an Impasse', *New Testament Studies* 26, 1980, 1–17. For this reason in recent studies scholars have again returned to the question of the origin of the canonical Gospels and the way in which the early church handed down the Jesus tradition. Cf. H.Koester, *Ancient Christian Gospels. Their History and Development*, London and Philadelphia 1990; G.Theissen, *The Gospels in Context: Social and Political History in the Synoptic Tradition*, Edinburgh 1994.

12. For a survey see e.g. K.Barth, *Protestant Theology in the Nineteenth Century*, London 1972; P.Tillich, *Perspectives on Nineteenth and Twentieth Century Protestant Theology*, London and New York 1967.

13. Albert Schweitzer gives a sketch of the life and work of Ernest Renan in Chapter 13 of his *The Quest of the Historical Jesus*, London [3]1950, 180–92. On the occasion of the centenary of Renan's death on 1 October a new biography appeared which showed how topical Renan's thought still is: P.Barret, *Ernest Renan – Tout est possible, même Dieu!*, Paris 1992.

14. E.Renan, *Life of Jesus*, London 1927.

15. Renan's scholarship was not up to date. As we have already seen, the dilemma 'John or the Synoptic Gospels?' had already been raised at the beginning of the nineteenth century.

16. See e.g. *RGG* I, 1848, and Schweitzer, *Quest of the Historical Jesus* (n.13), 222ff.

17. This information is provided by G.R.Beasley-Murray, *Jesus and the Future. An Examination of the Criticism of the Eschatological Discourse, Mark 13, with Special Reference to the Apocalypse Theory*, London 1954, 20.

18. Timothée Colani did not hesitate to regard certain texts or even pericopes as later additions or interpolations on the basis of literary-critical arguments. So he can be regarded as the 'inventor' of the thesis that Mark 13 is not the words of Jesus but that this apocalyptic discourse is based on a 'little apocalpyse' or an apocalyptic pamphlet. See T.Colani, *Jésus Christ et le croyances messaniques de son temps*, Strasbourg 1864.

19. Schweitzer describes the tragic life of D.F.Strauss in Chapter 7 of his *The Quest of the Historical Jesus* (68–77). He begins this part of the book, entitled 'David Friedrich Strauss. The Man and his Fate', with the words: 'In order to understand Strauss one must love him. He was not the greatest, and not the deepest, of theologians, but he was the most absolutely sincere. His insight and his errors were alike the insight and the errors of a prophet. And he had a prophet's fate. Disappointment and suffering gave his life its consecration. It unrolls itself before us like a tragedy, in which, in the end, the gloom is lightened by the mild radiance which shines forth from the nobility of the sufferer.'

4. A Vain Quest for the Life of Jesus

1. His *The Quest of the Historical Jesus* was published in 1906 when he was a lecturer in New Testament in the University of Strasbourg, first under the title *From Reimarus to Wrede*. It appeared in a considerably revised form in 1913 under the title *Die Geschichte der Leben-Jesu Forschung*, with many additional chapters. The English translation was made from the first edition, and sadly the additional chapters have never appeared in English.

2. 'These pictures of Jesus are very different. The rationalist depicts Jesus as a moral preacher, the idealist as an embodiment of humanity, the aesthete praises him as the brilliant orator, the socialist as a friend of the poor and a social reformer, and the countless pseudo-scholars make him a romantic figure. Jesus is modernized. These lives of Jesus are mere daydreams. The result is that each age, each theologian, each author discovers his own ideal in the personality of Jesus. Where do they go wrong? Without being aware of it, they replace dogma with psychology and fantasy.' Thus J.Jeremias, 'Der gegenwärtige Stand der Debatte um das Problem des historischen Jesus', in H.Ristow and K.Matthiae (eds.), *Der historische Jesus und der kerygmatische Christus*, Berlin 1961, 12–25:14.

3. See Chapter 21 of the German edition of Schweitzer's *The Quest, Die Geschichte der Leben-Jesu Forschung* (n.1 above), where he says how much he was stimulated by the work of Johannes Weiss (1863–1914).

4. Albert Schweitzer, *My Life and Thought*, London 1933.

5. E.g. SyrBar 70; cf. Schweitzer, *Quest*, 361 n.1.

6. The last sentences of the chapter on 'Thoroughgoing Scepticism and Thoroughgoing Eschatology' mentioned above are as follows: 'At midday of the same day . . . Jesus cried aloud and expired. He had chosen to remain fully conscious to the last' (395).

7. See A.Schweitzer, *The Kingdom of God and Primitive Christianity*, London 1968.

8. The number of real followers is limited. In Switzerland 'the Bern school' formed, making discussion of the meaning of consistent eschatology a theme of the history of dogma and dogmatics: cf. F.Buri, *Die Bedeutung der neutestamentlichen Eschatologie für die neuerer protestantischen Theologie*, Zurich 1935; M.Werner, *The Formation of Christian Dogma*, London 1957. However, they had their critics: W. Michaelis, *Zur Engelchristologie I. Urchristentum. Abbau der Konstruktion Martin Werners*, Basel 1942; F.Flückiger, *Der Ursprung des christlichen Dogma. Eine Auseinandersetzung mit Albert Schweitzer und Martin Werner*, Zurich 1955; O.Cullmann, 'Parusieverzögerung und Urchristentum', *Theologische Literaturzeitung* 83, 1958, 1–12. For the situation in the Anglo-Saxon world see N.Perrin, *The Kingdom of God in the Teaching of Jesus*, London and Philadelphia 1963, 37f.

9. E.Grässer, *Albert Schweitzer als Theologe*, Tübingen 1979.

5. From Optimism to Scepticism

1. The origin of this name is uncertain. It is usally supposed that Q is the abbreviation of the German *Quelle* (= source). It is difficult to say who introduced this letter. H.J.Holtzmann was certainly the first to attempt to reconstruct the second source which Matthew and Luke had in common. However, he did not speak of Q but of 'Lambda' (= Greek L for Logia), H.J.Holtzmann, *Die synoptischen Evangelien. Ihr Ursprung und geschichtlicher Charakter*, Leipzig 1863, 140–61. Johannes Weiss (1863–1914) first used the abbreviation in 1890, but suggested that he had taken it over from his father Bernhard Weiss (1827–1918).

2. Much has been published about Q in the course of almost 150 years. See e.g. R.A.Edwards, *A Theology of Q. Eschatology, Prophecy and Wisdom*, Philadelphia 1976; A.Polag, *Die Christologie der Logienquelle*, WMANT 45, Neukirchen-Vluyn 1977.

3. His daughter Agnes wrote a fascinating biography, A.von Zahn-Harnack, *Adolf von Harnack*, Berlin ²1951 (it first appeared in 1936).

4. His theological views also led to a deep rift with his father, the practical theologian Theodosius Harnack, for whom see M.Seitz and M.Herbst, 'Theodosius Harnack', *TRE* 14, Berlin and New York 1985, 458–62.

5. For more information about the dispute over the Apostles' Creed, see H.-M.Barth, 'Apostolisches Glaubensbekenntnis II' , *TRE* 3, 560–2; Gerd Lüdemann, *Heretics*, London and Louisville, Ky 1996, 184–92.

6. In 1988, fifty years after his death, a biography appeared which sheds

light on the topicality of his thought, available in English as W.Neuer, *Adolf Schlatter*, Grand Rapids 1995; meanwhile a much enlarged new version has been produced in German by the same author.

7. F.Schleiermacher, *On Religion. Speeches to its Cultured Despisers*, reissued New York 1958.

8. It is interesting that Harnack himself realized this only later. In the preface to the first German impression he could still write, 'The question has been raised and discussed in purely historical terms'. Later, however, towards the end of his life, he conceded that apologetic had been his deepest motive: 'I see that my real interest was apologetic, but at the time I did not realize it.'

9. A.von Harnack, *Sprüche und Reden Jesu, Die zweite Quelle des Matthäus und Lukas. Beiträge zur Einleitung in das Neue Testament* 1/2, Leipzig 1907.

10. Here is an attractive and evocative example from *What is Christianity?*, London 1901, reissued New York 1957, Lecture 7: 'It is a high and glorious ideal, and we have received it from the very foundation of our religion. It ought to float before our eyes as the goal and guiding star of our historical development. Whether mankind will ever attain to it, who can say? But we can and ought to approximate to it, and these days – otherwise than two or three hundred years ago – we feel a moral obligation in this direction. Those of us who possess more delicate and therefore more prophetic perceptions no longer regard the kingdom of love and peace as a mere Utopia' (113–14).

11. Another typical quotation: 'He (Jesus Christ) came into immediate opposition with the official leaders of the people and in them with ordinary human nature in general. They thought of God as a despot guarding the ceremonial observances in His household; he breathed in the presence of God. They saw Him only in His law, which they had converted into a labyrinth of dark defiles, blind alleys and secret passages; he saw and felt Him everywhere. They were in possession of a thousand of his commandments, and thought, therefore, that they knew him; he had one only, and knew Him by it. They had made this religion into an earthly trade, and there was nothing more detestable; he proclaimed the living God and the soul's nobility' (*What is Christianity?*, 50f.).

12. A.von Harnack, *Marcion. Das Evangelium vom fremden Gott. Eine Monographie zur Geschichte der Grundlegung der katholischen Kirche*, Leipzig ²1924, reissued Darmstadt 1985.

13. Ibid., 217: 'To reject the Old Testament in the second century was an error which the mainstream church rightly rejected; to retain it in the

sixteenth cenutry was a fate which the Reformation could not yet avoid; but to preserve it since the nineteenth century as a canonical document in Protestantism is the consequence of a religious and ecclesiastical paralysis.'

14. Cf. e.g. G.R.Beasley-Murray, *Jesus and the Kingdom of God*, Grand Rapids 1986, 286–7: 'It is extraordinary that a man of Schweitzer's intellectual brilliance could not bring himself to accept the simple fact that the discourses of Matthew were constructed by the evangelist from sources available to him. It needs no more than a synopsis of the Gospels to convince humbler students of that.' For a recent example of the literary-criticism of Matt.10 see D.J.Weaver, *Matthew's Missionary Discourse. A Literary Critical Analysis*, Sheffield 1990.

15. Some examples are: J.A.T.Robinson, *Jesus and His Coming. Did the Early Church Misinterpret the Original Teaching of Jesus?*, London 1957, 96–7; W.Pannenberg, *Jesus – God and Man*, London and Philadelphia 1968; James M.Robinson, *A New Quest of the Historical Jesus*, London 1959 (the section 'The end of the original quest', 32–4); N.Perrin, *Rediscovering the Teaching of Jesus*, London 1967, 215–18; J.Moltmann, *The Crucified God. The Cross of Christ as the Foundation and Criticism of Christian Theology*, Munich 1972, 110–12; R.H.Hiers, *The Historical Jesus and the Kingdom of God. Present and Future in the Message and Ministry of Jesus*, Gainesville 1973, 1–10; W.Kasper, *Jesus the Christ*, London and New York 1977; J.Macquarrie, *Jesus Christ in Modern Thought*, London and Philadelphia 1990, 275–8.

16. K.L.Schmidt, *Der Rahmen der Geschichte Jesu. Literarkritische Untersuchungen zur ältesten Jesusüberlieferung*, Berlin 1919 (Darmstadt ²1969); R.Bultmann, *The History of the Synoptic Tradition* (1921), Oxford ²1968.

17. I have added this sentence deliberately. It will emerge in due course that it is in no way my purpose to claim that the Gospels had no biographical interest at all. Opinions are shifting in this sphere, too. Recently more importance has been attached to their biographical aspects. They cannot be compared with modern biographies, but there are parallels with Hellenistic biographies, cf. G.N.Stanton, *Jesus of Nazareth in New Testament Preaching*, Cambridge 1974, 117–36. Thus, with due caution and reserve, the term 'Jesus biography' can be used', e.g. by M.Hengel, *Acts and the History of Earliest Christianity*, London and Philadelphia 1979, 16.

6. The Kerygmatic Christ

1. W.Wrede, *The Messianic Secret in the Gospels* (1901), Cambridge 1971.
2. J.Wellhausen, *Einleitung in die drei ersten Evangelien*, Berlin 1905, ^{2}1911.
3. R. Bultmann, *Die Erforschung der synoptischen Evangelien, Aus der Welt der Religion*. Neutestamentliche Reihe 1, Giessen 1925, ^{5}1966.
4. K.L.Schmidt, *Der Rahmen der Geschichte Jesus. Literarkritische Untersuchungen zur ältesten Jesusüberlieferung*, Berlin 1919 (Darmstadt ^{2}1969).
5. See H.J.Kraus, 'Kähler', *TRE* 17, 511–15.
6. English translation Philadelphia 1964. In 7 August 1891 Kähler lectured on vthe same topic to a group of preachers in Wuppertal. The book first appeared in 1892.
7. M.Kähler, *Jesus und das Alte Testament. Bearbeitet und mit einer Einleitung versehen von Ernst Kähler*, Neukirchen-Vluyn 1965.
8. Thus J.M.Robinson, *A New Quest of the Historical Jesus*, London 1959.
9. See W.Schmithals, *An Introduction to the Theology of Rudolf Bultmann*, London 1968.
10. English translation, R.Bultmann, *Jesus and the Word*, reissued London 1962.
11. 'To be sure, the predictions of the passion foretell his execution as divinely foreordained. But can there be any doubt that they are all *vaticinia ex eventu?*' (Rudolf Bultmann, *Theology of the New Testament* 1, New York and London 1951, 31).
12. 'It was soon no longer conceivable that Jesus' life was unmessianic – at least in the circles of Hellenistic Christianity in which the synoptics took form. That Jesus, Christ, the son of God, should have legitimated himself as such even in his earthly activity seemed self-evident, and so the gospel account of his ministry was cast in the light of messianic faith' (ibid., 33).
13. See the intertestamental work Psalms of Solomon 17 and 18.
14. For an extended discussion of this question see the attractive volume edited by H.Ristow and K.Matthiae, *Der historische Jesus und der kerygmatische Christus*, Berlin 1961.
15. See R.Bultmann, *Faith and Understanding* (1933), London and New York 1969, 220–46; id, *Theology*, 238; Schmithals, *Theology of Rudolf Bultmann* (n.9), 213f.
16. Cf. C.K.Barrett, *A Commentary to the Second Epistle to the Corinthians*, London 1973; R.Bultmann, *Der zweite Brief an die Korinther*, Göttingen 1976.

17. 'Paul did not know Jesus of Nazareth. That is an important difference between him and Peter and the other Jewish Christians, but it corresponds, say, to the position of Barnabas, Timothy and Titus or the community in Damascus and Antioch. Anyone who wants to claim the opposite for Paul is moving in the sphere of fantastic speculations. So it is also historically unjustified to presuppose in Paul an overall impression of piety and personality to explain the development of Pauline christology from this starting point. Even if Peter passed on such information to him afterwards, there is no indication of this fact in Paul. That alone is decisive and carries weight. A statement like Heb.5.7–10 (cf. 2.17f.; 4.15) that Jesus was open to temptation yet resisted it would go against the style of Pauline christology' (J.Becker, *Paulus. Der Apostel der Völker*, Tübingen 1989, 119–31: 125.

18. Bultmann, *Faith and Understanding* (n.20), 240.

7. Renewed Interest in the Historical Jesus

1. R.Bultmann, 'New Testament and Mythology', in *New Testament and Mythology and Other Writings*, ed. Schubert M.Ogden, Philadelphia and London 1985, 1–44.

2. See e.g. G.R.Beasley-Murray, *Jesus and the Kingdom of God*, Grand Rapids 1986.

3. 'The message of Jesus is a presupposition for the theology of the New Testament rather than a part of that theology itself', R.Bultmann, *Theology of the New Testament*, London and New York 1952, 3.

4. The following criticism is apt: 'It is on this question of eyewitness that Form-Criticism presents a very vulnerable front. If the Form-Critics are right, the disciples must have been translated to heaven immediately after the Resurrection. As Bultmann sees it, the primitive community exists *in vacuo*, cut off from its founders by the walls of an inexplicable ignorance. Like Robinson Crusoe it must do the best it can. Unable to turn to any for information, it must invent situations for the words of Jesus, and put into His lips sayings which personal memory cannot check,' Vincent Taylor, *The Formation of the Gospel Tradition*, London [2]1935, 41.

5. Though he already proved remarkably restrained in drawing conclusions, for example, about the 'redactional' and theological activities of the evangelist Matthew. Thus he pointed out 'that this easy juxtaposition of conflicting traditions is almost characteristic of Matthew: cf. 10.5f. with 28.18–20; 23.3a with 16.6; 24.20 with 12.8; 6.16–18 with 9.15a; 8.12 with 13.38; 9.13b with 10.41b. That is also one of the

reasons why so far there has yet to be a satisfactory redaction-critical analysis of the first Gospel', J.Jeremias, *New Testament Theology. Volume I. The Proclamation of Jesus*, London and New York 1971, 291.

6. The term docetism is derived from a Greek word *dokein* which means 'seem'. In a docetic christology the humanity of Jesus functions merely as appearance.

7. 'We are in process of giving up the statement "The Word was made flesh" and dissolving the history of salvation, the action of God in the human being Jesus of Nazareth and in his preaching. We are approaching docetism, the idea of Christ. We are in process of replacing the message of Jesus with the preaching of the apostle Paul', J.Jeremias, 'Der gegenwärtige Stand der Debatte um das Problem des historischen Jesus', in H.Ristow and K.Matthiae (eds.), *Der historische Jesus und der kerygmatische Christus*, Berlin 1961, 17–18.

8. See especially M.Black, *An Aramaic Approach to the Gospels and Acts*, Oxford ³1967.

9. Jeremias, *New Testament Theology* (n.5), 36; id., 'Abba', in *The Prayers of Jesus*, London 1967, 11–65.

10. J.Jeremias, *The Eucharistic Words of Jesus*, London and New York 1966.

11. See E.Schillebeeckx, 'Jesus' original Abba-experience, source and secret of his being, message and manner of life', *in Jesus. An Experiment in Christology* (1974), London and New York 1979, 256–68.

12. A consensus is never complete. For critical voices see M.R.D'Angelo, 'Abba and "Father". Imperial Theology and the Jesus Traditions', *Journal of Biblical Literature* 111, 1992, 611–30; J. Barr, 'Abba isn't Daddy!', *Journal of Theological Studies*, 39, 1988, 28–47.

13. Jeremias, *Der historische Jesus und der kerygmatische Christus* (n.7).

14. Ibid., 24.

15. Ibid., 25.

16. 'The preaching of the church is not itself revelation. If one may be allowed to put it pointedly, revelation does not take place on Sunday between ten and eleven. Golgotha is not everywhere. There is only one Golgotha: in front of the gates of Jerusalem', ibid., 34.

17. Ibid., 25.

18. E.Käsemann, 'Blind Alleys in the "Jesus of History" Controversy', in *New Testament Questions of Today*, London and Philadelphia 1969, 23–65.

19. The meeting took place in Marburg from 20 to 23 October 1953. Käsemann's lecture was published in 1954: English translation 'The Problem of the Historical Jesus', in *Essays on New Testament Themes*, London 1964, 15–47.

20. '... there are still pieces of the Synoptic tradition which the historian has to acknowledge as authentic if he wants to remain a historian at all' (ibid.,46).
21. I can agree with Käsemann in this sense, that the earthly Jesus is the criterion of the kerygma and legitimates it', R.Bultmann, *Glauben und Verstehen* IV, 1965; for this discussion see J.M.Robinson, *A New Quest of the Historical Jesus*, London 1959, 12–21.
22. Cf. E.Fuchs, 'The Quest of the Historical Jesus', in *Studies of the Historical Jesus*, London 1964, 11–31.
23. 'Thus for Fuchs, Jesus' conduct is the key to understanding his message', Robinson, *New Quest* (n.21), 15.
24. In this connection Jeremias has also pointed out: 'In reality, the "founding meal" is only one link in a long chain of meals which Jesus shared with his followers and which they continued after Easter. These gatherings at table, which provoked such scandal because Jesus excluded no one from them, even open sinners, and which thus expressed the heart of his message, were a type of the feast to come in the time of salvation (Mark 2.18–20). The last supper has its historical roots in this chain of gatherings', *New Testament Theology* (n.5), 290.
25. Cf. Robinson, *A New Quest* (n.21), 16: 'in the message and action of Jesus is implicit an eschatological understanding of his person, which becomes explicit in the kerygma of the primitive church'.
26. Though it was not complete. Books were also written about Jesus between 1926 and 1956. For a survey see Robinson *New Quest* (n.21), 9 n.2.
27. G.Bornkamm, *Jesus of Nazareth*, London and New York 1960.
28. See e.g. F.Gogarten, *Christ the Crisis*, London 1970, 30–2.
29. Cf. e.g. H.Conzelmann, *An Outline of the Theology of the New Testament*, London and New York 1969, 124–7.
30. G. Ebeling, 'Jesus and Faith', and 'The Question of the Historical Jesus and the Problem of Christology', in *Word and Faith*, Philadelphia and London 1963, 10–46, 288–304.

8. A Jewish Rabbi

1. J.Maier, *Jesus von Nazareth in der talmudischen Überlieferung*, Darmstadt 1978.
2. The classic study on this story of Jesus, *Toledoth Yeshu*, is S.Krauss, *Das Leben Jesu nach jüdischen Quellen*, Berlin 1902.
3. For the text see H.Chadwick (ed.), *Contra Celsum*, Cambridge 1953.
4. See W.Seiferth, *Synagoge und Kirche im Mittelalter*, Munich 1964;

I.Willi-Plein and T.Willi, *Glaubensdolch und Messiasbeweis. Die Begegnung von Judentum, Christentum und Islam im 13. Jahrhundert in Spanien*, Neukirchen-Vluyn 1980.

5. J.Salvador, *Jésus Christ et sa doctrine*, Paris 1838.

6. See G.Lindeskog, *Die Jesusfrage im neuzeitlichen Judentum. Ein Beitrag zur Geschichte der Leben-Jesu Forschung*, Darmstadt 1973.

7. See e.g. S.Ben Chorin, *Jesus in Judentum*, Wuppertal 1970; P.Lapide, *Ist das nicht Josephs Sohn? Jesus im heutigen Judentum*, Stuttgart and Munich 1976.

8. For Richard Wagner see L.Poliakov, *Le mythe aryan*, Paris 1971, 314–36.

9. Ibid., 324–30.

10. J.Klausner, *Jesu han-Nosri*, Jerusalem 1922: English Translation *Jesus of Nazareth*, London 1925.

11. The famous New Testament scholar Gerhard Kittel (1888–1948) was particularly notorious here, see R.P.Ericksen, *Theologians under Hitler: Gerhard Kittel, Paul Althaus, Emanuel Hirsch*, New Haven 1985.

12. See the title of Chapter 1 of Ernst Käsemann, *Jesus Means Freedom. A Polemical Survey of the New Testament*, London 1969, 'Was Jesus a "liberal"?'.

13. 'For the gospels do not leave us in the slightest doubt that Jesus, judged by the standards of his religious environment, was indeed liberal and that it was probably that fact that sent him to the cross', ibid., 17.

14. Cf. Lapide, *Ist das nicht Josephs Sohn?* (n.7).

15. See R.E.Brown, *The Birth of the Messiah. A Commentary on the Infancy Narratives in Matthew and Luke*, New York and London 1979.

16. S.Ben-Chorin, *Bruder Jesus. Der Nazarener in jüdischer Sicht*, Munich 1967; D.Flusser, *Jesus*, Hamburg 1968; S.Ben-Chorin, *Mutter Mirjam. Maria in jüdischer Sicht*, Munich 1971; cf. also G.Vermes, *Jesus the Jew. A Historian's Reading of the Gospels*, London 1973; E.P.Sanders, *Jesus and Judaism*, London 1985.

17. Flusser, *Jesus* (n.16), 20.

18. See e.g. R.Riesner, *Jesus als Lehrer. Eine Untersuchung zum Ursprung der Evangelien-Überlieferung*, Tübingen 1984, especially the section on Jewish education, 97–245.

19. For what follows see J.Bowker, *Jesus and the Pharisees*, Cambridge 1973; J.Westerholm, *Jesus and Scribal Authority*, Lund 1978.

20. C.G.Montefiore, *Some Elements of the Religious Teaching According to the Synoptic Gospels*, London 1910, reissued New York 1973; id., *The Synoptic Gospels*, London 1927, reissued New York 1968.

21. For what follows see P.Winter, *On the Trial of Jesus*, Berlin 1961; C.Cohn, *The Trial and Death of Jesus*, Jerusalem 1972; D.Flusser, *Last Days in Jerusalem. A Current Study of the Easter Week*, Tel Aviv 1980.
22. For the most recent, critical study of the resurrection see G.Lüdemann, *The Resurrection of Jesus*, London and Minneapolis 1994.
23. Ben-Chorin, *Bruder Jesus* (n.16).
24. See Hyam Maccoby, *The Mythmaker. Paul and the Invention of Christianity*, London 1986.

9. Nag Hammadi and Qumran

1. A fascinating story in the *Church History* of the fourth-century church historian Eusebius (I.13) reports a correspondence between Jesus and King Abgar of Edessa, but sadly this must be dismissed as a legend, cf. W.Bauer, *Orthodoxy and Heresy in Earliest Christianity*, Philadelphia and London 1968, 1–7.
2. See M.A.Knibb, *The Ethopic Book of Enoch*, London 1978.
3. Cf. for an account of apocalyptic D.S.Russell, *The Method and Message of Jewish Apocalyptic*, London 1964.
4. Paul Billerbeck (1853–1932) made an important contribution to the opening up of early Jewish and rabbinic literature. Over many years he collected texts from the Talmud and Midrash which in one way or another could be of importance for the interpretation of the New Testament. The result of his efforts was finally set in order and published in H.L.Strack and P.Billerbeck, *Kommentar zum Neuen Testament aus Talmud und Midrasch*, Munich 1922–1928; see J.Jeremias, 'Paul Billerbeck', *TRE* 6, 640–2.
5. See E.Hennecke,. W.Schneemelcher and R.McL.Wilson, *New Testament Apocrypha* (2 vols.), Louisville and Cambridge 1991, 1992.
6. See H.R.Smid, *Protevangelium Jacobi. A Commentary*, Assen 1965.
7. See e.g. Marina Warner, *Alone of All Her Sex*, London 1976.
8. See J.Jeremias, *Unknown Sayings of Jesus*, London 1964.
9. See A.F.J.Klijn, *The Jewish-Christian Gospel Tradition*, Leiden 1992.
10. For an account of this development see e.g. J.D.G.Dunn, *The Partings of the Ways Between Christianity and Judaism. Their Significance for the Character of Christianity*, London 1991.
11. For further information see G.Strecker, 'Judenchristentum', *TRE* 17, 310–25.
12. For a more extensive discussion see 'Appendix I: The Gospel of Peter – A Noncanonical Passion Narrative', in R.E.Brown, *The Death of the Messiah. From Gethsemane to the Grave. A Commentary on the Passion*

Narratives in the Four Gospels, New York and London 1994, 1317–49.

13. For a brief introduction see H.M.Schencke, 'Nag Hammadi', *TRE* 23, 741–6.

14. For translations of these writings see J.M.Robinson, *The Nag Hammadi Library in English*, Leiden and New York 1988.

15. For an introduction see R.McL.Wilson, *Gnosis and the New Testament*, Oxford 1968.

16. For a convenient collection of the Gnostic writings commented on by the church fathers see Bentley Layton, *The Gnostic Scriptures*, New York and London 1987.

17. For what follows see also H.Koester, *Ancient Christian Gospels. Their History and Development*, London and New York 1990, 75–128.

18. A.Guillaumont, H.-C.Puech and G.Quispel (eds.), *The Gospel According to Thomas. Coptic Text Established and Translated*, Leiden 1959.

19. Cf. C.Tuckett, *Nag Hammadi and the Gospel Tradition. Synoptic Tradition in the Nag Hammadi Library*, Edinburgh 1986.

20. For a brief survey see Bauer, *Orthodoxy and Heresy* (n.1), 16–42.

21. See W.L.Peterson, 'Tatian's Diatessaron', in Koester, *Ancient Christian Gospels* (n.17), 403–40.

22. Cf. H.Koester and J.M.Robinson, *Trajectories through Early Christianity*, Philadelphia 1971, 114–43.

23. G.Quispel, *Markus, das Thomasevangelium und das Lied von der Perle*, Leiden 1967.

24. See Martin Hengel, 'Jakobus der Herrenbruder – der erste "Papst"?', in *Glaube und Eschatologie, FS. W. G. Kümmel*, Tübingen 1985, 71–104.

25. J.Jeremias, *The Parables of Jesus*, London and New York 1972 (the first edition of the book appeared in 1947).

26. For an attractive account of the finding of the Dead Sea Scrolls see Millar Burrows, *The Dead Sea Scrolls*, [3]1994.

27. See D.T.Runia, *Philo in Early Christian Literature. A Survey*, Assen and Philadelphia 1993.

28. For Josephus see T.Rajak, *Josephus*, London 1983.

29. For a discussion of the Qumran community see Geza Vermes, *The Dead Sea Scrolls*, London [3]1994.

30. Much literature has appeared on this theme: for a good introduction see O.Betz and R.Riesner, *Jesus, Qumran and the Vatican*, London and New York 1994.

31. This has, of course, now happened. See Geza Vermes, *The Dead Sea Scrolls in English*, Harmondsworth [3]1987 (a fourth edition is in preparation); F.Garcia Martinez, *The Dead Sea Scrolls Translated. The Qumran Texts in English*, Leiden 1994.

32. R.Eisenman and M.Wise, *The Dead Sea Scrolls Uncovered*, Dorset 1992.
33. B.Thiering, *Jesus the Man*, London 1992 (US title *Jesus and the Riddle of the Dead Sea Scrolls*, San Francisco 1992).

10. New Pictures of Jesus

1. For a survey of modern portraits of Jesus in literature and art see K.J.Kuschel (ed.), *Der Andere Jesus. Ein Lesebuch moderner literarischer Texte*, Munich 1987; W.Hamilton, *A Quest for the Post-Historical Jesus*, London 1993.
2. A.N.Wilson, *Jesus. A Biography*, London 1993.
3. Of Belloc, Scott, Milton, Tolstoy and C.S.Lewis.
4. G.Vermes, *Jesus the Jew. A Historian's Reading of the Gospels*, London 1973 (the sub-title is typical).
5. Reproduced with commentary in G.Rombold and H.Schwebel, *Christus in der Kunst des 20.Jahrhunderts. Eine Dokumentation mit 32 Farbbildern und 70 Schwarzweiss-Abbildungen*, Freiburg 1983, 134–6.
6. Cf. R.Batey, *Jesus and the Forgotten City. New Light on Sepphoris and the Urban World of Jesus*, Grand Rapids 1991.
7. R.Eisler, *Iesous Basileus ou basileusas. Die messianische Unabhängigkeitsbewegung vom Auftreten Johannes des Taufers bis zum Untergang Jakobs des Gerechten nach der neuerschlossenen Eroberung von Jerusalem des Flavius Josephus und der christlichen Quellen* I/II, Heidelberg 1929–30.
8. J.Carmichael, *The Death of Jesus*, New York 1962.
9. In an earlier study he had defended the view that the earliest community in Jerusalem had joined the Zealots on the outbreak of the revolt against the Romans and had been annihilated in 70 on the destruction of the city. See S.G.F.Brandon, *The Fall of Jerusalem and the Christian Church*, London 1957. In the 1960s he went further and also attributed a pro-Zealot attitude to Jesus; cf. also S.G.F.Brandon, *Jesus and the Zealots*, Manchester 1967; id., *The Trial of Jesus of Nazareth*, London 1968.
10. M.Hengel, *Was Jesus a Revolutionist?*, Philadelphia 1971; O.Cullmann, *Jesus and the Revolutionaries*, New York 1970.
11. For an extensive testing and challenging of Brandon's ideas see E.Bammel and C.F.D.Moule (ed.), *Jesus and the Politics of His Day*, Cambridge 1984.
12. M.Machovec, *A Marxist Looks at Jesus*, London and Philadelphia 1976.
13. G.Gutierrez, A *Theology of Liberation*, Maryknoll and London [2]1988; L.Boff, *Jesus Christ Liberator. A Critical Christology for Our Time*, New York 1978; Jon Sobrino, *Christolgoy at the Crossroads, A Latin American Approach*, Maryknoll and London 1978.

14. See A.B.Cleage, *The Black Messiah*, New York 1969; Theo Witvliet, *The Way of the Black Messiah*, London 1987.
15. For the influence of Mary Magdalene in the history of church and theology see S.Haskins, *Myth and Metaphor*, London 1994; E.Moltmann-Wendel, *The Women around Jesus*, London and New York 1982, 61–92.
16. Of course this was not a new idea. According to the art historian Leo Steinberg, *The Sexuality of Christ in Renaissance Art and in Modern Oblivion*, Oxford 1983, some mediaeval painters depicted Jesus' genitalia to emphasize the reality of the incarnation. However, this was a negative verdict on sexuality: the suffering of Jesus begins with the incarnation and is expressed by showing his sexual parts.
17. See E.Maeckelberghe, *Desperately Seeking Mary. A Feminist Appropriation of a Traditonal Religious Symbol*, Kampen 1991.
18. E.g. E.Moltmann-Wendel, *The Women around Jesus* (n.15).
19. See e.g. Carol Christ and Judith Plaskow, *Womanspirit Rising*, San Francisco 1992.
20. Harvey Cox, *Feast of Fools*, Harvard, Mass. 1969.
21. See e.g. E.Drewermann, *Tiefenpsychologie und Exegese* 1/2, Freiburg 1991.
22. E.C.Prophet, *The Last Years of Jesus. On the Discoveries of Notovitch, Abhedananda, Roerich, and Caspari*, Livingston, MT 1984.
23. Cf. H.Kersten, *Jesus Lived in India. His Unknown Life Before and After the Crucifixion*, Shaftesbury 1987.
24. For a critical evaluation see G.Grönbold, *Jesus in Indien. Das Ende einer Legende*, Munich 1985.

11. Back to Jesus?

1. J.Moltmann, *The Crucified God. The Cross of Christ as the Foundation and Critique of Christian Theology*, London and New York 1974.
2. J.B.Metz, *The Emergent Church. The Future of Christianity in a Postbourgeois World*, London and New York 1981.
3. F.-W.Marquardt, *Die Gegenwart des Auferstandenen bei seinem Volk Israel. Ein dogmatische Experiment*, Munich 1983; *Das christliche Bekenntnis zu Jesus, dem Juden. Eine Christologie* (2 vols.), Munich 1990–1991.
4. H.Berkhof, *Christian Faith*, Grand Rapids 1990.
5. E.Schillebeeckx, *Jesus. An Experiment in Christology*, London and New York 1979.
6. H.Küng, *On Being a Christian*, London 1974.
7. Ibid., 155f.

8. Schillebeeckx, *Jesus* (n.5), 75.

9. E.Käsemann, 'Blind Alleys in the "Jesus of History" Controversy', in *New Testament Questions of Today*, London and Philadelphia 1969, 23–65.

10. He arrives at five 'characteristics of the *ipsissima vox Jesu*': 1. the parables of Jesus; 2. the riddles; 3. the reign of God; 4. Amen; 5 Abba, cf. J.Jeremias, *New Testament Theology Part One. The Proclamation of Jesus*, London and New York 1971, 29–37.

11. 'It is generally recognized today – despite the need for a critical analyis of every single parable and the history of its tradition – that the parables belong to the bedrock of the tradition about him' (ibid., 30).

12. See D.Flusser, *Die rabbinischen Gleichnisse und der Gleichniserzähler Jesus. 1 Teil: Das Wesen der Gleichnisse*, Bern 1981, who concludes: 'One central recognition is that the parables of Jesus are testimony which represents the literary genre of the rabbinic parables.'

13. 'We can only count on possessing a genuine parable of Jesus where, on the one hand, expression is given to the contrast between Jewish morality and piety and the distinctive eschatological temper which characterized the preaching of Jesus; and where on the other hand we find no specifically Christian features', R.Bultmann, *The History of the Synoptic Tradition*, Oxford [2]1968, 205.

14. N.Perrin, *Rediscovering the Teaching of Jesus*, London 1967, 39, uses the term 'the criterion of dissimilarity' and formulates this as follows: 'the earliest form of a saying we can reach may be regarded as authentic if it can be shown to be dissimilar to characteristic emphases both of ancient Judaism and of the early church'.

15. Thus e.g. E.Käsemann,' Was Jesus a "liberal"?, in *Jesus Means Freedom*, London 1969, 16–41.

16. For these see Schillebeeckx, *Jesus* (n.5), 81–100.

17. There is a survey of the discussion in M.E.Boring, 'The Historical-Critical Method's "Criteria of Authenticity"', *Semeia* 44, 1988, 9–44.

18. Cf. R.Schnackenburg, *Jesus Christ in the Gospels. A Biblical Christology*, Louisville 1995.

19. Cf. especially the views of John A.T.Robinson, *The Priority of John*, London 1985.

20. Lucas Grollenberg, *Jesus*, London 1978, 46.

21. P.Sigal, *The Halakah of Jesus of Nazareth according to the Gospel of Matthew*, Landham MD 1986.

22. See the well-documented book by R.Reisner, *Jesus als Lehrer. Eine Untersuchung zum Ursprung der Evangelien-Überlieferung*, Tübingen 1984.

12. The Return of the Historical Jesus

1. C.A.Evans, *Life of Jesus Research. An Annotated Bibliography*, New Testament Tools and Studies 13, Leiden and New York 1989.
2. There is an attractive survey in A.Wessels, *Images of Jesus*, Grand Rapids and London 1990.
3. See. M.J.Borg, 'Portraits of Jesus in Contemporary North American Scholarship', *Harvard Theological Review* 84, 1991, 1–22; id., 'A Renaissance in Jesus Studies', *Theology Today* 45, 1988, 280–92; J.D.Crossan, 'Divine Immediacy and Human Immediacy. Towards a New First Principle in Historical Jesus Research', *Semeia* 44, 1988, 121–40; P.Hollenbach, 'The Historical Jesus Question in North America Today', *Biblical Theology Bulletin* 19, 1989, 11–12; for a critical voice from the German-speaking world see E.Schweizer, 'Jesus – made in Great Britain and USA', *Theologische Zeitschrift* 50, 1994, 311–21.
4. See S.Neill and T.Wright, *The Interpretation of the New Testament 1861–1986*, Oxford and New York 1988; E.Hurth, *In His Name. Comparative Studies in the Quest for the Historical Jesus. Life of Jesus Research in Germany and America*, European University Studies, Series 23: Theology 367, Frankfurt and Bern 1989.
5. See above all B.Gerhardsson, *Memory and Manuscript. Oral Tradition and Written Transmission in Rabbinic Judaism and Early Christianity*, Uppsala 1961; H.Riesenfeld, *The Gospel Tradition and Its Beginnings. A Study in the Limits of 'Formgeschichte'*, London 1957.
6. J.A.T.Robinson, *Honest to God*, London and Philadelphia 1963.
7. Id., *Redating the New Testament*, London 1976.
8. J.O'Callaghan, 'Papiros neotestamentarios en la cueva 7 de Qumrân', *Biblica* 53, 1972, 91–100.
9. See e.g. B.Estrada and W.White, *The First New Testament*, Nashville and New York 1978.
10. Thus C.P.Thiede, *The Earliest Gospel Manuscript? The Qumran Fragment 7Q5 and its Significance for New Testament Studies*, Exeter 1992.
11. Id., 'Papyrus Magdalen Greek 17 (Gregory-Aland P674). A Reappraisal', *Tyndale Bulletin* 46, 1995, 29–42.
12. G.N.Stanton, *Gospel Truth? New Light on Jesus and the Gospels*, London 1995.
13. Cf. C.A.Evans, 'Life-of-Jesus Research and the Eclipse of Mythology', *Theologische Studien* 54, 1993, 3–36.
14. Cf. e.g, Stevan L.Davies, *Jesus the Healer*, New York and London 1995; G.H.Twelftree, *Jesus the Exorcist. A Contribution to the Study of the*

Historical Jesus, Tübingen 1993; M.Smith, *Jesus the Magician*, London 1978.

15. E.P.Sanders, *Paul and Palestinian Judaism. A Comparison of Patterns of Religion*, London and Philadelphia 1977.
16. Cf. also the following studies: *Paul, the Law and the Jewish People*, Philadelphia 1983; *Jesus and Judaism*, London and Philadelphia 1985; *Jewish Law from Jesus to the Mishnah. Five Studies*, London and Philadelphia 1990; *Judaism, Practice and Belief, 63 BCE – 66 CE*, London and Philadelphia 1992.
17. Id., *The Historical Figure of Jesus*, London and New York 1993.
18. Ibid., 5.
19. At the beginning of his attractive biography *Alexander the Great*, London 1973, Robin Lane Fox writes: 'This is not a biography nor does it pretend to certainty in Alexander's name. More than twenty contemporaries wrote books on Alexander and not one of them survives. They are known by quotations from later authors, not one of whom preserved the original wording . . . Alexander left no informal letter which is genuine beyond dispute and the two known extracts from his formal documents both concern points of politics . . . It is a naive belief that the distant past can be recovered from written texts, but even the written evidence for Alexander is sparse and often peculiar. Nonetheless, 1,472 books and articles are known to me on the subject in the past century and a half, many of which adopt a confident tone and can be dismissed for that alone . . . This book is a search, not a story, and any reader who takes it as a full picture of Alexander's life has begun with the wrong suppositions' (11).
20. 'Their general approval of Jesus shows how well the authors of the gospels did their job', Sanders, *The Historical Figure of Jesus* (n.17), 7.
21. Ibid., 280.
22. 'The resurrection is not, strictly speaking, part of the story of the historical thus but rather belongs to the aftermath of his life', ibid., 276.
23. 'In the process they (his disciples and followers) created a movement, a movement that in many ways went far beyond Jesus' message', ibid., 280.
24. Ibid., 238–49.
25. Ibid., 249–75.
26. M.J.Borg, 'What Did Jesus Really Say?', *Biblical Review* 5, 1989, 18–25.
27. Id., *Meeting Jesus Again for the First Time. The Historical Jesus and the Heart of Contemporary Faith*, San Francisco 1994.

28. The results of the voting in the Jesus seminar can be found in the following articles: 'The Jesus Seminar. Voting Records. Sorted by Gospel, Chapter, and Verse', *Forum* 6, 1990, 3–55; 'Voting Records. Sorted by Weighted Average', *Forum* 6, 1990, 139–91; 'Voting Records. Sorted by Gospels, by Weighted Average', *Forum* 6, 1990, 25–98; 'Voting Records. Sorted by Grouped Parallels, by Weighted Average', *Forum* 6, 1990, 299–352; 'Voting Records. Sorted by Clusters, by Weighted Average', *Forum* 7, 1991, 51–104; 'Voting Records. Sorted Alphabetically by Title', *Forum* 7, 1991, 105–58.

29. R.W.Funk (ed.), *The Five Gospels: The Search for the Authentic Words of Jesus*, New York 1994.

30. Cf. J.M.Robinson, 'The Study of the Historical Jesus after Nag Hammadi', *Semeia* 44, 1988, 45–55.

31. For a survey see W.D.Stroker, *Extracanonical Sayings of Jesus*, Atlanta 1989; also id., 'Extracanonical Parables and the Historical Jesus', *Semeia* 44, 1988, 95–120.

32. See the influential study by H.Koester, *Ancient Christian Gospels. Their History and Development*, Philadelphia and London 1990.

33. See S.L.Davies, *The Gospel of Thomas and Christian Wisdom*, New York 1983, 1–17. B.Chilton, 'The Gospel according to Thomas as a Source of Jesus' Teaching', in D.Wenham, *Gospel Perspectives. Volume 5. The Jesus Tradition outside the Gospels*, Sheffield 1985, 155–75, is more cautious.

34. Koester, *Ancient Christian Gospels* (n.32), 86.

35. R.Pesch, *Das Markusevangeliumn. 2.Teil*, Herders Theologischer Kommentar zum Neuen Testament, Freiburg 1977, 1–27, is an important advocate of this theory.

36. C.J.den Heyer, *De messiaanse weg III. De christologie van het Nieuwe Testament*, Kampen 1991, 405.

37. Cf. J.L.White, 'The Way of the Cross. Was There a Pre-Markan Passion Narrative?', *Forum* 3, 1987, 35–49.

38. See e.g. R.E.Brown, *The Birth of The Messiah. A Commentary on the Infancy Narrative in Matthew and Luke*, New York and London 1979.

39. Koester, *Ancient Christian Gospels* (n.32), 224.

40. Thus, in addition to Koester, above all J.D.Crossan, 'The Cross that Spoke. The Earliest Narrative of the Passion and Resurrection', *Forum* 3, 1987, 3–22; id., *The Cross That Spoke. The Origins of the Passion Narrative*, San Francisco 1988. For a critical reaction see e.g. A.J.Dewey, '"And an Answer was heard from the Cross . . ." A Reponse to J.Dominic Crossan', *Forum* 5, 1989, 103–11; id., '"Time to Murder and Create." Visions and Revisions in the Gospel of Peter', *Semeia* 49, 1990, 101–27.

41. For criticism see e.g. R.E.Brown, 'The Gospel of Peter and Canonical Gospel Priority', *New Testament Studies* 33, 1987, 321–43; J.B.Green, 'The Gospel of Peter: Source for a Pre-canonical Passion Narrative?', *Zeitschrift für die Neutestamentliche Wissenschaft* 78, 1987, 293–301.

42. New York 1991. The cover of the book described it as 'the first comprehensive determination of who Jesus was, what he did, what he said', and even remarked '*The Historical Jesus* reveals the true Jesus'.

43. San Francisco 1994. Crossan dedicated it 'To Robert W.Funk and my fellow members of the Westar Institute's Jesus Seminar for their courage, collegiality, and consistency'. Funk founded the Jesus Seminar in 1985.

44. San Francisco, 1994; it had been preceded by id., *Jesus. A New Vision. Spirit, Culture and the Life of Discipleship*, San Francisco 1987.

45. Ibid., 42–44.

46. Crossan, *The Historical Jesus* (n.42), 58.

47. Ibid., 70.

48. Borg, *Meeting Jesus Again* (n.44), 88.

49. Cf. e.g. M.J.Borg, 'A Temperate Case for a Non-Eschatological Jesus', *Forum* 2, 1986, 81–202; B.L.Mack, 'The Kingdom Sayings in Mark', *Forum* 3, 1987, 3–47; J.R.Butts, 'Probing the Polling. Jesus Seminar Results on the Kingdom Sayings', *Forum* 3, 1987, 98–128; J.G.Williams, 'Neither Here nor There. Between Wisdom and Apocalyptic in Jesus' Kingdom Sayings', *Forum* 5, 1989, 7–30; W.S.Vorster, 'Jesus: Eschatological Prophet and/or Wisdom Teacher?', *Hervormde teologiese studies* 47, 1991, 526–42.

50. Borg, *Meeting Jesus Again* (n.44), 35.

51. Crossan, *The Historical Jesus* (n.42), 254–26.

52. R.Riesner, *Jesus als Lehrer. Eine Untersuchung zum Ursprung der Evangelien-Überlieferung*, Tübingen 1984.

53. Crossan, *The Historical Jesus* (n.42), 122.

54. Ibid., 117.

55. Sanders, *The Historical Figure of Jesus* (n.17), 262.

13. Jesus has Many Faces

1. This was spelt out in Chapter 11 of Schweitzer's *The Quest of the Historical Jesus*, 'Bruno Bauer', 137–60, and two further chapters on the denial of the historicity of Jesus which did not appear in the English translation of this book: see A.Schweitzer, *Geschichte der Leben-Jesu Forschung*, Tübingen 1966, 402–50 and 451–99.

2. See the extensive account of the life of Jesus by *J.P.Meier, A Marginal Jew. Rethinking the Historical Jesus.* A trilogy is planned of which the first two volumes have appeared: *The Roots of the Problem and the Person*, New York and London 1991 (484pp.), and *Mentor, Message, and Miracles*, New York and London 1994 (1118pp.).

3. See Chapter 6 above, 'The Kerygmatic Christ'.

4. See ibid., the section on 'The "So-Called" Historical Jesus'.

5. R.Zuurmond, *Verleden tijd? Een speurtocht naar de 'historische Jesus'*, Baarn 1994, 183–9.

6. See Chapter 7 above, 'Renewed Interest in the Historical Jesus'.